Collins, Aukai.

My jihad.

$22.95

DATE			

My Jihad

My Jihad

The True Story of an American Mujahid's

Amazing Journey from Usama Bin Laden's Training Camps

to Counterterrorism with the FBI and CIA

AUKAI COLLINS

The Lyons Press
Guilford, Connecticut

AN IMPRINT OF THE GLOBE PEQUOT PRESS

A note on the text:

Some of the individuals in this text appear under assumed names to conceal or protect their identities.

Before publication, the publisher attempted to clear the manuscript with
the executive branch of the federal government in order to give the government an opportunity to remove any sensitive or classified information.
The Publications Review Board of the Central Intelligence Agency respect-
fully declined to review the text, saying that they were unaware of any pre-
publication review requirement.

—Ed.

Printed in the United States of America

Book and jacket design by Casey Shain

1 3 5 7 9 10 8 6 4 2

The Library of Congress Cataloging-in-Publication Data is available on file.

To Saifudeen, my beloved "monster head"

And to Muhammad Zaky, Abu Zubair, Luqman Uthman, Field Commander Zaid, Abu Talha, Abu Hafs, and all the others who have already joined the caravan. Not a day goes by that I don't think about you.

Abu Hurairah, may Allah be pleased with him, reported:

The Messenger of Allah (may peace be upon him) was asked: What deed could be an equivalent to Jihad in the way of Allah, the Almighty and Exalted? He answered: You do not have the strength to do that deed. They repeated the question twice or thrice. Every time he answered: You do not have the strength to do it. When the question was asked for the third time, he said: One who goes out for Jihad is like a person who keeps Fast, stands in the Prayer (constantly), (obeying) Allah's (behests contained in) the verses (of the Qur'an), and does not exhibit any lassitude in Fasting and the Prayer until the Mujahid returns from Jihad in the way of Allah, the Exalted.

—Islamic Hadith

CONTENTS

ACKNOWLEDGMENTS .... *ix*

INTRODUCTION .... *xi*

Part One

From San Diego to Afghanistan Through Frankfurt,
Vienna, Pakistan, and Kashmir 1993 3

Afghanistan WINTER 1993-94 23

First Trip to Chechnya 1995-96 41

Part Two

Youth 133

Part Three

How the CIA Betrayed Me 1996-99 147

Chechnya Revisited 1999-2000 217

September 11, 2001 247

ACKNOWLEDGMENTS

My most sincere thatnks go out to Robert Young Pelton. Without you this book would have never happened. I owe you an incredible debt and will gladly "take one" for you any day. You kick ass!

And to Jonathan "Blood and Guts" McCullough at the Lyons Press. Thank you for all the time and effort you put into this book. No doubt you went above and beyond the call of duty.

INTRODUCTION

This is the story of how I converted to Islam, entered the world of the mujahideen, and fought jihad in faraway lands. It's also the story of how I became an undercover operative in a counterterrorism unit on behalf of the U.S. government. I had many successes and many failures, and I have more than my share of regrets. But this has been my life, and what I offer here is my first-hand experience with the world of the mujahideen and what was the U.S. government's war on terror.

Islamic fundamentalism, jihad, and the mujahideen are nothing new to the world. Nor are terrorism, kidnappings, and murder. But since September 11, 2001, these have loomed in the public imagination as new phenomena. Worse yet, they have been presented to the public as though they were intertwined, and that the war on terror—and those we'd wage it against—is very simple, very clear cut. Unfortunately, the world just isn't that simple. Being an Islamic fundamentalist does not mean that you support or engage in terrorism. Fighting jihad as a mujahid doesn't mean that you kidnap people or murder civilians. Yet many Americans fear Islamic fundamentalism, jihad, and the mujahideen as a national security threat, and that fear stems from the fact that few actually know about Islam, or who the mujahideen are, or why they fight jihad.

The Arabic word *jihad* means to strive or struggle against something. In the West, it has been translated as "holy war" because it is used in the Holy Qur'an almost exclusively in the context of war. Although the word is used frequently, perhaps now more than ever, jihad is not something to be taken lightly. Muslims cannot just fight or kill anyone or anything and call it a jihad. For a jihad to be declared, any given situation must meet several criteria as stipulated in the Holy Qur'an. To put it simply, when a Muslim land is being attacked and Muslims are being killed there is the need for jihad. In this case it becomes a duty for all able-bodied Muslims to come to the aid of the people being attacked. But even then jihad has many rules. It is forbidden to kill non-combatants. Crops and trees cannot be destroyed, and livestock cannot be killed. It is even forbidden to destroy the houses of worship of other faiths, and Muslims cannot force a person to convert to Islam.

As an example, consider the war in Bosnia. The Serbs murdered over two hundred thousand Muslims there. On one day in the city of Sebrenicia, over six thousand Muslims were slaughtered as U.N. peacekeepers looked on. During the war in Afghanistan more than a million Muslims lost their lives to the Soviet Union. In the tiny republic of Chechnya, in a war that still rages at this writing, the Russian army brutally killed at least another two hundred thousand Muslims. These are *hundreds* of thousands of lives, not thousands.

So who are the mujahideen? They are the Muslims of the world who answer the call of jihad and fight to defend the people of Bosnia, Chechnya, Afghanistan, and elsewhere as required. There are more than one and a half billion Muslims in the world, so it would stand to reason that of this number a million, or perhaps five hundred thousand, answer the call of jihad. No one knows for sure, but the mujahideen generally agree that there are actually fewer than ten thousand of us spread out throughout the world. Most of them are currently in Chechnya fighting the Russian army, but even there, their number is less than five thousand. Fifteen years ago many in the West considered these mujahideen to be heroes, valiant "freedom fighters" who dared to take on the Soviet Union despite being outnumbered and out-gunned. More recently they were the heroes of Chechnya, defending the tiny republic against the same army that tried to annihilate Afghanistan. So when the stakes are this high and the odds against them are this long, does it really make sense to impugn them with one broad brushstroke and say that they hate freedom?

The events of September 11 and everything that came after it were truly regrettable, and I would have done anything to have stopped it, not only because so many lives were lost, but also because it set back the jihad movement at least two decades. Regardless of whether they had anything to do with September 11, or any terrorism, the mujahideen have been tried in the court of public opinion and have been found guilty by association. This will have dire consequences for Muslims in war-ravaged lands, and will undoubtedly make it even more difficult to save the thousands of innocent lives that will inevitably be lost to state-sponsored terrorism, as in Chechnya. A life is a life, and the loss of thousands diminishes us all, whether they are lost in a spectacular attack on downtown New York City, or cumulatively in mop-up operations in a little village in Chechnya.

As an American citizen and a Muslim I feel our government cannot solve the problem of terrorist threats until they understand that Christian, Jewish and non-religious groups all pose threats. I have front-line combat experience with jihad in several countries overseas, and I also have front-line counterintelligence experience here at home as an asset of the CIA and FBI. But for years the U.S. government's ignorance of Islam, its people, and its history has fostered a culture of paranoia and xenophobia.

These racist philosophies have led to a tunnel-vision campaign of oppression similar to the fear of communism in America during the 1950s. My experience with the CIA and the FBI has convinced me that they have not only a misguided "witchhunt" mentality, but an agenda that turns them away from the real problem of transnational terrorist threats and toward degrading individuals within the American Muslim community. As you will see, I tried to both the FBI and the CIA how to infiltrate the terrorist cells in the United States and abroad, but as bureaucracies they do not have the capacity or motivation to actually confront and contain Islamic terrorist elements anywhere.

They don't want you to know that there is no real fight against terrorism. They don't want you to know that some of the highjackers of September 11 were known to the FBI as early as 1999. Now more than ever people need to know the facts because misunderstanding and fear will do nothing but destroy us all.

–AUKAI COLLINS
MAY 2002

Part One

From San Diego to Afghanistan Through Frankfurt, Vienna, Pakistan, and Kashmir

1993

MASJIDUL NOOR WAS THE FIRST MOSQUE I ever attended. It was in the ghetto of Fiftieth Street and University Avenue in East San Diego and had formerly been an old house. Black, Asian, and Hispanic gangs roamed at all hours of the day, but the immediate area around the mosque was a bustling Islamic community of Pakistanis, Kurds, Somalis, and Afghans. When I first walked in, I thought that the other Muslims might regard me with suspicion or amusement, but no one gave me a second look. I approached one of the men there when he'd finished praying and asked him for the Imam. He told me that the Imam wasn't there yet, but that I could speak to someone in a little house next to the mosque, which is where I found Khamil.

Khamil, a young and very friendly Pakistani, took an interest in me as a new Muslim. I hung out with him until *Salaatul Maghrib*, the prayer made just after sunset, and then he introduced me to Ibrahim, a very large man in his forties or fifties with a big, gray beard and an intimidating demeanor. When we spoke, I found him genuinely friendly and kindhearted. The Muslims at this mosque were called Tabliqis and Ibrahim was the emir, or leader. I told him about myself, and he could see that I was sincere about Islam. When I mentioned that I didn't know where I would be living in San Diego, he suggested that I rent a room in Khamil's little house next to the mosque. This pleased me; I would be around other Muslims and have the mosque just next door.

I fell into a comfortable routine with the Tabliqis. Every morning before sunup I would awaken to one of the guys outside making the *azan*, or call to prayer. After prayer we would get ready to go to work, and after work we would hang out in front of the mosque.

On the weekends the Tabliqis would send out *jamats*, or groups of the faithful, to mosques in other cities. Sometimes we would drive up to Los

Angeles and meet with fellow Muslims, and as I began to learn more about Islam, I adopted traditional Islamic dress. In a while I became a regular feature of the area—the guy with the big red beard and turban walking down the street.

After about four months I became concerned about the war in Bosnia, where the Serbs were slaughtering Muslims by the tens of thousands. Not only had the United States refused to help the Bosnians, but we had placed an arms embargo on them as well. Perhaps the most disturbing fact was that the more I learned about the situation, the less it seemed the Muslims around me cared about it. No one in the mosques talked about the war, and when I asked questions they seemed unconcerned.

Finally I went to Ibrahim, the emir, and told him that although I was new to Islam, I'd learned a great deal in the past four months and felt that I was ready to defend our religion. To my surprise, he didn't understand what I was saying, so I told him that I wanted to go to Bosnia for jihad. His response was even more surprising. He told me that because the majority of the Muslims in the world weren't practicing the religion properly, there was no jihad at the present time. I couldn't believe what I was hearing. This sounded like a cop-out to me. Jihad is an established principle of Islam, and when Muslims are being attacked and killed, it is the duty of every adult male Muslim to go to their aid. Yet Ibrahim was telling me that since most Muslims didn't practice Islam properly, I shouldn't concern myself with whether they lived or died.

Later I discovered that the Tabliq was basically a pacifist movement that had originated in Pakistan. Many people, myself included, believe that the movement had actually been started by colonial Britain to pacify the Pakistanis. Britain's imperial dreams would have turned to nightmares if the Islamic scholars had declared a jihad, so the British had fostered a movement within Islam that didn't include jihad.

Although I continued to stay around the Tabliqis, I became very disillusioned. One night, while sitting in front of the mosque, I met a man named Abdullah. Originally from Panama, he'd fought the Soviets in Afghanistan and the Serbs in Bosnia. I was drawn to him immediately, and asked him whether someone could get into Bosnia. He told me that a friend of his had just left for Bosnia, but that he would be back in a month and might be able to help.

I saw Abdullah at the mosque about a month later; he told me that his friend had just returned from Bosnia. The next night a man asked for me at the mosque. His name was Muhammad Zaky, and he was a large older man with a tough-looking face and a long red beard; during our conversation I learned that he'd been born in the United States of Egyptian parents. When he asked if I wanted to go to Bosnia, I leapt at the chance. He said it wouldn't be a problem, although it would take him a couple of weeks to make arrangements.

This was exhilarating: not only would I be able to help the Muslims of Bosnia but I would also complete my own faith. Jihad is the highest act of faith in Islam. The prophet Muhammad, peace and blessings be upon him, said that if a Muslim dies without making jihad, or at least having had the intentions to make it, then he dies with a form of hypocrisy in his heart.

I spent a lot of time with Muhammad Zaky as he made the arrangements for my trip to Bosnia. He was very intelligent and had spent many years fighting jihad. Like Abdullah, he had fought first in Afghanistan against the Soviets and then in Bosnia against the Serbs. Although he never spoke about it, some said that he had testified before the House of Representatives about the mujahideen in Afghanistan, and that his testimony had been instrumental in ensuring that the United States sent Stinger antiaircraft missiles to the mujahideen. Muhammad Zaky had a wife, two teenage daughters, and a son named Umar, a bright kid of about eleven or twelve who wanted to go to jihad like his father. As I became acquainted with Muhammad and his family, I never imagined that I'd end up bringing Muhammad's final words back to his son, after he'd died in a place I'd never heard of yet, called Chechnya.

Muhammad lived a simple life in San Diego when he wasn't fighting on the battlefields of faraway lands. He had a window-tinting business to pay the bills and ran the Islamic Information Center of the Americas out of an office in downtown La Jolla. I spent most of my time with him there, surrounded by piles of Islamic literature and shelves filled with videocassettes about the jihad in Afghanistan and Bosnia that were stacked all the way to the ceiling. We spent hours watching combat footage of the war against the Soviets.

The night before I left, Muhammad and the guys in his weekly jihad class threw a small going-away party for me. We sat together and drank tea and ate Arabic sweets. It was a joyous occasion, and at the end everyone hugged me and wished me well. Then Muhammad Zaky and I returned to his apartment, where we stayed up most of the night going over our plan. I'd fly to Frankfurt, where an Arab would pick me up, give me some papers, and put me on a train to Vienna. Once I reached Vienna, other contacts would transport me to Zagreb, the capital of Croatia. I would present myself as a journalist at the United Nations headquarters in Zagreb and obtain an UNPROFOR pass, or official U.N. pass. Until recently, the route into Bosnia had been wide open for mujahideen from all over the world, but conditions had changed, and by the time I was ready to go entrance was nearly impossible. One of the few points of entry was the U.N. flight into Sarajevo, and to get on that flight I would need an UNPROFOR card.

Muhammad Zaky took me to Lindbergh Field to catch my flight to Frankfurt. As I boarded the plane I looked back and saw him smiling at me. But when I arrived in Frankfurt and cleared customs, nobody was waiting for me. I tried calling the Arab man, but I wasn't able to get through. I wasn't able to reach Muhammad Zaky either, so I made my own plan. I traveled to Vienna by train and tried to call my contacts there; again, I couldn't reach anyone. However, I did have an address for my contacts' mosque, so I took a cab there.

Once I found my contacts at the mosque, everything went more smoothly. I stayed with them in Vienna for almost a week. I was supposed to take another train from Vienna to Zagreb, but just before I was to leave one of the guys found three Arabs from a relief organization who were driving to Zagreb, so I caught a ride with them. The customs agents at the Croatian border gave one of the Arabs a hard time, but eventually we were able to get through. We arrived in Zagreb early in the morning, and the Arabs dropped me off at an office, where I met two of Muhammad Zaky's contacts.

Both were from the Sudan. They were running a relief organization for the Bosnians. They had no problems with letting a fighter sleep in their office, but they wouldn't have anything to do with getting me into Bosnia. I rested for a day and then went down to the U.N. headquarters for my UNPROFOR card. One of Muhammad Zaky's friends had given me a forged letter saying that I was a reporter for the "La Jolla *Tribune*," but when I sat down in front of the U.N. official to get the pass, he nearly laughed at me. I must have made a humorous figure—some dumb nineteen-year-old kid with a big red beard and a shaved head claiming to be a reporter with nothing more than a forged

BOSNIA AND SURROUNDING AREAS

letter to back him up. The official gave me a list of items I needed to prove I was a reporter, which included three sample articles. Needless to say, I walked out of the office feeling stupid.

I went back to the Sudanese and told them what had happened. They said that another organization in Zagreb needed someone who spoke English. This organization also had one of the last land routes into Sarajevo, and when I went to its office the director offered me a job. But I was naive and looked at everything in terms of black and white. I told him that I'd left America only to fight in Bosnia and asked if the organization would give me a ride on one of its convoys that was scheduled to leave soon. The director told me that this was impossible; they would have nothing to do with helping mujahideen enter Bosnia.

It's interesting to note that at this writing, these same organizations, which wouldn't help a single fighter enter Bosnia, are being shut down by the U.S. authorities for supposedly aiding terrorists. Most mujahideen would view these organizations as disgraceful because they refuse to aid the jihad in any way. Despite this, they are being shut down by the FBI.

None of my plans were working out, so I called Muhammad Zaky. He told me to go back to Vienna and wait for him there; he would be arriving in a couple of weeks. Back in Vienna, however, I became more and more frustrated and impatient with the situation. In retrospect, I know that waiting somewhere for a couple of weeks is nothing, but at the time it seemed impossible. A couple of days after I'd retreated to Vienna, an African-American Muslim named Laith came to the mosque. We started to talk, and he told me that if I wanted to make jihad, he could put me in touch with some of his friends in Pakistan, who in turn could get me into Kashmir. My primary goal was to help Bosnia, but I was too impatient to wait, so against Muhammad Zaky's advice I took off for the Pakistani city of Karachi.

The customs officials at Karachi International Airport must have thought I was joking when I asked, "What visa?" It was the first time I'd been outside America, and I'd never heard of a visa. But I was wearing the traditional clothes of the Tabliq and I told them I'd come to Pakistan for *carouge*, a pilgrimage that Tabliqis make, so they relented and gave me a seventy-two-hour visa. To my surprise, somebody was actually waiting for me when I left the airport. He drove me to the office of Harakat-ul Jihad, a Pakistani jihad group. The next day the group took me to one of the Tabliq schools in Karachi to meet one of the emirs. Although the Tabliqis are opposed to jihad, the emir agreed to give me a letter to take to the Pakistani immigration officials for an extension on my visa, and as a result I was able to stay for three more months.

I was supposed to leave Karachi the next day, but the night before my flight to Islamabad I awoke with incredible pain, fever, and uncontrollable shaking. By morning I was almost delirious with pain, and my head felt as if it was going to explode. Every ten minutes or so I stumbled to the bathroom for an exhausting bout of diarrhea. The Harakat-ul Jihad office didn't know what to do; after much discussion I managed to persuade them to take me to the hospital, where the doctors wouldn't touch me until I'd paid them. Three days and an IV later, the doctors told me that I had a bad case of dysentery and instructed me to return to the States. As soon as I was strong enough to walk, I took the flight to Islamabad.

As usual, no one was waiting for me at the airport. It was late at night and all I had was the address for the Harakat-ul Jihad office, so I hailed a taxi. The driver had to stop three times to ask directions for sector 19-4, and when we finally found sector 19-4, he couldn't find the house. He stopped and asked a passerby, who also didn't seem to know the location of Harakat-ul Jihad. When the man looked into the back of the taxi and saw my my big red beard, his eyes lit up.

"Are you a mujahid?" he asked.

At first I didn't know what to tell him, but I thought, What the hell, I'll take the risk. "Yes?" I replied hesitantly.

"O-kay," he said. He pointed to a large three-story house at the end of the street. "That one. That is the house of the mujahideen." Apparently what went on there wasn't a big secret.

The taxi driver rang the bell at the gate of the house, and a bearded man came out. When the driver said something to him in Urdu, the man looked at me. "Abu mujahid," he said. "I am sorry, we didn't have a car to take you from the airport."

The next morning I met with Mufti Shaheed, who was the emir of Harakat-ul Jihad. I told him my story through a translator. When I'd finished he smiled and said they were happy to receive me, and that he would send me to Kashmir right away. That was easy, I thought; at the time I didn't know that Kashmir was also known as the "one-way jihad."

Harakat-ul Jihad was a Pakistani jihad group whose primary goal was to annex Kashmir or form a separate emirate. It also sent its mujahideen to other conflicts, such as those in Afghanistan and Tajikistan. The leadership (and the dozens of other jihad organizations) was supposed to have a sort of loose confederacy with Al Qaeda. At the time I visited—four years after the Soviets had been pushed out of Afghanistan—American influence and support for the mujahideen had waned and other anti-Communist and anti-Western influences, such as Dr. Abdullah Azzam and his wealthy protégé Usama Bin Laden, had stepped in. Where they got their funding, what confederacies they had, how their organization was composed, were all things I didn't consider or ask about. In 1993 the mujahideen were still the "freedom fighters" of

Reagan administration lore, and nobody outside the circle of active mujahideen knew about Usama Bin Laden.

I stayed for a few days in Islamabad. Every day, the mujahideen took me out to see the city, where we had a good time. Whenever we got on a bus one of my escorts would announce to everyone who would listen that I was an American mujahid. The whole bus would turn and stare at me, smiling. At first I found this discomforting, but after a while it was just amusing.

When it was time to go, one of the English speakers said he would ride to the Harakat-ul Jihad camp with me. Since we didn't warrant one of the group's vehicles, we left from the central bus station. There we caught a van for the long, exhausting trip to the border. Every time I thought that the van couldn't possibly get any fuller, the driver would stop to pick up another passenger. Finally the guy traveling with me yelled at the driver, saying there wasn't any more room for passengers. Five minutes later, the driver stopped to pick up someone else.

The narrow, snaking road to Kashmir threads its way through the mountains. Occasionally a vehicle would come from the opposite direction, instigating a negotiation between the two drivers about who would back up to a part of the road that was wide enough for one of the vehicles to pass. At sundown the driver stopped, and most of the passengers got out to pray on the side of the road. We arrived in the last city before the border late that night and went to the Harakat-ul Jihad office to spend the night. The camp was up in the mountains, just past the border, and the leader was staying at the office that night. Commander Khalid, an Afghan war veteran, was a serious-looking man with a full dark beard and a hard face. He was missing one of his legs below the knee and had a prosthetic, but he usually moved around with crutches and continued to participate in operations. My traveling companion and I sat down on some pillows with him, and another man brought us chai. For all his seriousness, Commander Khalid greated us genially and wanted to know all about me. I told him about my life and how I had accepted Islam. When I'd finished he told my translator that he had seen many mujahideen come and go over the years. Some were killed quickly; others kept fighting for ages. He said that I had the look of one of those who would die quickly. For many people, this would seem like bad news, but for a mujahid it is a blessing. I made an extra prayer that night and asked for it to be so, but Allah only chooses the best among the mujahideen for such an honor, and I am still waiting.

The next morning I set out for the camp in one of Harakat-ul Jihad's four-wheel-drive Toyotas, along with Commander Khalid and my translator from Islamabad. After about forty-five minutes of zigzagging back and forth up the steep and bumpy mountain passes, we stopped at a ninety-degree bend in the road. There two men in camouflage combat fatigues had AK-47s slung over their shoulders, so at first I thought we'd come to some type of Pakistani military checkpoint. Commander Khalid hopped out of the truck on one leg, grabbed his crutches, and introduced me to the two men. They seemed amused to have an American visiting them. When I tried to put on my backpack, one of the men grabbed it and carried it for me.

We formed a single file and walked along a steep trail that ran up into the mountains. The forest was dense, and within a few minutes we couldn't see the road. I found the trail steep and difficult, and I was amazed at how Commander Khalid was able to manage it with just his crutches.

We had been hiking up the trail for about half an hour when suddenly I noticed a group of armed men perched on rocks all around us. My translator looked at me and said "Don't worry; they are mujahideen." Apparently Commander Khalid had been away from the camp for a while and this was the welcome wagon. As we followed the path between two enormous rocks that loomed over us, one of the men shouted *Takbir!* and everyone chanted *Allah-u-Akbar!*—Allah is great. Then the men perched on the rocks started to fire their weapons into the air. They had AKs and a PKM light machine gun, and one of the guys even had an RPG (rocket-propelled grenade launcher), which he fired off toward the top of the mountain. If I'd been a journalist on a tour of the camp it probably would have scared me shitless, but when Commander Khalid turned around to see my reaction, it was a big smile.

The camp itself was perched on a flat outcropping between two ravines. It consisted of two large tents and a smaller tent. The clearing let daylight into the camp, but the ravines and tree-covered hills around the camp prevented detection, and it would have been extremely difficult to spot the camp from the air. Just above the tents the mujahideen had carved out a flat area for training that was about twenty meters long and ten meters wide. A natural spring supplied water to the camp just below the tents. It was a perfect place for a camp.

The camp had a festive atmosphere. Everyone was happy about the return of the commander, who was obviously well loved by this group, and they also seemed excited to have an American Muslim in the camp. They'd created a lounge area between the tents by laying blankets on the ground inside a circular dirt berm. The mujahideen sat on the blankets and leaned on the berm to chat and drink tea. The camp had about fifteen men, and everyone except those on guard duty sat down in the lounge area. Commander Khalid invited me to sit next to him to relax and chat. One of the soldiers spoke English better than my translator from Islamabad, and he fielded questions from everyone. What part of America was I from? Was I married? How is life in America? Why had I come here?

When some of the others went off to do their chores, Commander Khalid told me about the camp and what they were doing there. Some of soldiers were veterans of the war with the Soviets, and others were just new recruits here for basic training. The camp took part in combat operations against the Indian army, so the basic training was very hands-on. He asked whether I had any military experience and I told him not really but said I was familiar with firearms. He asked me if I wanted to go on any operations and I told him of course. What about the language barrier, he wondered. I told him to just teach me how to say *fire* and *cease-fire* in Urdu and I would be okay. After the evening prayer, dinner, and the night prayer, I settled in for my first night in Kashmir.

During the next few days Commander Khalid put me in a loose class, where we learned about the AK-47 and other light arms. After morning prayers everyone sat around reading the Qur'an for about an hour, followed by an hour of exercises and a run up one of the ravines. I particularly enjoyed the runs because the Pakistanis were so comical. None of them were very agile, and they would stumble and trip their way up to the peak of the ravine. The run down was hilarious. Everyone shouted at the top of their lungs as they ran balls-out full speed down the slope that led back down to the other ravine and to the camp. It was supposed to be a sort of war cry, but they sounded like a pack of braying donkeys with a flock of cawing crows.

Since I'd lost one of my bags on the flight from Vienna I had only the *shawal kamece* outfits that I'd bought in Karachi. These are the traditional knee-length-shirt-and-pants combinations that men wear in that part of the world. But after a day or two Commander Khalid gave me a set of American woodland-pattern BDUs (battle dress uniforms). After I put them on, all the guys cheered. I'm still not sure why they did this, but it had something to do with me looking like an American soldier and fighting on their side.

In a few days I'd familiarized myself with my comrades and the surrounding area, and Commander Khalid asked me to go on one of the daily patrols. He gave me an AK-47 and a utility belt and called someone over to translate something in Urdu: "Have fun," he said.

I set out with a small group of the guys and we started up the mountain. This had to be one of the most beautiful places on earth. For as far as I could see, the green, tree-covered mountains were shaped like nearly perfect steps, and walking up and down them and the valleys and gorges was like walking up and down an endless row of bleachers. Small rivers and waterfalls were everywhere. One of the English speakers explained that this was the westernmost section of the Himalayas, just inside the Pakistani border with Kashmir. I had been here only a few days and was still trying to adjust to the high altitude and thin air.

While on patrol we would hike for several hours without seeing a single soul; then we'd suddenly come across a mud house atop a peak, where an entire family would be sitting out front. Occasionally one of the guys would stop and chat with the people, but every time they did the conversation was almost always about me. I wasn't the first American to ever hike these mountains—just the first American to do it in a uniform, carrying an AK-47.

At the time I didn't understand what we were looking for on our patrols or what was going on in Kashmir. Later I figured out that we were just playing the routine games that characterize the dispute in Kashmir. The Indian army would occasionally send Sikh commandos across the border to kill and harass the local civilians. Instead of risking a conflict with India, the Pakistani ISI (Inter-Services Intelligence) would allow mujahideen to operate freely in this region and defend against any possible Sikh attacks. This was mutually beneficial in that Pakistan could defend its border without risking a major conflict with India, and the mujahideen got valuable experience and training.

One day I was sitting on one of the big boulders at the edge of the camp when one of the guys walked over to me. He motioned that Commander Khalid wanted to see me in his tent. Oh, I thought, this must be important for him to call for me. When I entered the tent, Khalid was sitting against some pillows with his assistant.

"Sit down." The commander spoke seriously, in English. I wondered if I was in some kind of trouble.

"Yes," Khalid said.

Yes what? I thought. Yes. I decided to smile.

He nodded his head and raised the stump of his missing leg. It was sheathed in a black sock with two white eyes drawn on it. It looked just like the head of a sheep. As the commander raised his stump, his assistant started to sing.

"Ba, ba, black sheep, have you any wool?" he sang with a heavy Urdu accent. As the assistant sang, Khalid flexed his stump back and forth as if the sheep's head were singing. "Yes, sir, yes sir, three bags full!"

I just sat there staring at the two strange men sitting in front of me. When the assistant finished singing their eyes lit with merriment and they howled with laughter. They were enjoying themselves immensely and had obviously done this to other visitors before.

Although I was having fun and learning a lot, sitting around the camp became boring. Once, I almost had an opportunity to enter Kashmir with a group of mujahideen. The commander promised that I could go, and I got ready for the trip with about thirty other fighters. As we prepared, one of the young mujahideen started to cry. It was an emotional, conflicting moment for all of us; no one wants to die, but for the mujahideen it is an honor. The young mujahid's crying started what can only be described as a chain reaction, and others started crying. Soon the entire group of thirty was quietly sobbing. When it was time to go I wiped my cheeks and followed the others but was held back by the commander. He did this because the Pakistani ISI didn't want the Indian army to see any foreign mujahideen among the dead, and on that mission there were to be many dead. It turned out that there was a traitor among us. A few days after the group took off, Sikh commandos surrounded them. An enormous firefight erupted, and my young comrades fought until they ran out of ammunition. All but one or two were killed.

But I'd been left behind, and it was starting to irritate me. As time passed, I complained endlessly to Commander Khalid's assistant, because

AFGHANISTAN, PAKISTAN, AND KASHMIR

Khalid had gone elsewhere. When the assistant finally got tired of listening to my constant bitching he told me to get my bags and go down the mountain to the office.

The next morning the guys in the office called Harakat-ul Jihad in Islamabad and I spoke with the man who had traveled with me originally and had acted as my translator. He told me that he had brought my problem up with Mufti Shaheed and that I should come down to talk, so I caught a van to Islamabad the next day.

I expected to see the mufti right away, but instead I was made to wait for three days. On the third day I walked into his office unbidden. Although he was busy speaking to some other people, I asked him what the hell was going on. He looked surprised at my rude entrance, but instead of getting angry he asked me what was wrong, in broken English. One of his other visitors spoke

English and translated for us. When I told him that the guy on the phone had told me to come back to Islamabad to speak with him, the look on his face changed. He immediately called for the guy.

When he came into the office the mufti started speaking to him in a harsh tone. It turned out that he had never spoken to the mufti about my problem and had just made up the stuff about me coming down to Islamabad. After a long conversation, Mufti Shaheed said that if I wanted to fight I could go to Tajikistan, but first I should do more training at one of Harakat-ul Jihad's camps in Afghanistan. This suited me, so I agreed to go to Afghanistan.

A couple of days later a driver showed up. Outside of Islamabad, we stopped at a house, where I met a couple of big, middle-aged African-American Muslims. They were Vietnam vets and were going to go to the camp to teach military techniques like rappelling. The driver from the Harakat-ul Jihad office left, and I waited with the two Americans for their driver. After a couple of hours a white older model Suburban showed up, and we left.

The drive was boring but much more comfortable in the spacious Suburban than in the cramped Pakistani van to Kashmir. When we got to the border of the North-West Frontier Province (NWFP), we were greeted with a big sign in English that said NO FOREIGNERS BEYOND THIS POINT! In the NWFP, a portion of Pakistan governed mainly by Pashtun tribal elders, daily life is marked with tribal rivalries, blood feuds, and constantly changing alliances. Despite the ominous greeting at the border, our driver appeared to have good contacts, and we were able to pass through the checkpoint without any problems. From there we drove to the outskirts of a town called Miram Shah, where we stopped at a compound. Two large crossed AK-47s were painted on the compound's front brick wall, along with the words HARAKAT-UL JIHAD. We stayed the night at the compound and left for the Afghan border the next morning, following a dry riverbed that ran between two mountains.

When we reached the border crossing—nothing more than a mud building with guards loitering around—our driver got out and chatted with the authorities. Harakat-ul Jihad was supposed to have some sort of arrangement with the border guards, but as our driver was speaking to them, one of them saw me. This was two or three years before the Taliban came to power, and any traveler in the NWFP could expect to be robbed, beaten, sodomized, or murdered. The local warlords would sell border crossings and checkpoints to their bandit buddies as a sort of concession, and the bandits would then harass anyone who came along the road. The sodomy had become so prevalent that the locals jokingly referred to it as "teasing." The Taliban eventually came to power in large part because the people of Afghanistan were tired of the constant harassment. The Taliban movement started when some students from a *madrasah*, or religious school, ambushed a particularly heinous checkpoint and hanged the culprits from the barrel of a tank that was parked nearby. But that was still in Afghanistan's future.

The border guard who confronted me was nothing more than a pimply-faced kid with an AK-47. He walked over to the rear passenger door and said something I didn't understand. When I didn't answer, he opened my door and motioned for me to get out. The driver of the Suburban tried to intervene, but the other guard said something to him and he shut up. The pimply kid then motioned for me to walk with him to the mud building.

My eyes adjusted to the light inside the small building. A man who was sleeping on a cot sat up. He was obviously some kind of senior officer, napping on his post. The officer had an exchange with the pimply kid, and, thinking I was an Arab, the officer tried talking to me in Arabic. My cover for the border crossing was that I was from a province in the north of Pakistan where the people spoke what sounded to me like gibberish, so I played dumb. After Arabic, the officer switched to English. He must have sensed a subtle change as he asked questions, because he was more persistent with the English. Once again I played dumb, but this only seemed to annoy him. After a few minutes he hissed something to one of his men, who in turn motioned for me to follow him back to the Suburban. I got in the back seat, the kid got in next to me, and the older guy got into the front and said something to the driver, who turned the vehicle around. Then we headed back toward Miram Shah.

When we reached Miram Shah the two guards escorted us to what was obviously some kind of police station. There were about ten old men with big beards and turbans standing around outside. They all had the traditional shawl wrapped around their shoulders, and I could see AK-47s poking out from underneath. As I passed by I noticed that one of them was eyeballing the two guards. The expression on his face reminded me of an experience I had had back in East San Diego when a cop was roughing up someone on the street.

A man in uniform sat at a desk in the next room. The two other Americans and I sat in chairs opposite him. One of the guards from the border was considerate enough to lean his AK-47 up against the wall next to me, and I started to form a contingency plan in case things went sour.

Without wasting any time, the cop started speaking to us in English. The two black guys played it cool and sat there staring at the ceiling. They didn't appear to be worried about a thing, but I wasn't feeling as confident. I must have been born under an unlucky star, because I've had problems with officials at borders from that day forward. The cop started to direct his attention toward me.

"So," he said, "it is all right if you speak to me in English."

I felt him scanning my face for any kind of reaction, but I just stared at the far wall as though I didn't know he was talking to me.

"It's not as if we are going to torture you or anything if you speak to us in English," which I found peculiar. If the situation hadn't been so grave I would have thought he was trying to imitate a Hollywood villain. I still gave no indication that I understood a word that he was saying.

I was starting to wonder how this would end when the cop's threats became less subtle. I couldn't speak for my two traveling companions, but I wasn't game for not being tortured or anything if I spoke to him in English. As I was debating whether or not to grab the AK-47 leaning against the wall, the door opened and the old man from outside strolled in. He looked at me as though we were in his living room and smiled, then looked over at the cop behind the desk. Until now the cop had been chilly, almost arrogant toward us, but when the old man looked at him his expression began a fascinating transformation. First he became visibly nervous. The old man sat down in an empty chair without saying a word.

The cop summoned another officer, who brought us tea a few minutes later, and we went from torture candidates to tea-party chums. No one said anything. The old man sat there and casually drank his tea. When he was finished he simply got up and walked out. As he passed by me he rested his hand on my shoulder briefly. I took the gesture to signify that we were under his protection.

There wasn't much else for the cop to do with us. To save some kind of face he tried to regain his composure by speaking to us in an official tone. "I am *werry busy* today," he said. "You are free to go, but you *must* go back to Pakistan." And that was that.

The two border guards stayed behind as we got into the Suburban, drove away from the police station, and headed back toward Pakistan. After crossing through the checkpoint with the NO FOREIGNERS sign, we stopped at a small town. The two other guys had a friend who was the head of a *madrasah* inside the town. We ate dinner with them and then discussed our options. We decided to try a different crossing in the morning, but after our talk the two African-American Muslims went off to use a phone, and when they came back they said their boss had called them back to Islamabad. They added something about being sent to Africa, and after saying a quick good-bye they left in the Suburban with the driver. The *madrasah*'s headmaster didn't speak English, and I had no idea how I would get into Afghanistan. Figuring that fate would sort things out in the morning, I went to sleep.

I was napping after the morning prayer when the headmaster motioned for me to follow him to a Toyota pickup in the schoolyard. It had a canvas shell over the bed, and it was full of smiling teenage students, all boys. The headmaster indicated that I should sit all the way in the front of the bed, next to the cab. When I squeezed between the students and sat down, one of them handed me an Afghan shawl to drape over my head. The students giggled and joked with one another as though they were on a field trip to a local museum, but we were headed toward the NWFP checkpoint again. My fellow Americans must have made arrangements for the head of the school to smuggle me back into Miram Shah using the religious students and their teacher as cover. Again we crossed the first checkpoint with no problems, and we were headed to the Harakat-ul Jihad office past Miram Shah. The truck stopped at the compound and let me off. The students smiled as they waved good-bye, and the truck drove off. That left the issue of crossing the Afghan border, but I figured that somebody had that planned out as well.

I'd been sitting in the compound for about an hour when an older Afghan man told me to come with him to an uncovered white Toyota pickup, where he introduced me to his son and his son's friend. Someone from the Harakat-ul Jihad office who spoke a bit of English explained that this man would sneak me across the border. I got in the back with the Afghan and we set off for the dry, dusty riverbed that led to the border. I wondered what I was doing riding in the back of an open pickup, which was even worse than being in the Suburban, but the driver stopped the truck as we came to a bend in the riverbed just before the border post. The older man jumped out and motioned for me to follow him.

A side channel of the riverbed was separated from the main channel by a small bank. I followed the older man as he scrambled over the bank and down the other side. The pickup left shortly after that, and I understood hat we were going to try to sneak past the border post using the riverbank for cover. I remembered from the day before that the border guards were less than a hundred meters away. The dry channel was full of large, smooth stones that made lots of noise as we walked over them, and I wondered how in the hell were we going to pull this off. The older man was running hunched over in front of me when all of a sudden he stopped and looked at me as if he'd just had a brilliant idea. He pulled off his shawl and motioned for me to drape it over my head. That's clever, I thought; instead of letting the border guards think that a foreigner is sneaking over the border, we'll let them think it's two Afghans sneaking over the border. But after about a hundred meters my crafty Afghan guide decided that he looked better with the shawl and took it back from me. He alternated between walking and jogging slowly, but he couldn't make up his mind about whether he wanted me to follow next to him or behind him. He would motion for me to move up next to him, then he would motion for me to get behind. Then he decided that I should wear the shawl after all.

When we reached the point where the border post was directly across from us, I noticed that we would have to crawl if we wanted to stay completely out of sight of the guards, but Afghans would rather get shot than crawl on their bellies. My fearless guide just kept jogging along in front of me, then beside me. When I looked over to the border post, I saw that one of the guards was looking in our direction, but he either didn't see us or didn't care. We continued this way for another half a mile; then all of a sudden the older Afghan man ran out into the middle of the main riverbed and started flapping his arms up and down. I just stared in amazement. The border post back down the riverbed was clearly visible. I hoped that his arm flapping was some kind of signal for his son, who must have been watching from a discreet location, but when I looked up and down the riverbed I didn't see anyone coming. The older guy also looked back and forth, and he didn't seem surprised when the border guards started to jump up and down, pointing in our direction and shouting. Within a minute or so they were in a pickup truck and coming toward us, so he started to walk in the opposite direction.

Just beautiful, I thought. The old tribal leader from the day before had better be hanging out in front of the police station again today.

When the border guards were within a couple hundred meters, the Afghan's son came flying around a bend in the riverbed, and we jumped into the white Toyota and took off.

The truck kicked up a giant plume of dust as the driver raced down the riverbed. The border guards were very close now, and I couldn't help but chuckle to myself. It was like the TV show *Cops*, but set in Afghanistan. I expected them to start shooting at us, but they just kept trying to catch up. A couple of miles later our driver veered off the riverbed onto a dirt road that ran up the bank, and when I l glanced back the border guards had stopped in their tracks. Their sudden reluctance to follow us puzzled me until I looked around and saw a set of mud structures farther up the road. The border guards were afraid to follow us into the training camp of the mujahideen.

Some people called the camp Jihadwal, others called it Khalid Bin Whalid. It was situated in a valley and was actually three separate camps—one camp for the Pakistanis, one for the Afghans, and one for the Arabs. I never imagined at the time that American cruise missiles would strike this valley one day or that I would be invited back by Usama Bin Laden while I was working with the CIA.

Afghanistan

I AWOKE TO SOMEONE gently shaking me.

As salaatul khairune minanaum, the kind voice was telling me. Prayer is better than sleep.

I opened my eyes to see one of the older commanders whom I had met the night before. Most of the new recruits in the camp slept outside in tents, but the commanders had taken a liking to me and had invited me to sleep in one of the only permanent structures in the camp. It was a small building with three rooms, mud walls, and a sod roof. We'd been sleeping in the main room, which was about the size of an average American bedroom. The floor was hard-packed earth, and we slept on wool blankets, shoulder to shoulder like sardines. It wasn't the Hilton, but it beat the hell out of being in the frigid cold outside.

The word *cold* can't begin to describe December in the mountains of Afghanistan. I had experienced cold as a kid in Indiana. I'd even gotten in trouble one time for going out and playing in the middle of a blizzard. But this was a different kind of cold. It seemed to penetrate my skin and bones. Even when the actual temperature wasn't that low it still hurt.

I eagerly got out of bed despite the cold. This was going to be my first full day in Afghanistan, and I didn't want to miss a thing. Answering the call of nature was the first priority on my mind; the night had been so cold that I put off relieving myself till the morning. First I had to get a *loti,* which was sort of like a plastic watering can, and fill it with the freezing cold water from a tank outside the house. I made my way in the dark to the hillside behind the building, where there was a designated "toilet" area. There we could shit anyplace someone else hadn't already gone. In Afghanistan, even outhouses are something to hope for in the future.

It was just before 5:00 A.M. and *Salaatul Fajr,* or the morning prayer, would be made before the first thread of light appeared in the sky. Everyone had to prepare for Salaatul Fajr by performing *wudhuu,* or ablutions. This is a Muslim cleansing ritual where the faithful wash their arms, hands, and feet, rinse their mouths, and wipe their hands over their heads. I'd gone to sleep wearing just about every piece of clothing I'd carried with me, including my big down winter jacket on top of it all. Now I had to peel away enough of the layers in order to roll up my sleeves and start washing for prayers. There were no washing accommodations in the building, so all of the washing had to be done outside. I stripped down, stepped out into the cold, and washed. The freezing water felt like acid as I poured it onto my skin.

The *azan,* or call to prayer, is made before a *jamat,* or group of Muslims, gathered together to pray. The camp woke up about half an hour before the *azan,* then *salaat* (prayer) was performed about fifteen minutes after the call. I had just finished my ablution when the *azan* started. Prayer occurs five times a day, according to Islamic custom, and it was an especially important part of the daily routine for the mujahideen.

The camp was spread out along a valley between two large mountains running from north to south, and a dry riverbed ran through the middle. A few permanent structures dotted the valley, one being the mosque where we prayed. It was a few hundred meters below the commanders' building, between the riverbed and the hillside. When the *azan* sounded over the loudspeakers, the seemingly deserted camp came to life. Mujahideen streamed out of the tents and mud shacks all over the camp to create a sort of rush-hour traffic headed toward the mosque. Some walked and chatted in little groups, while others made their way alone.

Once inside, the mosque looked like any other mosque in the world, with one important exception. Muslims usually empty their pockets when they pray, and before prayer you'll usually see a little pile of car keys or a cell phone next to each person. Here, however, it was an AK-47 or perhaps an old Russian SKS rifle. Some men sat quietly and recited the Qur'an while others said optional prayers before the Salaatul Fajr. Fifteen minutes or so after the call to prayer the Imam would get up and everyone would perform Salaatul Fajr.

The camp would be quiet for at least an hour or so afterward. Many of the mujahideen sat in groups of three or four to recite verses from the Qur'an. The commanders went to discuss their plans for the day, and as time went on I frequently attached myself to this group.

After the groups broke up, most of the mujahideen went to get breakfast at the "chow hall," a large mud structure. Inside were strange-looking earthen ovens with open fire pits. I went inside this place only a couple of times because it gave me the creeps. It seemed like a place where the Sand People in *Star Wars* might like to throw a party, roasting Ewoks before eating them.

The food—if that's what you want to call it—was served outside of this structure. Everyone sat on the ground in front of long plastic sheets and ate from pots of food in the middle. Breakfast was usually bread and *dhal*, crushed lentils with Pakistani spices. It looked and tasted like spicy green porridge, and I hardly ever ate it. Most mornings I would chew on a few pieces of hard bread and smile at everyone as they ate. More often than not, hard bread was all that was served anyway.

Many men would go back to bed after breakfast, but the more enthusiastic would hold an impromptu class and try to get one of the older commanders to teach them something. These sessions were a haphazard basic training, after which the trainees would be packed into Toyota trucks—the unofficial vehicle of Afghanistan—and shipped up to fight the Communists in Tajikistan. The government there was, and still is, among the most repressive in the world. Although most of the country is Islamic, the government was cracking down on Muslims who might offer other citizens a viable alternative to its rule. Russian troops are still in Tajikistan.

The camp commanders were all Soviet-era war veterans who had fought almost ten straight years against the Red Army and kicked ass. Now in 1993, four years after the Russians had left, they were still dedicated to the life of jihad. As I went back up the trail to the commanders' building, I thought about what kind of program I would start. One of the three rooms there was an armory; it was bigger than the sleeping quarters and had no windows. Inside was the most fascinating assortment of weapons that I have ever encountered. One of the walls had racks from floor to ceiling, filled with rows and rows of AK-47s. They were to be issued to the recruits in the event of an attack. The other walls and every bit of available space on the floor were packed with such a wide variety of different weapons that it looked like a firearms museum. In the rifle category there were G3s, FN FALs, bolt-action Enfield 303s, Colt M-16s, WW II-era Russian PPSs, and Dragunov sniper rifles. In the light- and general-purpose machine-gun category there were PKM

7.62 x 54s, FN MAGs, and tripod-mounted Degtyarev 30s. In one corner of the room was an assortment of Russian mortars and grenade launchers. In another there were RPGs—rocket propelled grenades. Every space in between was filled with Russian army ammo crates containing 7.62 x 39s, 7.62 x 54s, and several other types of ordnance. Heavier weapons just lay around in various places outside the building, such as DShK 12.7mm heavy machine guns and Shilka 23mm antiaircraft guns mounted on tripods. Stowed behind the water tank in front of the building was an old Soviet artillery piece, probably a 155.

I'd had a long-standing love for weapons, but now that I had every conceivable variety available to me, I wanted to learn how to use almost any weapon currently manufactured. I wanted to do it all, and this place was ideal for just that. There was no set curriculum here. If you wanted to waste your time, like the guys who went back to bed after breakfast, you could. And if you wanted to benefit from your stay here, you could do that, too.

I sat down with a couple of the commanders and told them what I had in mind. They already liked me, but after I told them what I hoped to get out of the camp, they seemed even more pleased with me. The older commander who had woken me that morning told me that he would be thrilled to share whatever knowledge he had and that he would provide whatever he could to help me accomplish my goals.

I spent the rest of my first day touring the camp with a guide, who told me that an incredible battle had taken place in the valley in 1986 or 1987, when the mujahideen were fighting the Soviets. The Russian army had inserted about three thousand Spetsnaz-aided paratroopers in an attempt to advance all the way to the Pakistani border, just a few kilometers away. About three hundred Pakistani commandos teamed up with five hundred mujahideen and fought the Spetsnaz for twenty-seven days; not a single Russian left the valley alive.

The valley was filled with all kinds of Russian equipment from that era. A Russian military truck sat a few hundred meters down the trail from the building where I slept, next to a small hill. It had a standard six-wheeled troop-carrier chassis with the large box cab often found on special vehicles, like radio trucks. This particular vehicle was outfitted with a full machine shop in the cab. The shop was immaculate and had a drill press, a lathe, and what appeared to be a thorough assortment of other tools and materials to make parts for weapons and vehicles. They could probably have built an AK-47 from scratch, but one day I came across a group of Afghans and Pakistanis who were trying to pry the casings off artillery shells so they could gain access to the explosives. Instead of using the tools from the machine shop, the evil masterminds had gathered an impressive array of rocks and were beating on the ordnance.

Further up the trail was a BRDM armored reconnaissance vehicle, and beyond that was the last building in the camp. My guide told me that the mujahideen who slept there were into special tactics. They were off somewhere in the camp training, so I peeked through one of the windows of their building. I was a little surprised to see five or six 90mm tripod-mounted recoilless rifles around their sleeping area, which was a small room. This would definitely be an interesting group to meet.

Past the last mud building the valley narrowed to a kind of V with steep sides. Before the valley became hard to navigate, there was an opening to a very long tunnel carved into the mountainside. Nobody seemed to know whether the Russians or the mujahideen had carved out this tunnel, but it was evident that the Russians had used it at one time. The tunnel was at least a couple of hundred meters long and filled all the way to the entrance with giant tractorlike tires for the BTR, a common eight-wheeled armored personnel carrier used to transport Russian infantry. They were so new that they still had the little rubber spikes on the treads.

I observed some of the mujahideen in their classes as I wandered around the camp. They would sit on the ground in a loose semicircle around one of the older commanders. One group was learning how to strip an AK-47 in the field. Another group was being instructed in the basics of handling a Russian Makarov pistol. When the *azan* sounded, everyone would drop whatever they were doing and make their way to the mosque.

Not every training camp had a mosque, and a mosque isn't necessary for making prayers. Some of the subjects taught at the camp were how to observe religious duties under battlefield conditions, how to clean yourself when no water was available, what constituted a suitable place to pray, and how to make the five mandatory daily prayers even when under direct fire from an enemy. Islam governs a person's life down to minute details, and jihad is the highest level of faith in Islam. Mujahideen are extremely careful to observe their religious duties.

One of the rules in the camp was that if you repeatedly missed *Salaatul Jama'a*—daily group prayers as opposed to individual ones—the camp commanders would lock you in an old jail for a day that used to house Russian POWs. Everybody in the camp was there by choice and made their prayers willingly—they wouldn't have come for jihad if they didn't pray—so the punishment wasn't severe, it was more of a reminder. While with friends, I went to see what the place was like. It was dug into the side of one of the mountains and had cells with iron bars. A young guy who had missed his prayers on more than one occasion was locked up for the day when I went. The place was dark and dank and gave me the creeps.

Over the next few days I settled into a kind of training program, most of which I devised myself. I attended some of the classes already available, but usually I would make a list of topics that I wanted to study and then bug the hell out of the older commanders until I felt like I was catching on. Most of it was weapons training. I would first study the technical principles of a weapon, observing how it worked and by which action. Then I would study its operation and actually use it. After I could proficiently operate, strip, clean, and maintain the weapon, I would move on to something else. I was eventually able to take almost any manually operated weapon system on the face of the earth—whether I was familiar with it or not—and be able to operate it proficiently, break it down, and reassemble it within five minutes.

In between weapons training I also took advantage of the incredible combat experiences that the older vets had, to focus on tactics. I learned about flanking maneuvers and enfilades. Although conventional armies wouldn't be impressed with the level of training, the instructors taught knife techniques and hand-to-hand combat. Most likely, they'd read about it the day before, or had once seen an instructional video about judo. I also took advantage of the opportunity to learn about counterintelligence. A gang of two or three would practice tailing someone, subtly "passing the baton" from one to another until the target noticed he was being tailed. This would prove useful to me later on.

One of the classes was about conventional and improvised explosives. It was during one of these explosives classes that I would see the first death of a fellow mujahid. One of the older guys was teaching a small group about the construction and use of improvised booby traps. He'd made a small bomb using the explosives salvaged from an old Russian artillery shell. Everyone took cover as the teacher attempted to detonate the bomb, but nothing happened. After waiting a moment to avoid a delayed explosion, Khalid—I will never forget his name—walked up to the bomb and picked it up. He had just started to say something when it went off. Everyone instinctively ducked. When they looked up, Khalid was cut nearly in two.

Islamic burial rituals are very simple and rapid, compared to those of the West. But the burial of a *shaheed*, or martyr, is even simpler and more rapid than that of a regular Muslim. Normally when a Muslim person dies, his or her body goes through the purification process and is buried within twenty-four hours. First, the body is washed in a certain way. The stomach is pressed on to force any waste out, after which cotton is inserted into all of the body's openings and the mouth is tied shut with a strip of cloth. Then perfumed oils are applied to the body and it is wrapped in a white cloth. All the Muslims of his or her community gather together and perform *Salaatul Janazah*, the funeral prayer, before the body is placed in the grave.

But the burial for a *shaheed* is different. One of the hadiths, or sayings of the prophet Muhammad, states that when a mujahid who leaves his home to go out in the path of jihad dies or is killed before returning, he will be accepted by God as a *shaheed*. It is believed that *shuhadaa* (plural of *shaheed*) go directly to Heaven upon their death. All previous sins are forgiven, so there is no need for a funeral prayer or for the body to be washed. The usual practice is to bury the mujahid immediately and in his uniform.

But it really all depends on time and circumstance, and only Allah knows who is a martyr and who isn't. We weren't on the front lines, so the elders of the camp decided to go ahead and wash Khalid's body and make the funeral prayer, even though we considered his death to be that of a martyr.

The body was taken to the room in the commanders' building where I slept. Outside, a temporary screen was set up to cover the body as it was washed and prepared for burial. Muslims value modesty even in death, and the screen was to prevent people from seeing the private parts of the deceased person, whose body was to be washed only by someone of the same sex.

After being prepared and wrapped in a white winding sheet, the body was placed on a bier that resembled an old wooden four-poster bed that had been turned upside down. He was taken to the edge of the large field at the base of the camp. Easily over two hundred men had lined up for the prayer, which was a very large congregation for a regular daily prayer. The two prayers are similar, but the difference is that after the first *raka'at,* or section, a prayer is said for the Prophet. The third raka'at asks Allah to have mercy on the deceased, and the fourth asks Allah to have mercy on the world.

After the prayer was finished, one of the older commanders gave a brief talk with a bullhorn, saying something to the effect that this was the way of jihad, and that when your time is up, it's up. Our brother Khalid had fought the might of the Soviet military without so much as ever receiving a scratch, but today his number had obviously come up. When the commander was finished, Khalid's friends saluted him by firing short bursts with their AKs.

The body was to be buried a half a mile or so away, at the edge of an area that was used as a kind of loose rifle range. I had been practicing advanced tactics there that very morning. I forget the reason why, but everyone wanted to carry the body to the grave, and only about eight guys could fit under the wooden bier. So in the light of the late afternoon sun, more than two hundred men shuffled along, kicking up a large cloud of dust. When the eight pallbearers were pushed out of the way, they jogged around to the back of the procession, so that eventually everyone worked their way to the front at least once.

A Muslim's grave might seem unusual to Westerners. It looks like a standard grave but no coffin is used, and a small niche is carved out of the side facing the *qibla,* or direction of the holy city of Mecca. The body is interred on its right side facing Mecca. The niche is then sealed off from the main part of the grave, and then the grave is filled in with earth.

As the teacher was placed in the grave and it was sealed with wooden planks, I bid him farewell but couldn't help but feel the irony of all this. Here I was just entering the life of jihad, and here this man was just leaving it. I wondered about my fate—what would become of me in this life of never-ending wars and conflicts? Would I lie bleeding to death on some forgotten battlefield someday? Or would I stand as an old man in front of the graves of the many fallen brothers and comrades that were sure to come over time, and ask them how they fared on their journeys into the next life? The contemplation of fate can easily become overwhelming, and it might have been too much for me had I known at the time that within weeks I would be sitting next to another body of another fallen brother, this time his death giving me life.

◆

Life in the camp became routine. I started to comprehend and speak Urdu, the language of the Pakistanis, and continued to learn the skills of war. But I was suffering from the ill effects of life in Afghanistan. By now I wasn't eating enough to keep a child alive, let alone myself. To begin with, there wasn't enough food to go around. To make matters worse, I couldn't stomach what little there was. The dysentery I'd contracted in Pakistan was starting to catch up with me again. Because I suffered from constant diarrhea, I was succumbing to dehydration, and I couldn't take in enough fluids because the water was what caused the diarrhea in the first place. Sometimes the camp "store" had some small food items which probably kept me alive. Every few days I was able to buy an egg or two and maybe a potato. Some of the guys noticed how bad I was looking and would try to bring me an egg when they could. It was about all that I could manage to hold in. At some point I must have become delirious with hunger. A couple of mongooses would occasionally poke around behind the building that I slept in. One day I was so hungry that I grabbed an AK off the front porch and began shooting at them. I chased them all the way up the hill behind the building, firing an entire magazine at them without any luck.

To me this was rational. I was hungry and wanted to eat. But the older commanders didn't see it that way. They insisted that I visit the camp doctor. After checking me out, the doctor informed me that I wasn't in good shape and recommended that I go back to Harakat-ul Jihad's headquarters in Islamabad. This wasn't acceptable; I'd come to Afghanistan for more than training. The leader of Harakat-ul Jihad back in Islamabad had promised me that I would be sent to the front in Tajikistan after training. I wasn't about to let something silly like malnutrition, dehydration, and chronic diarrhea stop me from my goals. I decided to tough it out.

After a while, a man named Umar showed up. He was Pakistani by blood but had been born and raised in the United Kingdom. It had been quite some time since I had been able to have a decent conversation in English, and his arrival cheered me up considerably. We got along well together right from the beginning and were side by side throughout the rest of my stay in the camp.

Umar was an interesting guy. He wore a full beard—as we all did—and he had bulging forearms and was taller than the average Pakistani. He was a devout Muslim, but back in Britain, he'd been a professional arm wrestler. I thought that many of the guys in the camp were a little soft, but Umar was a tough guy. He also had Western sensibilities, and between the two of us we never ran out of ideas about how to stay busy.

Umar and I were probably a source of entertainment for some in the camp as we scurried around on our daily escapades. If we weren't bugging the guy at the armory who handed out the weapons to give us something bigger, we might be practicing our surveillance techniques by following an unwitting fellow student around the camp. Sometimes an explosion and a plume of smoke would reveal our whereabouts as we detonated homemade bombs behind one of the hills.

All in all, our daily routine was more comical than terrifying. Afghan traders used the dry riverbed that ran through the valley toward Pakistan's North-West Frontier Province to transport their goods to Miram Shah, the town just inside the NWFP border. They still used camels, which made their caravans resemble a scene from the Middle East. Umar and I found a ravine off the riverbed that we used as a pistol training area, and when we heard the caravans coming we would pretend that they were an enemy convoy. We would rush around to set up an ambush, and when the caravan of camels got close—usually led by some old guy with a giant beard and an even bigger turban—we would jump out from behind the rocks with sticks in our hands and make shooting noises. The old guys would just stare at us in bewilderment.

But not all of our training was childish. Sometimes Umar and I would sweep through the camp at night pretending to silently kill everyone along the way. As we "killed" individuals, we would get them to cooperate and play dead until we were finished. One night we took out a good portion of the camp before being discovered. Another night we talked to the ominous group of guys who lived in the last building of the camp. For the most part, they just stuck to themselves. At night, after the camp generator was shut down, they even guarded their own little area in shifts and wouldn't let anyone come near their building. So Umar and I decided that it would be a good idea to test our skills with these guys.

We agreed to a contest: if we could dispose of their sentries and take out the rest of the house, then we won. If they discovered us first or were able to repulse the attack, they won. Whoever lost had to take a shower at night in the freezing cold water, which I had already learned to fear. The only rules were that Umar and I had to strike before sunup and that it had to be at least partially stealthy; we couldn't just shoot a rocket and level the whole building. The building was backed up against a small outcropping of rocks, and if you were careful you could get onto the roof. Our game plan would be for one of us to approach the building from the rear and take out the roving sentry. The other one would then enter the door of the building overtly, posing as the sentry while the one on the roof would swing down and rush in behind the first, firing on everybody.

In the end there really wasn't a winner. We thought that we took out the sentry with a head wound from my mock silenced weapon, but he insisted that he was still capable of sounding an alarm.

After a while, the camp commanders started to get frustrated with our little circus show. We ignored their orders regularly, and we were always making a ruckus somewhere. One time we even organized an arm-wrestling contest in front of the mosque. Islam doesn't prohibit arm wrestling; on the contrary, sports like that are encouraged. The spectacle we created, however, irked the older men in the camp. They didn't appreciate the sight of a bunch of otherwise quite religious guys jumping up and down as they cheered for their friends who were arm-wrestling in front of the mosque.

This tension didn't go away. The older commanders started to subtly disrupt our little show by restricting our ability to check out weapons from the armory. When we tried to exchange a PKM machine gun for a couple of AK-47s, the guy at the armory told us that we couldn't have anything else. Umar asked him who had said this, and he replied that it was one of the commanders who had been giving us dirty looks lately. We left without turning in the PKM.

Nothing in these camps could ever be taken at face value, and Umar himself was an example. I'd assumed from the beginning that Umar had come to the camp the way I had, through the auspices of Harakat-ul Jihad. But when the tensions started to grow with the commanders he told me that he was affiliated with another Pakistani group, which I later found out was Harakat-ul Ansar, and that he was here on an exchange program of sorts. Harakat-ul Ansar was funded by Usama Bin Laden and was the same group that John Walker Lindh would later belong to. By running around with Umar and causing a ruckus, we were creating tension with the Harkat-ul Jihad guys. I didn't care really, but at least it was starting to make sense.

The next morning Umar and I decided to show the older commanders that we didn't like the disruption in our routine. Right after breakfast we set up the PKM on one of the hills that ran up the side of the valley. We'd used this hill before to practice long-range fire by shooting over the camp and across to the other side of the valley. There was nothing directly below us except the path that led from the commanders' building to the mosque.

Due to the lack of organization and supervision in the camp, it wasn't uncommon for people to do things like sit on one hill and shoot at rocks on another hill. I rested the PKM on a little pile of rocks and began firing across the valley. The commanders usually walked up to their building as a group after breakfast and were due to arrive shortly. After a few minutes Umar saw them coming and pointed. When they got a little closer I stopped firing to feed a new belt into the PKM and let them pass beneath us. I started firing again after they'd moved past. When none of them were looking back, I swung the barrel of the PKM over and fired a burst of rounds right up to within a few feet of the last guy in the group. The commanders jumped a little when the rounds kicked up the dirt behind them. They immediately glanced up at us with very sour looks. Umar and I both just smiled.

After that incident the tension really started to mount. I became increasingly frustrated, because I should have been sent to Tajikistan by now. Every day a fresh group of recruits left for Tajikistan, but every day the commanders had a new excuse about why I shouldn't go. Although he wouldn't tell me why, Umar was also getting frustrated over something. Both of us were getting into arguments with the commanders almost daily. When we finally managed to exchange the PKM for a couple of AK-47s, we carried them with us twenty-four hours a day.

Umar and I were sitting on the firing range near Khalid's grave a few days after the PKM incident. A group of guys were climbing the hill on the opposite side of the valley with an RPG, but we didn't think much of it. They were probably a hundred meters higher, and we figured that they were going to fire across the valley. But they also had something else in mind. I watched with mild interest as they fired the first round across the valley. I have always enjoyed the sound of an RPG. It makes a tremendously loud, hollow boom as the rocket leaves the tube, like a shotgun but ten times louder. Then the rocket makes a shrieking sound as it flies through the air, which is followed by a sharp boom at impact.

The first round impacted directly across the valley, about a hundred meters above us. Although that would probably have been a totally unacceptable distance by Western military standards, it didn't bother us in the slightest. What did bother us was when the next round slammed into the hill about twenty meters in front of us. First we felt the concussion of the blast, and then a shower of dirt fell on us. Had it been an antipersonnel round instead of a HEAT (high-explosive anti-tank), we would have been shredded with shrapnel. Either way, the point was well taken. Sooner or later, the arguments and tensions were going to escalate.

A couple of days later, while Umar was off somewhere in the camp, I was sitting near the commander's building when a cloud of dust appeared at the riverbed behind a vehicle that was traveling up the dirt road. Visitors didn't ordinarily go past the lower part of the camp to the commander's building, so I was a little surprised when a clean shaven Pakistani with a fresh *shawal kamece* came striding up the trail. He walked by me, then paused for a second. Instead of just coming straight out and asking if I was the American in camp, he decided that he would rely on his years of training as an agent for Pakistan's Inter-Services Intelligence agency, or ISI.

"Please be excusing me sir," he said in English with a cheesy Pakistani accent, "You don't happen to know anyone here who speaks English, do you?"

"No," I replied in Urdu. He cocked his head, confused.

"Are you sure?" he asked again in English.

"Very sure," I said in Urdu.

Obviously his whole game wasn't working the way he had envisioned it, and now he looked really confused.

"Where are you from?" he asked in English.

"What?" I said in Urdu. "I don't understand what you are saying."

"But you speak English, don't you?" he said.

"No, I don't speak English," I told him in Urdu.

"Well, then how are you answering my questions, because they are in English?" he asked.

"I'm not answering your questions, I'm telling you that I don't speak English."

"But you just did it!" he said.

"Did what?" I asked.

"I asked you a question in English and you answered."

"Yeah, but I answered in Urdu, so that means that I don't speak English."

"Aha," he exclaimed, "so you do speak English!"

I had seen and hidden from ISI agents since the first camp in Kashmir, but this was the first time that I had been confronted by one. I could have tried to avoid him, but no one had seen it fit to warn me that he was coming, so I didn't really care at this point. Once I stopped playing with the ISI agent, he started to ask me questions. He asked if I was American and I replied that I was a mujahid. He tried to pin me to the American issue, but I simply told him that he was in a camp for mujahideen; it wasn't important where I was from. He continued to ask more questions but eventually just left me alone.

I talked with Umar about the situation over the next few days. We'd benefited from the camp, but I wanted to call it quits if I had to sit around and wait instead of making jihad somewhere. Umar confided that he was here because he was planning to do something big. A group of British tourists or journalists was going to be in Kashmir. Someone in Harakat-ul Ansar wanted him to conduct a hostage operation there, and Umar asked if I would stick around long enough to join him. The idea of taking hostages, however, didn't appeal to me. Revolutionary groups and even governments resort to kidnapping, but it wasn't what I'd come to do. I wanted to make jihad on the front lines.

One day everything came to a boil. Umar and I sat down with the commanders and had a very candid discussion. I told them that I didn't care for the way they were treating me and that I hadn't came all the way from America to sit around and watch other mujahideen train and fight in Tajikistan. I tried to get a straight answer out of them about when they would send me to fight, but they were inscrutable. I was very angry by this time and made no attempts to conceal my frustration. Looking back on the situation, I think I pushed the camp commanders too far. They didn't conceal their anger either and told me to hit the road if I didn't like the way things were going. The catch was this: they wouldn't stop me, but neither would they help me in any way.

Getting past the NWFP tribal police and into Afghanistan with Harakat-ul Jihad's blessings had been dangerous and difficult. If they washed their hands of me and I left now—friendless, penniless, and foreign—getting out of Afghanistan alive would be next to impossible. I should have apologized to the commanders and continued to stick it out in the camp, but I was young and hotheaded and told them good-bye. I didn't give a fuck, either.

After the meeting I went to pack my things. Umar followed and told me he'd try to help me get across the border. He intimated that he had some sort of plan, but it later turned out that he was going to risk his own ass just so that I didn't have to go it alone. Umar and I said good-bye to a few of our friends in the camp, shouldered our backpacks, and headed down the dirt road to the riverbed that ran to the border where we'd made our mock ambushes on the camel trains. Along the way we talked about our options for crossing. Finally, Umar came up with a plan. He would play the Qur'an over his portable cassette player.

"And then?" I asked.

"And then *what*?" Umar said.

"What's next?"

"That's it." But Umar went on to elaborate, saying that we would just turn the Qur'an up loud and walk through the checkpoint. If the NWFP police tried to stop us, we would ignore them and keep walking. If they wanted to shoot us, then that's just the way it would be. Given the situation the plan didn't seem like the worst of our options, and the whole scenario was almost amusing. Umar and I joked about our plan as we walked down the road.

Shortly after we reached the riverbed, a flatbed truck came down the road from the camp. At first I thought that maybe the commanders had sent someone after us, but when the truck neared us it stopped, and we saw that no one on the truck had a gun. The driver, one of the guys from the camp, told us to get on the flatbed if we wanted a ride. We went to the rear to hop on and saw a body wrapped in a white winding sheet lying on top of a bier—the same one we'd used to take Khalid's body to the grave. Four or five other guys were also sitting in the back. Umar asked them what had happened. They explained that as we were leaving the camp a group of students had been out running in the riverbed on the other side of the camp. One of the students had fallen down and never gotten up. He simply fell over as he was running, and by the time the camp doctor got to him he was dead. One of the guys pulled the sheet back so that I could see his face. It was the young man whom I had seen locked up for missing prayers. They were taking his body to his family, over the border in Pakistan.

Riding in the back of the truck with his still-warm body, I couldn't help but wonder about fate. A few moments ago Umar and I weren't sure if we would make it through the day; now this brother's death would get us through the checkpoint. The people of Afghanistan respect the dead and grieving, and even the NWFP police wouldn't question anyone on a truck carrying a cadaver.

As we approached the checkpoint I simply wrapped a shawl around my face and put my head down. The NWFP police said a few words to the driver but barely glanced at the back of the truck when they saw the body. Less than a minute later we were on our way to the Harakat-ul Jihad office in Miram Shah. Although relieved to be over the border, I couldn't muster a cheery mood as we rode through the province with our morbid lifesaver.

The office in Miram Shah either didn't know or didn't care about my problems with the commanders back at the camp, so Umar talked with them and then told me that they would give me a ride back to the main office in Islamabad that evening. Umar asked again if I would go along for the Kashmir operation, but I said that I wasn't interested. When the truck was ready to leave I told Umar good-bye, wondering if I would ever see him again.

The first couple of days back in Islamabad were confusing. No one at the office wanted to give me any straight answers about what was going on, and my translator from the Kashmir trip (whom Mufti Shaheed had rebuked earlier) had an attitude with me. After about three days I finally talked to Mufti Shaheed. He didn't seem to be screwing around with me intentionally; rather, it appeared that no one in Harakat-ul Jihad knew if they were coming or going. There was a wide gap between what people said or intended to do and what actually got accomplished. Mufti Shaheed promised to send me to Tajikistan, and although I doubted it would ever come to pass I decided to stick around the office for a while. A couple of days later, events I had no control over would lead me in a different direction.

I'd been running every morning after prayers to stay fit and get out of the office. I would go to a park near the Harakat-ul Jihad office where the cricket players exercised. Islamabad is cold in the morning in winter, and I'd see the cricket players through the dense morning fog that hung over the field. The air in Islamabad always had a peculiar burning smell from the countless fires all over the city. People burned their trash and made fires to warm up or cook their food.

One morning I woke up and almost had a fit. As I came out of my sleep for the morning prayer, I lay there for a minute. When I tried to sit up, I found that my knees were extremely painful, swollen, and literally locked stiff; I couldn't move them an inch. The guys at the office seemed concerned, but it was two full days before I could convince them to take me to a hospital.

At the hospital the doctor jammed an extremely large syringe into one of my knees but came out with nothing; he informed me that I was suffering from "acute arthritis." The pain and stiffness became worse, so the next day I went to a better hospital. This time a doctor stuck a syringe into the right place in one of my knees and pulled out two or three vials worth of yellow fluid. I never did quite understand what was wrong with my knees, but it took a couple of weeks before I could even start to walk again.

By this time I'd had enough. I was ready to go back to America, only I didn't have a dollar to my name. I was so desperate that I would have gone to a terrorist organization with limitless finances to help me get back to the States, but such things exist only in the minds of "experts" on terrorism. Instead, I called my father and begged him to buy me a ticket home.

I left Pakistan defeated and disillusioned. Although I had learned a great deal about myself and about the world in my time away from America, I had never come close to my goal, which was to become a *shaheed*. Umar, also known as Ahmed Omar Saeed Sheikh, conducted his Kashmir operation in 1994 but was captured by Indian authorities and incarcerated in Bombay. He was shot, and as a result of improper medical care, he had lost the use of his arm. He was freed on January 1, 2000, when an Indian Airlines jetliner from Kathmandu bound for New Delhi was hijacked. As part of the Taliban-brokered deal, he was released in Afghanistan. At this writing he is on trial in Karachi for the kidnapping of a *Wall Street Journal* reporter named Daniel Pearl, who was abducted in Pakistan and killed.

Although my father helped me get a ticket back to San Diego, once I was home he now treated me as though I had a communicable disease, and the people at my old refuge, the mosque, were only slightly more receptive.

Although American Muslims weren't then in full denial of the jihad, as they are currently, I'd become someone to avoid. I'd begun to feel completely alienated when I got a letter from Tammy, an old girlfriend. We hadn't talked in over a year, but she had been looking for me ever since. The day after I called her I was on a bus bound for Arizona. I stayed with her for about a month, and in time she converted to Islam and we wed according to Islamic custom back in San Diego.

We lived near the mosque, where Tammy changed her name to Sumaya. She was befriended by the women in the Somalian community and was happy there. I worked for a while building custom yachts for an old friend's company. We went on like this for about a year, but I wanted to get back to the jihad.

First Trip to Chechnya

1995-96

THE FIRST TIME I HEARD OF the little republic of Chechnya was when I opened a newsmagazine and saw a picture of a Russian soldier in a muddy foxhole on the outskirts of Grozny. He was sitting behind a weapon that I was all too familiar with, a PKM light machine gun. The Chechens were trying to establish a breakaway republic in a region that the Russians felt was strategically sensitive, and the Russian army was poised to invade. There was no mention that the Chechens were Muslim, or that the Russians were committing atrocities as they smashed tiny Chechnya to pieces, or that the war was a jihad. But the bearded rebel soldiers looked to me like mujahideen, and I had a feeling about the place. As I read and reread the article, I knew somehow that Chechnya would haunt me for the rest of my days.

Soon after, I saw Muhammad Zaky. He'd been upset about the way I'd handled the trip to Bosnia, but he wasn't the kind of man to hold a grudge. He told me about the situation in Chechnya and said he was going there soon.

About a month later, in March 1995, I ran into my Pakistani friend Abbas, who asked if I had heard the news about Muhammad Zaky. He'd been killed in Chechnya. I was in shock. I'd just talked to him and didn't even know yet that he had left. Although we'd had our differences, he was a beautiful man and I'd admired him greatly. He was everything I could only hope to be and had now achieved what I had tried for unsuccessfully—martyrdom. I cried for three days, then made a vow that I would go to Chechnya.

Over the next month or so I began talking with a man named Kiffah. Kiffah was an associate of Muhammad Zaky's and was beginning to take over his work using Zaky's organization, American World Wide Relief. Kiffah was planning to send a shipment of humanitarian aid to Chechnya, and I asked him if I could go with the shipment. It took me a while to convince him, but he finally agreed. I went on many road trips with Kiffah as he raised money for humanitarian aid in Chechnya. We visited mosques up and down

California, showing videos and speaking about Chechnya. Kiffah could collect up to $40,000 at one time at some of the mosques, and he was very careful about how the money was used. He knew what I didn't back then—that the FBI had it out for Islamic groups, no matter how legitimate they were. For this reason he wouldn't even pay for my ticket to Chechnya with money from the mosques. Instead, he collected money from friends. The money he collected from the mosques was used strictly to buy such things as medicine and food for the people of Chechnya and to fund relief projects there.

I considered Abbas a close friend. I had first met him through another friend, Attiquallah, an Afghan who had fought under the legendary Afghan commander Golbudeen Hikmartry during the war with the Soviets. This was back in the golden age of the twentieth-century jihad, when people like Attiquallah could come to America after fighting heroically against the Soviets and put bumper stickers on their cars that read I SUPPORT THE AFGHAN MUJAHIDEEN.

Abbas was over six feet tall and probably 250 pounds. He was from an extremely rich Pakistani family that owned a marble factory in Peshawar. Abbas had come to America because of an incident with another prominent family back in Peshawar. He'd killed a member of the other family, which had started a blood feud, and his father had sent him to America to avoid the inevitable reprisal.

Abbas always talked about the jihad, but he'd never participated. He'd grown up in Peshawar, just over the border from the Soviet-Afghan war, which was raging during the 1980s, but had never joined the fight. This concerned me about him at first, but I figured, Who am I to judge?

Supposedly, Abbas hadn't gone to join the jihad during the war in Bosnia because he was waiting for U.S. citizenship and the American passport that came with it. Now he told me that his citizenship was about to go through and that he would follow me to Chechnya in three weeks. Because he would be fighting with me in Chechnya, we decided that it would be best for my wife, Sumaya, to go to Pakistan to live with his family, who had a house the size of a small fortress, surrounded by a high wall and guard towers. During my stay in Chechnya Sumaya did go to Peshawar to stay with Abbas's family, but three months later she was back in Arizona with her mother. At the time I didn't know why she left Pakistan, but if I had known I would have thought twice about my relationship with Abbas. Abbas promised to look after Sumaya until she left for Pakistan, but as soon as soon as I was gone he started coming on to her. Sumaya reprimanded him and left it at that, but Abba's wife called the family and told them that Sumaya had come on to Abbas. As a result, Abbas' family treated Sumaya poorly. Abbas never went to Chechnya that year.

I was ready to go by the beginning of June 1995. I was excited to be going and had purchased all of the equipment I would need for the trip. Sumaya didn't say much about my leaving. She knew that it was something required by our faith and, aside from the fact that she would miss me, I think she supported the idea. I would be leaving from Los Angeles and traveling first to Newark, New Jersey. Kiffah wanted me to stop there and meet with a woman called Umme Muhammad, who was coordinating humanitarian aid for Chechnya. Her father was a Chechen field commander and religious scholar, and her husband was a fighter. Kiffah told me that she had some boxes that I would be taking to Chechnya with me and also some things for her father. I said good-bye to Sumaya, and Abbas drove me from San Diego to Los Angeles to catch my flight.

Once in New Jersey I found that "some" boxes were actually twelve big boxes, which I would be carrying as far as Azerbaijan, after which someone else would get them into Chechnya. Most of the boxes contained medical supplies and items to be used in hospitals in Chechnya. Umme Muhammad also gave me a small plastic bag that had personal items for her father, along with some letters for him. I stayed the night with a local Muslim guy in Newark and then was off for Istanbul the next day.

On the way to the airport I wondered how I was supposed to get twelve boxes plus my own luggage onto the airplane, but it turned out that Umme Muhammad knew somebody who worked for Turkish Airlines who could get everything checked in without any extra charge or hassle. She also gave me some final instructions and the names of contacts in Istanbul and Azerbaijan.

When I arrived in Istanbul, a Chechen picked me up at the airport. The Chechens have a vast diaspora in the area as a result of the reign of Josef Stalin, who murdered thousands of people and deported hundreds of thousands of others during World War II. Many Chechens live in Turkey, Jordan, and elsewhere. Their fight for an independent republic was caused in part by this diaspora, because they wanted a homeland.

The Chechen man who picked me up lived in Istanbul, where I stayed for a couple of days before going on to Azerbaijan. Later on I discovered that he and his brother were major players in the Chechen war. They'd originally dealt with Muhammad Zaky before he was killed, but the contact had continued through Kiffah and Umme Muhammad.

We were just passing the coastline of the Caspian Sea when our plane lined up for its final approach. As we descended I could start to make out details on the ground. Even from the air it was apparent that Azerbaijan was a very poor county. I felt a sense of exhilaration as we descended toward our destination. I would experience this feeling many times over the years just before reaching a war, but none of them were as intense as the day I flew into Azerbaijan, bound for Chechnya.

I found the starkness and roughness of Azerbaijan shocking. The airport terminal looked like some kind of weird postapocalyptic outpost. The center of the terminal was a half-finished dome built from concrete slabs resting on a rusted steel skeleton. A rusting old crane stood over the steel and concrete like a sentinel. I looked around, almost expecting a character from *Mad Max* to appear.

As I entered the terminal with the other passengers, I felt out of place in the ill-fitting suit that Umme Muhammad had forced me to wear. Somehow she'd thought it would conceal the fact that I had a bald head and a red beard that went all the way down my chest. But in reality the suit made me look like somebody trying to hide something.

I was nervous about the customs officers. I was traveling with twelve boxes of equipment, a helmet, body armor, and night-vision goggles, but I didn't have a visa for Azerbaijan. As I came up to the customs officer, I saw two men who fit Umme Muhammad's description standing to the side. One was tall and had a red beard, and the other was a shorter Sudani with a ball cap and glasses. The Sudani tapped the customs officer on the shoulder as I presented my passport. The officer put it into his shirt pocket while the Sudani motioned for me to follow him. He spoke a little English and introduced himself as Abu Saifudeen. His associate spoke perfect English because he came from Irvine, California, and was working for Kiffah here in Baku. We walked to the baggage-claim area, where Abu Saifudeen grabbed four or five baggage handlers.

Chechnya and Surrounding Areas

As the luggage from the plane started coming around on the raggedy carousel, I pointed out all of the boxes that were ours. After getting all of the boxes off and stacked on the carts, we headed for the parking lot. In Azerbaijan you have to put your luggage through an X-ray machine before leaving the airport. When I saw this I thought that we were going to have some problems, but Abu Saifudeen motioned for the guys with the carts to go around the machine. I was impressed; he obviously had the right connections here in Azerbaijan.

As we drove toward the city of Baku I was shocked by the bleakness. Everything was constructed from unfinished concrete. We drove to a one-bedroom apartment, where I would spend the next two weeks with five Arabs. We were forbidden to go outside because we were obviously mujahideen, and the local cops would either shake us down for coffee money or do worse. One morning as I was preparing to throw my daily fit for being cooped up two weeks instead of going to Chechnya, we heard a knock on the apartment door. It was Abu Saifudeen, the guy who had gotten me through Azeri customs. After talking to some of the guys in the apartment in Arabic, he looked over at me.

"So, Mr. Mujahid," he said in English with a heavy Arab accent, "are you ready for your big trip to Chechnya?"

"Don't play with me," I said.

"What do you mean?" he said. He didn't seem to understand.

"Never mind. When am I going to Chechnya?"

"I just told you, now."

"Seriously? You mean right now?"

"Yes, of course. Are you ready?"

"Let's get out of here," I said.

I called my wife, Sumaya, to say a final good-bye and make sure that she was okay. She had news, too. She had just found out that she was pregnant with our first child, Asiya. I didn't know what to say or think. I wasn't going to scrub going into Chechnya, but it wasn't easy to continue on. I told Sumaya that everything would be all right and that I would see her again someday, insha'Allah—if Allah willed it.

Abu Saifudeen took me in his Lada Niva, a compact Russian SUV, to a house on the other side of town. There we met three Arabs who would also be going to Chechnya. Two were from Saudi Arabia and one was from Yemen. Abu Jaffar, the Yemeni, was a little guy, probably not more than five foot seven and not even 150 pounds. He was someone I was to become familiar with in Chechnya; he would eventually become a principal officer under Ibn-ul Khattab, the legendary Arab field commander. The other two guys were from the holy city of Mecca. Of the four of us who made the trip into Chechnya that day, I am the only one left alive.

We left Baku full of excitement on a beautiful, warm morning with no clouds in the sky. As Baku disappeared behind us, the van filled with laughter and the sounds of Arabic *nashids,* songs about jihad. We traveled north along the coast, with the Caspian Sea on our right and a plain that stretched into mountains on our left. When we reached the Azeri police checkpoints, our Chechen guides were able to get us through with ease.

We didn't have any problems until the early afternoon. The road we had been traveling on crossed the border into Dagestan, but instead we took another route northwest toward the mountains to an easier border crossing. We'd been driving through the mountains for about an hour when a car approached from the opposite direction. None of us thought anything of it, but as it went by we saw that the driver was a uniformed Azeri cop with three guys in plainclothes. When he saw the three Arabs and me in the back of the van, he did a quick U-turn. He drove up next to us and motioned for the Chechen driver to stop.

At first it seemed like he was just like any other Azeri cop who wanted a quick bribe, but then he started to get rough with the Chechens. He opened the side door of the van and stuck his head in. Of the four Arabs and myself, he decided to pick on me. He yelled at me for my documents. The Chechens said something to him in Russian, but he ignored them and yelled at me again. My passport was back in Baku for safekeeping, so I just stared at him with a blank look on my face.

The cop was either stupid or overly brave, because he leaned most of the way into the back of the van. He was getting pissed over my stupid act. The three guys in plainclothes sitting in his car appeared to just be friends who were riding around with him. Meanwhile, the Chechens had gotten out of our van and were standing behind the cop, trying to calm him down. I was a little surprised at the cop's anger. It looked as if he was going to try to drag me out of the van at any moment. The guys didn't know it, but back in Baku I had strapped a knife to my ribs, under my shirt. The cop was putting himself in the worst position possible, and I readied myself to stab him in the neck if he tried to grab me.

At that moment one of the Chechens touched him on his back to try to calm him down. He swung around and tried to draw his Makarov pistol. Russian police holsters are big leather affairs with a silly fastener on the flap, and he was having trouble getting it undone. Luckily the Chechens were able to calm him down a little before he got the holster unfastened. After a discussion with the cop, our driver asked me in broken English if I had any kind of documents at all. The only thing I had on me was a cheesy fake I.D. card from American World Wide Relief. I handed it to the Chechens, who pulled the cop to the side. After about ten minutes they shook hands, and he walked to his car and left. It turned out that our Chechen guides had given the cop fifty U.S. dollars and that was that. Maybe the cop used the fake I.D. as some sort of pretext to inflate the price.

We drove on through the mountains for about another hour. After crossing a river that looked as if it was going to wash us downstream, we came across a group of what appeared to be Azeri soldiers. But on closer examination I realized they were Russians; we'd crossed the border into Dagestan. The two Chechens stopped the van, and when the soldiers started to walk toward us I thought we were in for big trouble. But when our driver got out and shook hands with them, I realized that we were in a world where nothing is what it appears to be. I'd learn this lesson over and over again, and it would prove invaluable in the future dealings I would have with my CIA handlers.

The two Chechens walked up a small hill with a Russian officer. The rest of us sat in the back of the van, staring at one another and not really knowing what to think. The Russian soldiers stood around and talked with each other, occasionally glancing at us. After about twenty minutes our driver came down from the small hill and told the four of us to follow him back up the hill. We stood in front of the Russian officer without a clue as to what was going on. The two Chechens talked with him back and forth, but the officer kept gesturing toward me. Finally our driver pulled out $700 and gave it to the officer. After pocketing the money the officer smiled and patted me on the shoulder and said something in Russian.

As we walked back to the van, one of the Chechens translated what the officer had said: "Have a good time in Chechnya." He went on to explain that because of my build and my American combat boots, the Russian officer had thought that I was some kind of mercenary or something. He thought that the other mujahideen were Arab cannon fodder, so they weren't worth much when it came to bribes, but a mercenary going to fight in Chechnya was worth more to him.

The sun was just starting to set when we took off, and we drove for only about ten minutes more before the driver stopped. The four of us got out and the two Chechens told us to stay out of sight until they came back. We didn't have a clue as to what was going on. For all we knew, they could be dumping us here and not coming back.

It was dark by then and the moon was rising. We stood at the side of the road and watched the two Chechens drive toward our destination. There was a river on one side of the road and a hill on the other, with only light brush here and there. I told the Arabs that we should walk up the hill and lie under some bushes that were off in the distance. As we started to hike up the hill a set of headlights suddenly appeared around the bend in the road. We were too far away to get cover in the bushes, so we lay flat against the hillside and prayed that whoever it was couldn't see us. As the vehicle drove by we could tell that it was an Awazik, a Russian military jeep, but to our relief it didn't stop.

About half an hour later another set of headlights appeared from the same direction. This time the headlights slowed down as they neared our hiding spot. The van stopped and one of the Chechens yelled for us. We ran down the hill and jumped into the van. After less than five minutes floodlights illuminated the road ahead. As we got closer to the lights we saw a large checkpoint. Our driver stopped at the gate, and a Russian soldier opened it right away. That was way too easy, I thought, and I was right.

There were more lights about a mile down the road. This time there was an even bigger checkpoint. As we came to a stop it was clear that these Russian soldiers were more serious than the others we'd encountered along the way. They held their AKs at the ready and seemed to be scrutinizing us. After the two Chechens had left us on the side of the road, they had driven ahead and taken care of the bribes at the last checkpoint, but now it looked as if they hadn't known about this one. The Russian government was aware of the situation along the roads leading to Chechnya and was attempting to solve the problem. Most of the checkpoints would accept bribes, but every now and again the Russians were still able to man a few checkpoints with soldiers and officers who actually did their jobs. At the time, a few Arab mujahideen had been arrested and were being detained in a Dagestani prison.

The two Chechens got out to talk with the officer, but it didn't look good for us. Two soldiers immediately opened the side door of the van and started to look around inside. There couldn't be any doubt in their minds as to what we were, and I started to wonder what they would do with us. After a couple of minutes the Russian officer walked back over to the van with the Chechens. He poked his head in the side door and looked us up and down. Then he told our driver to take our bags out and ordered one of his soldiers to go through the bags. The soldier casually rooted around in the bags belonging to the Arabs, but the officer didn't pay much attention until they opened my bag. The first thing that the soldier pulled out was my Kevlar helmet. The officer rolled his eyes and said something to the Chechens that I inferred must have been "You guys have got to be kidding me."

The officer told the soldier to move and began to personally go through my bag. He pulled out my night-vision goggles and then my woodland-pattern BDUs, or Battle Dress Uniforms. When he got to my flak jacket he shook his head, stopped searching, and looked at the Chechens with amusement. The fact that we hadn't already been thrown on the ground or shot made me think that there might actually be some hope for the situation. Our driver continued to talk with the officer, who kept shaking his head as though he *just* couldn't *believe* the *whole situation*. It was no secret that mujahideen were entering Chechnya through this route, but I suppose that we weren't supposed to be so blatant about it.

Our driver was good at what he did and was eventually able to get the officer to accept $1,100 to let us pass. There must have been a problem with other soldiers at the checkpoint, because the officer called for his personal Lada Niva. We were quickly loaded into the vehicle, and the soldier who'd searched my bags drove off down a bumpy dirt track that ran parallel to the border. We'd traveled about half a mile to a field with some brush, when the driver suddenly stopped and told us to get out. We had no idea what to do when he did a quick U-turn and drove back to his checkpoint. We could still see the lights of the checkpoint behind us on the road.

I figured that we were supposed to travel parallel to the road and over the border, then make our way back to the road. The three Arabs didn't have any better ideas, so I just started jogging in the direction we needed to go and they followed. After a good half mile or so we came to a tree line that seemed like a good place to head back to the road. At a spot where the trees came right up to the road, we crouched down. From there I could just barely make out the lights of the checkpoint. Nothing had been explained to us since the trip had started, but this took the cake. How were the Chechens supposed to know where we were? Even if they assumed that we'd moved parallel to the road, how would they know where we were waiting?

After a few minutes a pair of headlights came from the direction of the checkpoint. If it was our van and we let it pass, we would be stuck here, but if we tried to signal and it turned out to be a Russian vehicle, we would be shit out of luck. The Arabs were discussing the same options as the truck got closer. None of us did anything as a Russian army truck rolled by. About twenty minutes more passed before another set of headlights came from the checkpoint. The vehicle was going extremely slowly and I figured that it had to be our van. As it was about to pass us I jumped out on the road and waved my arms up and down. Luckily it was our van, and the Chechens stopped.

We drove on for another hour and then pulled off the road. At first I thought that our driver was just stopping for a rest, but when he started maneuvering the van up a road that led into a residential area I assumed that he knew where he was going. We entered a neighborhood and a couple of minutes later stopped in front of a house. There was a lantern burning in the window, and our driver jumped out and went to the front door. In a moment, he came back to the van and told us to get our bags and come inside.

Inside the house was a husband and wife. Through an open door I could see two children sleeping on beds. The woman brought us hot tea and fresh bread with cheese. This was obviously a kind of Chechen underground railroad, and these people were putting themselves in danger so that we could go and fight the Russians. As usual, we didn't know what our plans would be, but the people told us to relax and get some sleep.

The next morning we woke for the morning prayer, but we couldn't get back to sleep afterward. Shortly after sunup our driver left; he reappeared half an hour later with a Dagestani cop car behind him. He came inside and told us to get our bags, and when we went outside he told us to get in the cop car. The three Arabs piled into the back and I got into the front. "No problem" was all our driver told us as we drove off, leaving him behind.

The cop didn't say anything to us as he drove out to the main road. A big fat guy with a mustache, he was obviously some kind of officer. He lit a cigarette and turned up his cheesy Russian disco music as we flew down the road in his little Lada, which he drove as if it were a Porsche. The cops manning the first checkpoint saluted the officer as we passed. God only knows what they were thinking when they saw three Arabs and a white guy with a chest-length red beard riding with him.

Our driver barely slowed down as we drove through another three or four checkpoints manned by cops. After a couple of hours we came to Makhachkala, the capital of Dagestan. The cop pulled off the road and cut the ignition. We sat there for more than an hour while the cop listened to the blaring disco music. Just when I thought I couldn't take any more, a familiar-looking van pulled up behind us. By this point I wasn't surprised when the two Chechens got out, walked up to the cop car, and told us to get back into the van. It was definitely a clever deal that they had set up with the cop.

The drive into the city was easy. We pulled up to a large house with a steel gate in the front. These steel gates are common in this part of the world. Our driver honked the horn and someone opened the gate. The guys inside had big beards and were obviously mujahideen. We cleaned up and rested until late afternoon. I assumed that we were going to stay the night, but our driver came in and told us to get our bags again.

This time there was a silver late-model Mitsubishi Montero with tinted windows waiting for us in the courtyard of the house. The driver and his buddy were well dressed with shiny leather jackets, and I got the impression that they were some kind of Mafia. We got in the Montero and started to drive west toward the Chechen border. We passed a couple of checkpoints with no problems; the cops didn't even want to look in the back, where we were sitting on fold-down jump seats. The Chechen Mafia is a very serious organization, and in Russia the cops fear the Mafia, not the other way around.

I got the impression that this vehicle would deliver us to the Chechen border in style, but as usual I didn't have a clue. After driving awhile, we stopped on the edge of a busy marketplace in a suburb west of Makhachkala.

Once again our first Chechen driver came out of the woodwork and told us to follow him. We got out of the Montero and into a microbus full of women, children, and a few older men. Everyone stared at us as we walked to the rear, but not in a bad way. They obviously knew where we were going and seemed more curious than anything. The bus took off over a bumpy dirt road that snaked through the mountains toward Chechnya. We came across only one checkpoint. A cop stuck his head in the door of the bus and saw us sitting in the back, but he didn't give us a second look.

After maybe forty-five minutes, most of the people had gotten off the bus at different spots along the way. The driver turned north to a road that ran parallel to the Chechen border. We stopped at a small village in the foothills of the mountains. Our first Chechen driver had been tailing us in a different vehicle and stopped with us. We got out of the bus, and it left. Our driver motioned for us to follow him, and we walked to the door of a little two-room house.

A couple and their children lived there, and they invited us in to take tea. The man was very friendly and tried to communicate with us. Between our driver's broken English and the little bit of Russian we'd learned in Baku, we pieced together an interesting conversation. The children played in the background, and would stop playing occasionally to stare at us.

In late afternoon, our driver left. The Arabs wanted to take a nap, but I was too excited to even think about sleep and did push-ups instead. Our driver reappeared as the sun was going down and told us to come outside, where a small Lada was waiting for us. The car drove us perhaps a kilometer and a half, then stopped at the bottom of a gorge. The driver told us to leave our bags because we had to walk across the border, and it was going to be difficult.

Just as the last light was fading we started hiking up a steep and muddy trail through a heavily wooded gorge. The Arabs were having a hard time getting traction with their cheap shoes, but I was moving easily with my Danners. One Chechen stayed in front of us and one stayed behind as we moved up the gorge. Occasionally the Chechen in front would raise his hand for us to stop, but it was so dark that I would run into him before seeing his hand. I knew we were getting close to the border and I was getting excited. I tried to control my breathing, but as I listened to the Arabs huffing and puffing behind me I felt better about it. Back in the apartment in Baku, they were amused with my push-ups and vitamins, but now they could hardly make it up the hill. Even the Chechen in front was getting frustrated with their speed.

After what seemed like forever, I could just barely make out the edge of the gorge. We crouched down as we came over the top, but I wasn't expecting the sight that awaited us. We were on the edge of a big field that was illuminated by a giant spotlight coming from a Russian base. The spotlight was for crazies like us who might try to sneak into Chechnya. I was even more surprised when our Chechen guide got up and started to walk along the edge of the field. The Arabs didn't seem to find anything wrong with this and got up to follow him. The Chechen in the rear also walked past me. I stood there for a minute, dumbfounded, before following. Great, I thought, I'm going to get shot from behind while walking under a spotlight before even getting into Chechnya.

But the Russians either didn't see us or didn't care enough to do anything about us, and we made it to the other side of the field without incident. We proceeded to a road that ran up the mountain in front of us. Occasionally we could hear bursts of heavy machine-gun fire from all directions in the mountains, the tops of which glowed eerily. Later I learned that the glow came from fires at the homemade oil refineries that were all over the mountains of Chechnya.

The moon had come out by now, and I sensed that we were in the bottom of a wide, shallow valley. Up ahead in the road were large rectangular concrete blocks that looked like giant sticks of clay staked to one side of the road. The first Chechen raised his hands wide and said, "Chechnya." And that was it.

As we walked past the blocks there were a couple of houses to our left, and a couple more up the road a short distance on our right. The road went up and over a hill, and the village of Zandak lay at the top. The Chechens led us to one of the houses on the right, where a man and woman and their infant child lived. It wasn't actually a house but more like a metal shipping container. Despite living in a box, the woman offered us food as soon as we sat down. They didn't have any type of stove but used a heating element to warm soup for us. Their electricity came from a generator behind their metal box.

The man who lived here was even friendlier than our last host, and he asked question after question. We stayed for about half an hour and then an

Awazik pulled up in front of the box with our Chechen driver, who always seemed to pop out of nowhere. This time he had an AK-74, a newer version of the AK-47 that fires a 5.45 x 39 round. We told the people who lived in the metal box good-bye, and when we left we found that the man's wife had cleaned our boots while the man had entertained us.

We piled into the Awazik and drove up the road to the house of a Chechen named Zakaria, who was part of the Jordanian diaspora of Chechens and who had lived in the United States before coming here. He was a short, thin man in his forties with a salt-and-pepper beard. When he greeted us at the door I had a strange feeling about him, the kind of vibes you get when somebody really bad looks you in the eye, and it was Zakaria's eyes that worried me. I couldn't put a finger on it, and I'm not an expert, but the way he held his body and moved seemed to indicate what could only be described as some sort of neurosis. As I monitored his rapid, jerky movements and the way he talked fast, it occurred to me that he was a dead ringer for a crystal meth addict on the streets of San Diego.

We sat down and discussed our plans. The Arabs were headed for the camp whose Arab commander was named Ibn-ul Khattab. I didn't have a plan, so Zakaria suggested that I hang out in Zandak for a couple of days. I asked him where I could buy an AK, but before I could finish my question he bounced off to another room and came back with a brand new AK-74, complete with a 40mm grenade launcher under the barrel.

"Here," he said, "take this one."

I'd been warned not to accept guns from Chechens. In the Chechen culture, if you borrow a gun and shoot someone, the person you borrowed the gun from is responsible. More importantly, if you buy your own gun, nobody can come back later and try to take it from you if you haven't obeyed his commands.

"How much?" I asked.

"Just take it, don't worry about the money."

"No. Kiffah gave me three hundred dollars for an AK, so just take the money."

"It's okay," Zakaria said. "It's yours, just take it."

I asked him if he was sure that it was mine, meaning that he was giving it to me and not loaning it, and he said yes. Against my better judgment, and the advice I'd been given, I was thrilled over scoring an AK-74, a brand-new one at that, with a grenade launcher.

The next morning a driver arrived in another Awazik to take the Arabs to Khattab's camp. I was excited to see Chechnya, so I went along for the ride. A light fog had enveloped the mountains, and everything was lush and green. The rainy season had made the road muddy and difficult to navigate, even with the four-wheel-drive Russian military Awazik. After a couple of hours we came to a raging river and water flooded into the cab, but we made it to the other side without getting swept away. I proudly held my new AK-74 between my legs as we traveled through the mountains. I was deeply moved when we drove through the villages. When the children along the road saw us they would all start yelling *Allah-u-Akbar*! It was exhilarating to be in Chechnya for jihad.

On the other side of the river there was a stand of trees at the bottom of a hill. Nestled between the river and the hill was Ibn-ul Khattab's camp. We stopped next to a six-wheel-drive Kamaz military truck with a cab on the back. The last place I'd seen these vehicles was the camp in Afghanistan. In this camp, mujahideen in mismatched Russian camouflage gear chatted and cleaned their weapons. When we entered, the mujahideen greeted me, but no one asked any questions. Our driver told me to hang out for a couple of hours, then he would bring me back to Zandak.

I wanted to know what Khattab was like, so I asked an Arab with U.S.-issue olive drab BDUs and a boonie hat if he spoke English.

"Yes, a little," he replied.

"Where is the commander?"

He looked around nonchalantly before saying, "I'm right here."

"You're the commander?"

"Yes."

Khattab had a full black beard and long, curly black hair that came out of his boonie hat in two braids and fell over the front of his shoulders. It almost looked permed. He was thin, probably from life on the front lines, but I could tell that he was muscular and would be much bigger in a less stressful environment. Khattab's right hand was bandaged in an Ace wrap, something I would never see him without. I found out later that he'd lost three fingers when a grenade exploded before he could throw it. The outside media think that Khattab is Jordanian born, but he's really from an eastern province of

Saudi Arabia, close to Dammam. Later in Baku, I'd meet his brother, who would tell me Khattab's story.

Khattab's well-to-do family wanted him to attend medical school in the United States sometime during the late 1980s. Two months before he was set to go he became interested in the Soviet-Afghanistan jihad. Within a couple of weeks the teenager was on the front lines fighting against the Soviet army. He was originally under Usama Bin Laden's command, but broke from Bin Laden later because he wanted to do his own thing, and his family sent money so that he could form his own group. The men under his command fought the Soviets, and when the Soviet army was defeated, in 1989, he took them to Tajikistan, where they fought the Communist government. In 1994, when the war started to brew in Chechnya, he moved his group there. By the time I arrived a year later, he'd already inflicted heavy losses on the Russians. The Chechens believed that God had sent Khattab to Chechnya, and the Russians said that it was the Devil. Either way, the man is the fiercest and most brilliant warrior I have ever seen.

Khattab was very polite and unimposing. I asked him for advice on what I should do in Chechnya, and he said that I should look around before deciding. He also said that I was welcome to join his group. There were a handful of Arabs in the camp at the time, but the rest were Chechens. While we spoke, some of the Chechens asked if I wanted to fire the grenade launcher under my AK, and I thought that would be fun. They asked Khattab if we could have a few 40mm rounds. He waved his hand like a busy, distracted father who tells his kid to have fun and keep quiet. The back of Khattab's six-wheeled truck was full of weapons and ammunition for the camp. One of the Chechens started climbing over piles of machine guns and rockets, searching for a bag of the 40mm rounds. On the way out he got an expression on his face like, Hmm, that looks good, I'll take some of those too. By the time he jumped out of the back of the truck the Chechen guy had handed us an RPG with three rounds, a PKM light machine gun with a full box mag, a Dragunov sniper rifle, and a Mukha disposable rocket.

I walked around the hill with five other Chechens and we started shooting. They were using me as a pretext to play war, but I didn't care because it was so much fun. Later someone told me that Khattab was working on something and had a fit when he heard the small war behind the camp. I left that afternoon for Zandak. My bag had arrived while I was gone and now I was free to go anywhere.

The next day I met a Chechen named Ulbi at crazy Zakaria's house. Ulbi had lived in New Jersey and spoke perfect English. He was of average height and build and had a sandy blond beard. If I'd met him on the street in San Diego I would have thought that he was just another American. He had two brothers, one of whom had been killed in the battle for Grozny a few months earlier. The other was operating in Baku, sending supplies and other things to Chechnya. Ulbi commanded a small group nearby that held a strategic road from the village of Nozhai-Yurt to Zandak. The road led to the mountains throughout the region of Zandak, so it was imperative that we hold the position.

Ulbi and I had a lot in common, and we immediately became good friends. He suggested that I come to the front line with him, saying that if I liked it, I could stay with them. This sounded good to me, but when Zakaria caught wind of it, he started acting even stranger than usual. He suggested that I meet Sheikh Fatih—Umme Muhammad's father—whose house was close by. Ulbi said it didn't really matter to him and that he would come back for me later.

The first of my many bizarre experiences in Chechnya began that day. Zakaria drove me the couple of miles to Fatih's house. Upstairs, we found an old man with a long gray beard sitting on the edge of a bed with a Krinkov, a short-barreled version of the AK-74, lying next to him. He introduced himself as Sheikh Fatih, a Jordanian Chechen who spoke Arabic, English, and, of course, Chechen. Fatih was in his seventies, and had fought against the Soviets during the war in Afghanistan. He'd come here to teach Islam and had become a field commander when the war started.

Zakaria explained that Fatih needed another bodyguard and that they wanted me to take the position. I wasn't opposed to the idea, as it would be an honor to protect any Chechen leader, but I couldn't figure out why they wanted me. Besides, I'd come to Chechnya to fight the Russian army at the front. I spoke with Fatih at length, but he never said outright what he wanted of me, and I felt a little confused when we eventually went back to Zakaria's house.

The next morning Ulbi came back and we left for his position, which, I found out, was just on the outskirts of Zandak. On the way, Ulbi pointed out a small graveyard with seventeen fresh graves in a row. These were for seventeen mujahideen who had died during a raid into Russia led by Shamil Basaiyev. Shamil, whom I would later meet, had taken a hundred men and started driving toward Moscow to attack the Kremlin. About halfway to their destination they ran out of bribe money and had to either turn back or make a stand. The police arrested them and took them to the police station in the city of Buddenovsk; there the Chechens overpowered and killed their captors. Shamil and his men set up in the police station, but after determining that it was a poor defensive position, they proceeded to take the hospital, along with over two thousand hostages. Russian Alpha troops tried unsuccessfully to retake the hospital three times over the next two weeks, killing many of the hostages. In the end, Shamil negotiated safe transit to Chechnya for his men and their dead.

The road forked just after the graveyard. To the left lay Benoi, Dargho, and Vedeno. We took the branch to the right and drove down a muddy road toward Nozhai-Yurt. Ten minutes later we were at Ulbi's position, where they'd blocked the road with a big dirt berm and a wide ditch in front of it. Trench lines and bunkers snaked out on either side, and the road sloped downward past the berm and curved left toward a steep slope that dropped down into the forest. A gently sloped hill with no cover came up from the valley on the right. If the Russians wanted to take the position, they would have to either approach from the curve in the road and make a direct assault up the middle, or make a long, vulnerable Pickett's charge up the gently sloping hill.

Ulbi told me that two companies of Russian soldiers were stationed just over the next hill and that they'd tried to come up the road a couple of times already. We stopped on the side of the road and parked the jeep under some trees for cover. Ulbi walked me around the position and introduced me to the men. Everyone was excited to meet an American, and I was just as excited to meet them. Before sundown Ulbi asked me if I wanted to go back to Zandak, but I was having too much fun and told him that I would stay on the line for a while. Ulbi left for Zandak, and I spent my first night on the front lines in Chechnya.

The lieutenant or captain of the position took me to a small area where some of the guys were sitting around a fire and drinking tea. He didn't speak English, but I understood that he was telling me that I would stay by his side until I got a feel for things. After the evening prayer I had my first meal on the front lines, a large piece of semi-stale bread. None of the guys spoke any

English, and I didn't speak any Chechen or much Russian at the time but somehow we all sat there for a couple of hours having a nice conversation. The questions were always the same. What city in America are you from? Are you married? Do you have children? Now, years later, after all the countries I've been to, and all the fighters I've met, I'm convinced that the world would have fewer problems if people would just sit down with one another and talk as friends.

After the final evening prayer the lieutenant took me to one of the bunkers to rest. I lay on the cold dirt floor and didn't bother taking off my magazine vest. I fell asleep almost instantly and was awakened some hours later by one of the guys shining his flashlight into the bunker. It was our turn for guard duty. I jumped up eagerly and was ready to go out in the trenches before the position commander was even fully awake. The Chechen who had woken us up gave a look that said "I bet you won't be that eager in about a week."

My first night on guard duty was uneventful, but I had never felt so alive. The next morning I volunteered to man one of the forward listening posts, really just a foxhole a couple of hundred meters off to the side of our position at the bottom of the steep hill. I'd been sitting there for about an hour and was getting bored when a twig snapped and someone coughed. I jumped in the foxhole, switched the selector on my AK to full auto, and sat there staring at the forest. My breathing sounded loud and irregular as my ears strained to hear what was out there. A minute or two later I slipped out of my hole and moved back up the hill quickly and silently. When I got within sight of one of the Chechens I signaled that I'd heard movement. Then I moved back down to the foxhole while he rounded up some other guys. The position commander came up from behind while I knelt with my AK at the high ready. I explained what I'd heard with hand gestures before we all moved out into the forest.

I almost ended my tour in Chechnya before it really started. We'd gotten about a hundred meters out when I looked down to see a wire running between a tree and a stake mine; another step would have been fatal. The other guys disarmed the booby trap. We searched the forest for another half an hour before heading back to the position. Ulbi later explained to me that the Russians often booby-trapped the areas around our positions, and that the Spetsnaz were specialists in this technique. Detecting traps would become a common experience during my stay in Chechnya, but eventually I wouldn't be as lucky as I was that morning.

Ulbi came back a couple of days later and we drove to the town of Benoi, where there was a field hospital. I visited all of the wounded fighters but was surprised to see how many civilians, including women and children, were recuperating there. I knew that the Russian army wasn't very careful in differentiating between civilian and military targets, but I was shocked when I listened to the stories about how the Russians indiscriminately raped and killed men, women, and children as they ran amok through the countryside. One woman told me of how her teenage daughter had been pulled out of their home by Russian soldiers who had come to town to "look for terrorists." She was raped repeatedly in the back of a BMP armored fighting vehicle and then publicly executed. As if that wasn't enough, the Russian soldiers drove a wooden stake between her legs to disgrace the girl. All in the name of looking for terrorists. As shocked as I was that first day to hear those stories, it was nothing compared to what I would see before leaving Chechnya.

As we drove back toward our position that afternoon, I wasn't feeling well. By the time we reached the position I had a terrible ache in my right side. That night as I was standing in the trench for guard duty I was hit with such a horrible pain that I fell over and couldn't get up. The position commander called Ulbi on the radio, and he came with the jeep. He took me to a small clinic in Zandak because it was closer than the hospital in Benoi. The doctor there examined me and told Ulbi that I would have to be moved to the field hospital first thing in the morning.

After an excruciating night in the clinic, things got worse: I thought that I'd die from the bumpy ride through the mountains. At the hospital, the doctors drew blood and examined me. Then they told me the last thing in the world I would have expected: my appendix needed to come out.

Wait a second, I thought. I wouldn't even want to have that operation back in the States, let alone in a Chechen field hospital. I tried to get up and leave, but I couldn't stand very well and the doctors sat me back down. They explained that I would die if I didn't have the operation, and they carried me to an operating room that looked like something out of *Sweeney Todd*. There was a wooden table with sidepieces for the patient's arms sticking out; big leather straps dangled off the sides. Crude instruments were strewn around the room on various trays and tables. Most notable was the absence of anything that might resemble anesthesia equipment.

I was stripped naked and laid on the table. I had hoped the leather straps were only for emergencies, but when one of the nurses started to fasten my arms down I became extremely uncomfortable. She looked at me compassionately as she cinched the straps tight.

"Hey, hey!" I said, trying to rationalize my way out of the situation. "Let's talk about this, guys. Maybe I just have really bad gas."

Some of the hospital staff spoke English, but no one paid any attention to my whining.

"There's a war going on, you know. If I'm not back by nine my commander is going to be *very* upset."

"Okay," one of the doctors said as he placed an IV in my arm.

My heart was racing and I desperately wanted to get away, but the real fun started when the first drops of the IV solution hit my vein. I suddenly felt as if a freight train was roaring through my head. There was a loud buzzing in my ears, and then it was silent. I felt as if I had passed out and then abruptly reawakened. I was lying there with my eyes half open and could hear music coming from a radio in the background. One of the nurses was laughing about something, and I wondered when the doctors were going to put me under for the operation. I noticed movement through my half-open eyes and realized that one doctor was standing over me. Then he put a scalpel to my belly and started to cut. My mind screamed for him to stop, but the medication had paralyzed me, and I was unable to lift a finger or even blink my eyes. Later I'd discover that the medication was some sort of horse tranquilizer, but as I lay there I could feel every little movement the doctor made inside me. There was a disconcerting feeling of something being tugged out of me, as though he were trying to pull out my very soul. Then there was a massive jolt of pain as he cut the thing he was pulling. I continued to feel every stitch as the doctor sewed me up. After that, the real pain began.

As my body slowly regained control, waves of agony flowed up my body from the area that had just been cut open. The more I regained control, the more I started to move. I began to freak out and became aware that people were trying to hold me down as I screamed and twisted around. A nurse was trying to squeeze between the people to give me some kind of injection, but when she put a tourniquet around my arm I thought that it was a snake and started to fight even harder. Eventually I passed out, either because of the injection or from exhaustion.

I awoke later feeling as if I had been stabbed in my stomach. The pain was so intense that I could barely even shift my body. I lay in bed for two days, unable to sit up. The agony might have been too great if not for the nurses, who would stop to sit with me and chat. They didn't speak English, but somehow I knew what they were saying. One nurse in particular, Leila, made my stay bearable. Leila was a beautiful and powerfully built woman. She reminded me of an extremely pretty Olympic power lifter. She was very frank and liked to joke about seeing me buck naked on the operating table.

After about three days I was frustrated and wanted to get back to the front lines. Ulbi had stayed at the hospital with me that whole time, but he wasn't in any hurry to leave because his cousin was there and he was having fun talking to all of the nurses. At some point during my hospital stay I met the infamous Shamil Basaiyev. He'd come to the hospital for some kind of treatment, but when he heard that there was an American fighter around he came to my room for a visit. Shamil was a polite and good-looking guy with a wide scar across the bridge of his nose; he'd received it in the battle for Chechnya's capital, Grozny. He had a full dark beard and wore a Russian special forces jungle hat. He showed me a trophy that he'd taken from a dead Alpha trooper during the raid at the hospital in Buddenovsk. It was a silenced Stetckin 9mm automatic pistol, something only the elite forces in the Russian military carried. When I told Shamil that he was famous in America as a result of the Buddenovsk operation, he laughed and said that he liked that. While recuperating, I also struck up a friendship with a doctor named Umar Khambiev, who was the Chechen Minister of Health. After four days in the hospital I couldn't take it anymore, so I told Ulbi that if he wanted to stay, I would make my own way back to Zandak. He didn't take me seriously until I'd put my gear back on, grabbed my AK, and headed out the door. About a hundred meters down the road I realized that I wasn't in any shape to be walking at all, let alone all the way back to Zandak. I couldn't swallow my pride and turn around, so I kept on going. After a half mile I was in terrible pain, and the weight of my gear was killing me. But fate has always had a funny way of stepping in at exactly the right moment for me and just when I was about to pass out from the pain in my stomach a car that had been approaching pulled over and stopped. There were three men in the car, all of them fighters. The biggest one got out.

"You American?" he asked.

"Yeah," I said.

"I am Luqman," he said. "What is wrong with you?"

"I just had my appendix out and I don't feel so good. I'm trying to get to Zandak."

"Luqman can take you there."

Relieved, I got into the car. A thought occurred to me. "Why did you ask if I was an American?"

"You wear American gear. I had American friend once. He lived in Sand Diego. His name was Muhammad Zaky."

It turned out that Luqman had been next to Muhammad Zaky when he'd been hit, and he told me the story of how Zaky had died. Luqman and Muhammad Zaky were part of a platoon defending the city of Vedeno. They were in the back of a six-wheeled truck and Muhammad Zaky was manning a large DShK 12.7mm machine gun. A Russian SU-24 bomber started to make an attack run on the city, and Muhammad Zaky opened up on it. The pilot saw where the fire was coming from and came back around to fire rockets at the truck. Everyone ran except for Muhammad Zaky and Luqman, who was feeding the belt into the DShK. The rockets impacted next to them but, other than throwing them from the truck, didn't do a lot of damage. Luqman said that he got up and told Muhammad Zaky that they needed to move, but Muhammad Zaky was on his hands and knees, and he just shook his head. When Luqman tried to help him up, he saw that Muhammad Zaky's intestines were spilling out of a gaping hole in his stomach.

Muhammad Zaky was still alive, and he might have lived, but on the way to the hospital, one of the guys made a terrible mistake and tried to pack his intestines back in, which can cause a fatal internal infection. After four days in the hospital it appeared that Muhammad Zaky would nevertheless recover, and the mujahideen made arrangements to move him to an Azeri hospital for Chechen soldiers. On the morning of the fifth day Luqman and other witnesses noticed Zaky staring at something. He raised his hand toward whatever it was he was seeing and Luqman asked Muhammad Zaky what he was looking at. "I see her. I see her," he replied. Luqman asked him what he was talking about, and Muhammad Zaky told him that he saw the hoor 'ain—the maiden of paradise. The room stilled as everyone held their breath. Luqman asked Muhammad Zaky what the hoor 'ain was doing. "She is telling me I will come with her but I must wait a short while first."

One of the people in the room asked Muhammad Zaky to describe the woman, but he said that he was unable to because words couldn't describe what he'd seen. Everyone present, including Muhammad Zaky, knew that he would pass on to the next life. It was just a matter of time.

Later that evening Muhammad Zaky asked Luqman to come near him. "Make sure that what I say now reaches my son, Umar," he said. "He must never abandon the jihad. I have seen what is waiting for us on the other side, and Allah's promise is true."

Many in the room wept, and moments later he simply looked up and said "*La illaha ilalallah, Muhammador rasulallah.*" There is no God except God, and Muhammad is his messenger. They are the last words that should pass a Muslim's lips, and shortly thereafter, Muhammad Zaky died. ·

When Luqman was finished telling the story I had almost forgotten about my pain. I wanted to get back to the front lines to follow Muhammad Zaky on his journey. He had set the example for me in life, and now he set the example for me in death as well.

Luqman was headed away from Zandak, and arranged for someone else to give me a ride there. Since I was having a hard time recovering from the surgery, eventually I went to Zandak to rest in a house that was used by Ulbi's group. While I was sitting outside one day, a man with a bushy brown beard and long hair coming out of an American boonie hat stopped by to talk with one of the guys. He looked more like a biker than a mujahid, but it turned out that he was Abu Muhammad from New Jersey, Umme Muhammad's husband. Abu Muhammad was fighting with Khattab's group, and I told him that I wasn't all that happy with Ulbi's group. Some of the men smoked cigarettes, which is contrary to Islamic law, and didn't strike me as being as religious as they should be. So I agreed to come with him to Khattab's camp.

The first few days in Khattab's camp were nice; I enjoyed being around the Arabs because they were more religious. Khattab had around a hundred guys in his group at that time but only four proper tents for all of them. Those who weren't in the tents made shelters for themselves however they could. Most had strung up plastic sheeting between trees, and the camp had the over-all appearance of a hobo jungle. I made my home in a tent that no one else wanted to use because it smelled like mildew. No one in the camp had built bunkers or trenches, so I dug a shallow foxhole next to where I slept in the tent. If the Russians should come and bomb us at night, my plan was to just roll over into my hole, but the Arabs found this hilarious and joked that I'd dug my own grave.

Aside from operations, life in Khattab's camp was thoroughly boring, so I tried to stay busy learning new things. Since many of the Arabs were Afghan veterans, I'd ask them to teach me whatever skills they had. One really neat toy was a Russian T-72 tank parked in the trees on the edge of the camp. It actually "belonged" to the guy who had captured it during the battle for Grozny, but he let Khattab use it. The man who captured it was a skinny, older Chechen with a scruffy beard who had been a tanker in the Russian army. He didn't look particularly fierce, but everyone said that he had killed the tank crew by himself on a street in Grozny, and had then proceeded to drive their tank into the mountains. I saw this as a golden opportunity and asked him to teach me everything he knew. He seemed thrilled that someone actually want-ed to hear what he had to say. After teaching me the start-up sequence, he showed me how to operate all the controls, which were fairly simple. Within an hour or so I had my finger over the starter button and was ready to go.

"Can I?" I asked. I could barely contain my excitement.

"Of course," he replied in Russian.

The tank shook and made an enormous roar as the engine came to life. The skinny guy adjusted the throttles for me as the tank warmed up, then climbed back into the turret. I put on the tanker helmet that he had given me which was equipped with an intercom headset. The Chechen seemed a little out there—maybe one too many tank rounds had gone off near him—but he made the entire production enormously fun. Through the intercom he rambled on and on in what seemed like Russian-English tank-commander technobabble about throttles and batteries and oil pressure. My only response to each of his comments was the word *"Da!"* in my best Russian-soldier accent. Finally, in what sounded like his best John Wayne accent, he said, "Let's go, pardner."

A T-72 tank has six gears. I dropped the clutch and mashed it into first. We did a tank version of burning rubber—which was really tossing mud—and I swung onto the road that led into the camp. I had the driver's hatch open and watched as all the Arabs ran out of their little plastic shelters to see what was the commotion. When I got to the middle of the camp I held one of the control sticks down while I pulled the other one back, which made the tank spin around and around in a circle. The Arabs had been eating watermelon when I made my dashing entry, and they started to throw the rinds at me.

"Enemy fire!" the crazy Chechen yelled into the intercom. "Shut door! Shut door!"

I buttoned up the hatch and drove back to where he'd originally parked the tank. When I went through the shut-down sequence by myself, the Chechen poked his smiling face into the driver's hatch and said "*Koroshey tankist.*" You're a good tanker.

Later that day Khattab returned to the camp to find tank tracks running through his camp. He threw up his arms and asked the Arabs who'd driven the tank all around camp. When they all pointed at me, I thought I would be in big trouble, but Khattab just kind of shook his head the way you might when confronted with a mischievous kid.

"*Please*, Abu Mujahid," he said, "don't drive the tank in my camp. Okay?"

"Umm, okay," I replied.

Every day brought something new for me in Khattab's camp, and the Arabs took to calling me Abu Mushakil, "Father of Trouble."

One day a new guy came into the camp. He looked like a Pakistani, but he walked up to me and asked in perfect English if I was Abu Mujahid. He introduced himself as Abu Turab, "Father of Dirt." His parents were Pakistani, but he'd been born in Texas. He'd spoken to Kiffah before he left the States, and Kiffah had told him about me. Abu Turab told me that Kiffah and my wife were worried about me because they'd heard that I'd been in the hospital, but they didn't know why.

Things really got fun when Abu Turab showed up. I had a new playmate, and it reminded me of the days back in Afghanistan when Umar and I had caused so much trouble. Khattab quickly got fed up with us and approached one morning as we were wrestling on the ground.

"Do you two want to go to the front lines?" he asked abruptly.

"Yes!" we both yelled in unison.

"Then get your stuff. The truck is leaving soon."

Abu Turab and I ran to our tent, the Mildew Inn, and started throwing stuff in our bags. Abu Turab was making little hooting noises and I was yelling "Yee-haw!" Soon we were on a Russian military truck bound for a position between the camp and the city of Vedeno, where Muhammad Zaky had died. The Russians had since taken the city. We drove for about an hour to a ridgeline in a thick forest. We could see a Russian helicopter base a couple thousand meters away, on the other side of the valley. We had a large DShK 12.7mm machine gun set up on the ridge in the event that the Russian helicopters tried to cross the mountains in this direction. Abu Turab and I jumped off the truck and ran up to Abu Zaid, the commander of the position, and shouted, "Reporting for duty, sir!" He regarded us with a blank look on his face as our driver said something to him about Americans. "Okay," he said with an incredulous half smile. He got us settled in his tent, which he shared with several other guys.

We spent some of the best times in Chechnya at that camp. There were about ten young, friendly guys at the position, one of whom I will always remember. He was young and muscular and had the sort of medium-length hair you'd expect to see on a surfer from California. He also had a surfer's serene, far-out-dude mannerisms and had somehow gotten an American-style long-sleeved flannel shirt; the kind surfers wear before they go out in the morning. To add to the image—unintentionally, I'm sure—he had a habit of walking barefoot around the position, as though he were just back from a jog on the beach.

Below the ridge, a trail led down to a river that ran through the forest. The river pooled there between two boulders and made an almost perfect place to bathe or sit back and relax. Whenever Abu Turab and I weren't manning the DShK we would hang out at the pool in the river. One part of our stay was nighttime guard duty. Abu Turab and I always stood guard together, despite the small amount of Russian we were able to speak. We joked that although we knew how to say "Stop, who's there?" for all we knew the reply might be "A Russian soldier who has come to kill you," to which we'd say "Okay."

Sometimes Abu Zaid would send us down the valley on patrol. During one of these patrols I noticed something that would eventually get me in trouble with Khattab. At the bottom of the valley there was a large clearing, maybe a couple of hundred meters across, and as we neared it we could see Russian soldiers sitting on top of a BMP at the edge of the trees on the other side. They were smoking cigarettes and sunning themselves while listening to music from a portable radio. For some reason this really irritated me. I told the guy who was in charge of the patrol that we should attack them right there, but he said we didn't have permission. The fact that the Russian cowards were sunning themselves and having a nice time in between raping Chechen women infuriated me.

After that day I often watched the clearing with a pair of binoculars. Every day the same BMP would come down the valley from the helicopter base and park there. The soldiers weren't concerned about whether or not they might get attacked, and this pissed me off even more. Shortly after that I went out on patrol with a couple of the more aggressive guys. I'd brought my Mukhas—disposable rockets—with me, and no one really noticed or asked why. When we approached the clearing I explained to the Chechens what I wanted to do. We would skirt the edge of the field with the Mukhas and hit the BMP broadside. The Chechens didn't seem to care about permission and said they were with it.

Slowly we made our way around the clearing. The BMP was about a hundred meters away when we got in line with it; a Mukha's maximum effective range is about two hundred meters, so we had a good chance of taking it out. I gave the Mukhas to the Chechens because they had more experience. They took a good firing position and looked at me. On the days that I had watched the BMP from the ridge I had always counted between seven and nine Russian soldiers. A BMP carries six troops in the back, plus three crewmen. On that day I counted seven, so that meant that somebody was getting lucky, somebody had stayed back at the base for whatever reason and would be sitting there that night contemplating fate.

Four of the soldiers were lounging on top of the BMP while three sat under a tree nearby. One of the soldiers under the tree got up and gestured with his hands, as though he was telling a story. I nodded to the Chechens, who yelled, "*Allah-u-Akbar!*" and then fired. At the sound of the yells the Russian storyteller spun around in our direction. Then the two rockets streaked past him, and both hit the BMP. One would have been sufficient, but I guess we just wanted to be sure. The impact wasn't all that dramatic, but it was loud. A couple of the hatches blew off and flipped up into the air; then fire came out of the compartment. The storyteller had been knocked down and started to pick himself up, while the other two ran for the treeline. One of the other Chechens had a PKM light machine gun and opened up on them. I also began to fire bursts from my AK-74 at the back of one of the soldiers. He dropped in a heap, and the other two did the same from the PKM fire. The four soldiers who had been sitting on top were scattered around the burning BMP not moving. I wanted to run out and grab some of their weapons but suddenly felt nervous and sensed that we should get out of there before the Russians came down the hill.

We heard helicopter gunships behind us as we ran through the forest toward our side of the valley. We dropped down and took cover for a minute and watched the choppers circle over the clearing. Their guns made noises like big zippers as they fired blindly into the forest around the edge of the clearing. We made it back to the position without any problems, but when we got there Abu Zaid was waiting for us. Luckily he didn't speak English, so he yelled at the Chechens instead.

A couple of days later the truck from Khattab's camp came to our position and the driver said that Khattab wanted to see me. Uh-oh, I thought, I'm in trouble now. Khattab was busy when we got to the camp, so I sat and talked to an Arab named Uthman while waiting. He spoke a little English and told me that he didn't like hanging out with a lot of people and did his own thing in Chechnya. He was the first of the "wanderers" I would meet; by the end there were four or five of us. We were always walking around the mountains of Chechnya by ourselves, looking for action. We didn't do this as a group, but we would occasionally see each other and spend a few days together.

I got tired of waiting for Khattab and left with Uthman before he could talk to me. As I walked out of the camp, some of Khattab's men looked at me in surprise and asked where I was going. "Be back later," I called over my shoulder. My Arab friend was taking me to a village called Cecin, where he made his temporary headquarters for an army of one. Cecin was situated next to a river at the bottom of a mountain. The Chechens were shorthanded there and had to protect both approaches to the village from the Russians, who were at the top of the mountain. The Russian base was so close that we could see it from the village. Uthman had volunteered to help the Chechens hold the road leading into the western side of the village, but he was doing it practically by himself.

We stayed in a house on a bank of the river that overlooked a bridge the Russians would have to cross if they wanted to enter the village. We had Mukhas and our AKs to stop them, and maybe the Chechens would get there in time to back us up, but we didn't really care. I had a lot of fun during my stay in Cecin and made friends with the commander there, whose name was Issa. He became a good friend and would end up saving my ass later on.

Neither Uthman nor I had any money, and the fighters of that district weren't bringing us any food. Finding meals became a daily problem, but the hospitality of the Chechen people always saved the day. Whenever strangers visit a Chechen's home and are invited in, they are always served food and tea. It wasn't an ideal situation for the Chechens we visited and who fed us, but we all knew that we were there for their protection. Sometimes when we approached a Chechen home, Uthman would pull my shirt up to show our prospective hosts my appendectomy scar. This almost always guaranteed us a meal, and more often than not, our boots were cleaned by the time we left.

One day I heard that there was fighting back near Zandak, so I decided to take the daylong trek there. In Chechnya we had a saying that there wasn't any such thing as *good-bye*, only *see you tomorrow*, so I told Uthman we'd meet again soon and started walking. I always enjoyed passing through each village along the road; the people were invariably amused by the lone American who walked through the mountains. I got lucky, and in the late afternoon a Lada Niva filled with Chechen fighters stopped to give me a ride.

I joined up with Ulbi's group again back in Zandak. There wasn't any major fighting yet, but the Russians were up to something on the border and everyone was on alert. A couple of mornings later one of Ulbi's men came running out of the house shouting for everybody to gear up, as the Russians were coming over the border from Dagestan. An instant adrenaline rush went through me. Everyone scrambled to get their gear on. We lined up on the road in front of the house as the last stragglers ran out. Once everyone had assembled, Ulbi did a quick head count.

"*Takbir!*" he yelled.

"*Allah-u-Akbar!*" everyone roared back, *God is great.*

"Sabilallah! Sabilallah!" one of the men shouted. *What is Allah's way?*
"Al jihad! Al jihad!" they yelled back. *Jihad is the way.*
"Tariqnah! Tariqnah!" *What does Allah say?*
"Al kital! Al kital!" *Kill! Kill!*

We double-timed it up the hill to the main road. The memory of it lingers with me: the sound of everyone's boots hitting the dirt as they ran, the clinking and clacking of loose gear as it bounced against our bodies.

"Hey, Muhammad," one guy shouted to another.

"What?" Muhammad replied.

"How many Russians are you going to kill today?"

"That depends on how many bullets I have with me."

"Allah-u-Akbar!" everybody chimed in.

As we ran I felt the blood coursing through my veins with every heartbeat, felt every breath I took, felt the sweat run down my face. I'd never felt so alive. This was real. There wasn't any other way than this. We were outnumbered and outgunned, and we ran to come head-on with our enemies. There was no hesitation, no pause.

The Chechens have a saying: If we die, we win. None of us would join what is called the caravan of martyrs that day, but we held the border.

I continued to stay in the area with Ulbi and his men, and during this time I actually became friendly with two Russian soldiers. It was common in Chechnya for Russian soldiers to go AWOL and surrender to the Chechens. Some simply laid down their arms and lived with Chechen families, while others joined the mujahideen and fought against their former comrades. Two such men somehow ended up with Ulbi's group, and the Chechens gave them religious names: Salaambeck and AsSalaambeck. Over a period of a few weeks they lived with Ulbi's guys and became interested in our prayers. At the time, only one Arab, Abu Zubair, was with the group. He spent a lot of time with Salaambeck and AsSalaambeck, and one day they approached all of us as we sat and drank tea.

"We are ready," they said.

"Ready for what?" someone asked.

"To do what all of you do," AsSalaambeck replied, making a gesture with his hands like the one Muslims make when they pray. Everyone just sat there for a moment, staring at the two Russians, and then someone shouted *"Allah-u-Akbar!"*

"*Allah-u-Akbar!*" everyone shouted back.

These weren't the first Russian soldiers to convert, and they wouldn't be the last, but it was important for me because I was there to watch as they took *shahaadat*, or the proclamation of faith.

"Repeat after me," Abu Zubair told them. *"Ashadu Allah illaha ilalallah, wa ashadu ana Muhammador rasulallah."* I bear witness that there is no God except God, and I bear witness that Muhammad is his messenger. After they'd repeated this, everyone hugged and kissed Salaambeck and AsSalaambeck. I became very close with AsSalaambeck, who was just a little younger than I. He taught me some Russian and I taught him English. His teenage life in Russia had been quite similar to mine in America, and we often contemplated the fact that we had both been steered toward Islam and were now in Chechnya. We would both fight for the Chechen people and, though we didn't know it yet, would eventually shed our blood for them as well.

Nothing is taken for granted in war. To prove their loyalty, Salaambeck and AsSalaambeck went with some of Ulbi's men to their Russian army base. Salaambeck hid with the Chechens in the forest outside the perimeter while AsSalaambeck walked into the base. There, he told the base commander that the four other soldiers who had gone AWOL with him were in the forest and were scared to come back to the base for fear of punishment. He said that if the commander would promise to go easy on them they would return their weapons. The commander wanted to gather some men and go talk with the AWOL soldiers, but AsSalaambeck said that they were afraid and might fight if they saw the commander coming with other soldiers. Eventually the commander agreed to come out by himself. When he got to the place where Salaambeck and the others were hiding, Salaambeck jumped out and hit him with the butt of his AK. Then they dragged him off a good distance from the base and killed him.

It may seem odd that soldiers would treat their officers this way, but there are many irregularities in the Russian army. Salaambeck and AsSalaambeck told me many stories about life in the Russian army. At night on Russian firebases throughout Chechnya, they said, the soldiers would consume massive amounts of alcohol and drugs and then hide in the bunkers. Each bunker thus became a bastion of insanity whose paranoid inhabitants would shoot at the slightest noise or motion. The bunker mentality was so severe that even base commanders didn't dare approach their own men at night. This was believable because on any given night when we were near a Russian base, we would listen as they shot off rounds and parachute illumination flares all night long, like the bridge scene in *Apocalypse Now*. Worse, Salaambeck and AsSalaambeck told stories about how Russian commanders would kill their own soldiers and then not report them as dead or missing so they could collect their pay and amass stockpiles of materiel for sale on the black market. One of the dirty little secrets of the war in Chechnya was that most of the guns and ammunition the Chechens bought were actually from Russian army officers. There were also stories about how the Russians would even fight themselves. One commander might try to intimidate another for fuel or food, and if the goods weren't forthcoming the commander would have his soldiers attack.

At some point during that period, I started to develop problems with Ulbi's second in command. He was one of the not-so-religious Chechens, and in peacetime he was probably some kind of gangster. We didn't have serious conflicts until the day I looked outside to find a Russian military jeep marked OMON. The OMON serves as the military police of the Russian army, and was responsible for many of the atrocities in Chechnya; it is rumored that OMON troops shot Russian army regulars when they tried to retreat from Grozny.

Zandak was close to the border, but I couldn't figure out why the OMON would be here sitting in front of our house. Then I realized that Ulbi's second in command was talking with them, so he must have invited them. I grabbed another Chechen and asked what the hell was going on. He told me that the second in command was discussing the issue of Salaambeck and AsSalaambeck. It appeared that the Russians wanted them back because they'd lured their commander to his death, and this fucker was actually trying to make a deal with them while Ulbi was away. Ulbi simply wouldn't have tolerated the proceedings. Salaambeck and AsSalaambeck were Muslims now, and to turn them over to the Russians would be nothing less than treacherous.

When I headed for the door, clearly incensed, the Chechen I was with tried to stop me, protesting that we shouldn't get involved. Fuck that, I thought. I grabbed an RPG lying nearby, slid a round into it, and marched out the door. The second in command was standing in front of the jeep with two

OMON officers. Two other OMON agents were sitting in the front of the vehicle. RPGs arm at a certain distance, so I kept enough space between us in case I had to use it. I raised the RPG to my shoulder and pointed it at the jeep.

"Hey, you fuckers!" I yelled in Russian. They swung around and looked at me in surprise. "What the fuck are you doing?"

The second in command yelled something back about official business that was none of my concern. I told him that Salaambeck and AsSalaambeck were Muslims and it was *haraam*, forbidden, to even think of turning them over. The two OMON officers outside the jeep started to move, but I motioned that I would fire if they continued, in which case their two other buddies would be shit out of luck because they wouldn't be able to get out in time. The second in command yelled something at one of his Chechen buddies, who then pointed his AK-74 at me.

"Fuck you," I shouted at him. "You are *munafiq*." A traitor.

We all stayed there like that for a moment, like a standoff in a spaghetti Western.

"Drop your gun or I blow the jeep," I said to the guy pointing the AK at me. Killing the OMONs would be a pleasure for me, and the second in command would have big problems if I did. He'd invited the OMONs here, and if it appeared that he'd set them up, other Russians would surely hunt him down. Zandak would probably also be bombed, which would also be his fault. The guy pointing the AK at me still wasn't dropping it, but then a couple more of Ulbi's guys came out of the house with their AKs. They pointed their guns at the second in command and started talking loud in Chechen. They were obviously telling him the same thing I was, because the other Chechen stopped pointing his AK at me. The second in command was visibly pissed off, but he couldn't do anything. The two Chechens who'd come to my defense told the OMON agents to take a hike, so they got in their jeep and left.

A big argument ensued between Ulbi's guys and the gangster and his buddies. When Ulbi showed up, he got into it too. Ulbi was pissed over what was going on, but for some reason he didn't do anything to the guy who'd invited the OMON and caused all the problems. My impression was that the second in command was some sort of serious gangster, and that he carried so much weight that Ulbi wasn't prepared to deal with the consequences. In the end, Ulbi reprimanded him and left it at that, but the problem continued to fester.

The so-called peace talks were going on at that time and there wasn't a lot of fighting, although both sides conducted operations here and there. Salaam-beck, AsSalaambeck, a Chechen, and myself took to hanging out together and became pretty close. One day we decided that sitting around was bullshit and we would make our own action. Salaambeck told us that two BTRs patrolled the border with Dagestan near our area. Each BTR had a full squad on board that always rode on top of the armored vehicles. Part of the area they patrolled was heavy forest, so we decided that an ambush was in order. We "borrowed" the RPG from the group and also got a couple of Mukhas. The Chechen had a PKM, and the rest of us had our AKs. Everyone was accustomed to seeing the four of us running around the hillsides in Zandak, so no one noticed when we all disappeared one day. We made good time and started looking for a suitable ambush site on the dirt road where the BTRs patrolled, and found a place with a steep embankment on one side and heavy trees on the other. We would use the RPG to take out the lead BTR and the Mukhas at the rear. The soldiers riding on top could run only in one direction because of the embankment, so we set up the PKM just inside the trees on the side of the road where they would run. Salaambeck knew what time the BTRs came through this area, and once we were set up we had time to spare. However, none of us relaxed. We didn't have an extra man to go down the road and warn us when the BTRs were approaching, so we stayed alert and listened for them.

As we heard the low rumble of the BTRs approaching, I felt a wave of nervousness wash over me. We'd decided that if there were just the two BTRs, as Salaambeck had predicted, we would go through with the ambush. If what came down the road deviated from this, we would scrub the operation. AsSalaambeck and I were lying together up on the embankment to take the lead BTR. He had the RPG, and I would cover him. Salaambeck was lying about fifty meters to our right with the Mukhas to take the rear BTR. The Chechen waited on the other side of the road with the PKM.

AsSalaambeck and I had the lead; if we didn't fire, the others wouldn't either. As the BTRs came into view everything looked like Salaambeck had said it would. They were even being nice enough to keep a very short distance between the front and rear BTRs. Each vehicle carried a squad of twelve plus three crewmen. Both squads sat on top of the BTRs, as they always did. AsSalaambeck wanted to hit the lead vehicle from the front. That wouldn't have been a good idea if it had been a tank or a BMP, but since it was only a BTR and we were above it, the shot was ideal. AsSalaambeck got into position and pointed right into the base of the small turret that was on top.

"*Bismillah Allah-u-Akbar,*" AsSalaambeck whispered. In the name of Allah, Allah is great. We'd taught him to say that before firing a weapon so that Allah would direct it to its target. Then he raised up and fired. The turret of the BTR popped off like a cork, and there was a tremendous explosion as the round impacted. The BTR continued rolling for a few more meters before coming to a stop. I threw two grenades between the BTR and the embankment, where some of the Russian soldiers had been tossed like rag dolls. Out of the corner of my eye I saw fire and then felt something whizzing past my head. The second BTR hadn't been hit and was firing at us with a heavy machine gun. The soldiers riding on top of it were jumping off it and running for the trees on the other side of the road. I couldn't see what was happening, but I heard our PKM open up. I was trying to figure out why Salaambeck hadn't hit the rear BTR when it, too, exploded. "*Allah-u-Akbar!*" our Chechen friend screamed.

AsSalaambeck and I shouted "*Allah-u-Akbar!*" I jumped down the embankment and rounded the lead BTR, which was burning now. The Chechen had cut down most of the Russians who'd run in his direction, but a couple were lying in the road and returning his fire. They didn't see me running at them, and I fired on both of them. AsSalaambeck had run along the embankment and was helping Salaambeck with the Russians who had managed to run behind the rear BTR.

Then it was over as quickly as it had started. "*Allah-u-Akbar!*" we shouted. The Chechen had a minor head wound, possibly from fragments of the explosions. We wanted to take weapons with us but needed to get out of there fast, and AsSalaambeck, Salaambeck, and I started to move into the forest. But the Chechen was jogging in the opposite direction, toward the bodies lying in the road.

"What are you doing?" Salaambeck called to him.

"Just wait a minute," he called back.

My heart was still racing and I wanted to get out of there. I remember thinking, "Oh great, *now* he wants to play." The Chechen pulled out a curious curved knife and started to cut the head off one of the bodies in the road. When he was done he took the head and laid it on the crotch of another dead Russian.

"See?" he shouted at us with a big smile on his face. "He is a dickhead."

We weren't able to make it back to Zandak by nightfall, so we slept in the forest that night. When we arrived the next morning, some unfamiliar Chechens were at the house where we usually stayed. They'd heard about the ambush, and since our little group had mysteriously disappeared, they correctly assumed that we were the perpetrators. You'd think that a few overzealous fighters in the middle of a war wouldn't be a bad thing, or that perhaps we'd catch a little flak for not listening to orders, but something funny was going on in that region. The village elders of Zandak and Nozhai-Yurt wanted to cooperate with the Russians, and we were bringing heat down on them; in effect, they were collaborators. No one could really say that we'd done something bad by destroying the Russian patrol, but bad vibes started to circulate around the village.

I spoke with Ulbi a couple of days later. He didn't really care about what the elders or anyone else thought. He was there to fight, not cooperate. As we were talking late into the night, a jeep pulled up to the house and one of Sheikh Fatih's people got out. Sheikh Fatih was Umme Muhammad's father, the old man who had wanted me to act as his bodyguard. Zakaria, the crazy Chechen who'd given me a gun, had introduced me to the sheikh. The sheikh's emissary told us that Fatih wanted to see us right away. I was suspicious, but Ulbi said we should go just to see what the old man wanted. When we picked up our AKs to get into the jeep, the driver said that we should leave them behind. That was very unusual.

"Why is that?" Ulbi asked him.

The driver started rambling about this and that and eventually his story became so fishy that we told him we'd changed our minds. He left, and Ulbi and I talked about what was going on. Half an hour later, two jeeps pulled up at the house. This time Fatih himself got out with three bodyguards and an additional jeep full of armed fighters. Fatih asked to talk inside, so Ulbi and I followed him in but kept our AKs in hand. Two bodyguards stayed outside, and one came in with Fatih.

We had a very strange conversation. Fatih talked about obeying leaders and not rocking the boat. Obedience is an important feature of the Islamic faith—*Islam* means "submission,"—and Fatih was a sheikh, or holy man, but Ulbi decided to ask Fatih just what the hell he was talking about. In addition, Fatih wasn't our leader, so we had no obligations to him. This angered Fatih, and he started getting off into subjects that I didn't understand. In the end, I think the old man was just trying to intimidate us, but it wasn't working. Ulbi knew too much, and I simply didn't give a fuck.

The problems, however, had just begun. I was lying down after breakfast a couple of days later when crazy Zakaria came up to the house with another big Chechen. I wasn't expecting any problems from them, but as soon as they got through the door the big Chechen grabbed my AK. I jumped up. "What the fuck," I said. I started to move toward the Chechen but he pulled out a pistol and pointed it at me. Zakaria launched into a bullshit lecture along the same lines as Fatih's and told me he that he was taking my gun back because he had only loaned it to me. He was lying, of course. We'd established that he'd given it to me and that it was my property. I told him that if he wanted to play this way I would come and get him when he wasn't expecting it. He replied that if I did anything he would tell the other Chechens that I had stolen the AK from him. Being a troublemaker was one thing, but an accusation of theft was entirely different; it wouldn't be easy to deal with. There wasn't much I could do other than give up the gun and vow to deal with the little bastard in the future; three countries and a year later he would escape me by only a couple of days.

I told Ulbi what had happened, but we had other problems to deal with at the time. Our group didn't have any extra guns, so for the time being I became the RGP operator. Not having an AK was dangerous; you can't carry an RPG around with you the way you would a rifle. Things settled down, nevertheless, until Ulbi had to go to Baku to do some business with his brother. The shit hit the fan the morning after he left.

The Chechen mafioso I'd stood down during the OMON fiasco was going somewhere with his buddies, and before leaving he sent one of them to me for the RPG. I told him that Ulbi had left it in my care and that it was my weapon for the time being. The mafioso didn't really need it. He was just look-ing for an excuse to make problems, and when he heard about my response he marched into the house, his face red and his veins bulging.

"Give it to me!" he said.

"No."

In a rage, he tried to rush me. We struggled for a few seconds until he backed me up against the wall. He was shorter than I but bigger and stronger and got me by my neck. He reached for the knife he always carried in the small of his back, but somehow it wasn't there. Meanwhile, I managed to get under his arm and throw him backward. He just kind of stood there, and so did I. I wasn't in a very good position, but for some reason he backed off.

"If you're still here when I get back," he said, "*I will kill you.*"

After he left, I didn't know what to do. I was sure that he meant to keep his threat, and since Ubi was gone, he could see it through. This was the prob-lem with groups that weren't completely religious; real mujahideen don't behave that way with one another.

I decided to go to my friend Issa in Cecin to see if he could help, so I bor-rowed an AK, a disposable Mukha rocket, and some grenades from one of Ulbi's Chechens and started walking. Because the road to Cecin had a lot of open stretches in the mountains, I had to be careful, since the guy that had just threatened me might be out there, waiting.

A few pro-Moscow bandit groups operated in various areas. They worked pri-marily for money, took orders from the Russian military, and conducted most of their kidnappings in Chechnya at the request of the Russians. At this time I wasn't really aware of these groups and assumed that all Chechens were on the same side, so I wasn't worried about the threats they might pose. But one day as I was walking through the mountains I got a crash course in Chechen sociology.

I had already been all over this area of Chechnya and had always been received warmly by the people. They always seemed amused by the American guy walking around the mountains by himself, asking for directions to the front lines. And in the event that I might run across some unfriendly people, I still had my usual combat load with me—assault rifle, disposable rocket, eight magazines, and three grenades.

One day, a Russian dump truck came down the mountain road as I was walking between villages. Four Chechen fighters were in the back, and at first they thought I was Chechen, but they quickly realized by my rudimentary Russian that I was foreign. They appeared to be friendly enough and invited me to their village for food. I didn't think much about it because it was customary, and because in a war you don't pass up a free meal. I hopped in the dump truck, and after we got under way I asked them where they lived. They told me an unfamiliar name, but I didn't think anything of it. After all, I didn't know the name of every village in Chechnya. The way they answered me seemed a bit odd, however.

After driving up into the hills for quite some time, we came to a village of just a few houses. The usual roadside stand selling candy bars and cigarettes wasn't there. We stopped at a house and the Chechens there sized me up carefully. They paid too much attention to my American combat boots.

As the four guys from the truck introduced me, I got the impression that these men weren't religious. There were about five other Chechens—all armed—in addition to the four from the truck. Another thing that worried me was the fact that all of these guys had on very neat and clean uniforms, and some even had expensive wristwatches; this unit hadn't seen combat anytime recently.

By this time I knew enough to want to get the hell out of there, but if I tried to leave there would probably be a shootout. They all invited me inside for food, so I went along with a definite sense of unease. When the hosts offered to take my rifle at the door—another custom, like taking someone's umbrella—I tried to refuse politely. But they insisted. It was another situation where pushing the issue would only make things worse and, since I wasn't in a position yet to do anything, I gave them my gun. Of course I kept my mag vest on, which still had my grenades and my knife. All I could do was take it moment by moment and wait for a chance to make a move.

We went into a typical Chechen living room, and the hosts brought tea. Little details seemed to confirm that I wasn't just being paranoid: there were no prayer rugs in the room, and I couldn't see a Qur'an anywhere. These aren't absolutely necessary in every Chechen household, but their absence was just another indication that this wasn't a religious group. They spoke in Chechen, which I couldn't understand, but I could tell from their tones and gestures that they were up to something. I went along with the situation as though everything were okay.

This would have been a good time for a sidearm, but I hadn't been able to get one yet. My knife wouldn't do me much good. I was relying on my grenades to deliver me from this mess. Fortunately, my hosts weren't in a hurry to do whatever they had planned for me. A group of them left the room after about ten minutes, which left four still sitting with me. They had also left their guns outside or in the entryway. I figured that now was as good a time as any to get out of there. Still unsure about my plans, I smiled at the Chechens in the room and pulled out an F-9 fragmentation grenade, which has a kill radius of 50 meters. Before they could do anything I yanked out the pin with my left hand. My grasp on the spoon of the grenade was the only thing keeping us alive.

Russian fragmentation grenades are no small threat. The grenades I carried had to be used with some kind of cover or obstacle between you and the target, because you can't throw one far enough to not kill yourself. I wasn't the first guy in Chechnya to use a grenade to get out of a tight situation, and my hosts did what most people do when faced with someone holding a live grenade: nothing. "So," I said in English, "I really have to be going now." None of them understood, of course, but I was speaking in English for psychological effect.

Next, I motioned for them to stand up. One of them started to say something to the others, but I raised my finger and shushed him. I used what little Russian I knew to inform them that if I'd a problem with dying I would have stayed home in America instead of walking around in wars by myself. I also told them that I wanted to kill a few Russians before dying, but that a group of Chechen thieves would do if today was my day to go.

Before the guys who had left the room had a chance to come back in, I motioned for this group to open the door and walk outside. I saw that my AK was leaning against the wall with several others at the end of the hallway. On the way out I grabbed mine and jammed the selector down to full auto. Following behind the last guy, I crouched down with my AK in one hand and the grenade in the other.

Outside, I scanned the area for the other five guys; they were by one of the vehicles, twenty feet from the door. They turned when they noticed us coming out, their AKs slung on their shoulders. At first they didn't spot the grenade in my hand and they looked confused; they hadn't planned to see their buddies coming out of the house or me with my gun. Before they could react or get away, I held up the grenade and shouted for them to drop all of their weapons and walk toward us quickly. I added that if any of them tried to run I would blow up all their buddies.

As the rest of the Chechens approached us I shouted for everybody to lie facedown on the ground. After they did this I kicked the guy nearest me and told him to run over and grab the weapons that his buddies just dropped on the ground. I covered him with my AK as he gathered the guns. When he'd dumped the guns in a pile I moved back toward the door and told him to grab all the guns lying against the wall just inside. Then I had him put all of the guns in the back of the dump truck.

Next I told my hosts that one of them would drive me out of there, and that if I saw anyone coming down the road after us, I would kill the driver before worrying about whoever was following us. To thank them for their hospitality, I told the commander that I liked his watch and that I would be taking it with me.

From there, things went smoothly. I'd memorized enough landmarks on the way to their house to make sure the driver got me back to where they'd picked me up. I wasn't out of the woods yet; if the hosts had a radio they could call their associates in the area to ambush us. But I was confident that unless the driver was extremely unpopular with his buddies, my threat to kill him would be deterrent enough.

We eventually made it back to the road without incident. I decided that it would be safer and easier if I had him drive me to Cecin because I knew that Issa, the commander, was there. I also considered that it might be a good idea to have my driver explain what they had planned to do to me; then I turned this over in my mind and decided that it might very well turn against me, since they hadn't actually done anything yet. Also, I didn't want to involve Issa in any messy disputes. We stopped at a fork in the road in the mountains outside the village. There was a shortcut to the village there, and the split in the road threw some doubt on my destination. I took off the watch and told the driver to give it back; I didn't need it and didn't want to be accused of stealing. Besides, I thought that they'd appreciate the message it sent. I took some shortcuts through ravines and valleys and stayed the night at Issa's house.

Issa was a good guy, and we got along well. He took me back to Zandak in his jeep to return the borrowed AK, and to demonstrate to the mafioso that I was under Issa's wing. This gave the signal that the mafioso and his crew risked conflict with another group if they tried to do anything to me. After taking care of the business in Zandak, we talked for a long time about my future. He told me that he understood why I was wandering around looking for action but that I would need to eventually settle down with one group. It was as though he were giving me advice about women. I agreed with what he had to say. Issa went on to tell me that he had a friend who was the commander of a group of misfits and who was, in Issa's words, "not normal." The group had fought in the battle for Grozny, and despite all the crazy things that had happened in Chechnya they'd somehow acquired a reputation for being a few sandwiches short of a picnic. Issa thought they might make a good home for me, and I agreed to give it a try.

A couple of days later Issa and I got into his jeep and set off for a nerve-racking trip to Juglarge. I sat in the back, with seven helicopter-gunship rockets piled up on the floor under my feet. They were 70 or 80 millimeters (about three inches) in diameter and as long as the jeep was wide. Their presence didn't really bother me, but they had safety caps on the noses and one of the caps was missing. That exposed the detonator. Whenever Issa made a right turn the rocket would slide across the floor of the jeep, so I had to stop it with my foot before the detonator hit the door.

It was a rainy day and the roads were muddy. We bumped and slid our way past the small houses of the village of Juglarge and stopped at the front of a long driveway that led to a house poking over a hill. A couple of armed fighters standing in the mud told us that the driveway was too muddy for the jeep, so we squished our way through the muck until we reached the two houses that made up a little compound. The walls were riddled with holes, and the windows had been blown out and covered up with plastic sheeting. A mujahid watched me as I took in the scene.

"The Russians like to say hello from time to time," he explained.

A short stocky guy with chiseled features came out of the house with the most damage. Issa introduced him to me as Musa, the commander.

Most of the mujahideen sat under a makeshift awning built between two parts of one of the houses. Musa introduced me to all of them. They were all young guys—the youngest was fourteen—but the rest were about my age, twenty-one. Most of them were strong and burly looking and two of them, Ruslan and AsSalaambeck, had been tae kwon do champions before the war. When we sat down Issa started to explain my problem to Musa and the rest of the guys. I didn't understand a lot of what he said because he was speaking in Chechen, but whatever he chose to tell them about me made them laugh out loud and stare at me. One of them pointed at me, slid his finger across his neck, and asked, "*Russkie soldat,* how many?" I pretended to concentrate and counted on my fingers the way a child might, and they laughed. Musa patted me on the back and said "You are welcome."

I could tell just by looking at them that these were my kind of guys. They all had that look in their eyes.

Issa ran off with Musa and left me to get to know the guys under the awning. We sat and joked and even tried to fix an AGS-17 30mm automatic grenade launcher that was sitting disassembled on the floor. After a while Issa came back and asked me if I wanted to stay or go back with him, but there was no question in my mind. This would be the first and only group I would find a bond with in Chechnya.

I had a good time with the guys in Juglarge. I taught them what I knew, and they taught me everything that they knew. After a few days Musa, Ruslan, AsSalaambeck, and I walked down the road that led to the town of Kerchaloy. The area was an active front, and there were signs of the war everywhere. Small parachutes with burnt-out illumination flares dangled from trees, and unexploded rockets and mortar rounds were buried halfway in the earth. Musa nonchalantly mentioned that the road was littered with mines, but said I shouldn't worry because they were only antitank mines that needed at least 150 kilograms, or 330 pounds of pressure to detonate. Suddenly I felt like I was walking on eggshells. When we came across two BTRs that had obviously hit some of the mines I was amazed at the destruction. The BTRs were literally split in half, as though some giant had come along, picked them up, and broken them in two. The forest nearby was littered with debris—a twisted hatch here, a wheel over there.

On the way to Kerchaloy a group of Chechen teenagers saw us and must have thought we were Russian soldiers. They looked at us with terrified expressions, then began to run. Ruslan called after them and when they stopped running both he and AsSalaambeck began rolling on the ground with laughter.

"You're not Chechens!" Ruslan called out to them. "You must be Azeris. *That's* why you run when you think you see Russians."

This must have really tickled AsSalaambeck's funnybone because the laughter really started then.

"No," one of the boys protested. "We were going to warn the others."

"Warn them how?" Ruslan asked. "With your wet pants?"

The kids knew we were giving them a good-natured ribbing and they walked with us to Kerchaloy, the first big Chechen city I'd seen. It was amusing how all the people looked at us when we entered the town. The men regarded us with respect and the women gazed at us with admiration. We strode through the streets like knights in dirty camouflage fatigues. Along the way I'd wondered about the purpose of our trip—was it some kind of reconnaissance? After all, we'd walked through the Russian lines to get here.

I found out that our mission was far more important. Kerchaloy still had a small television studio in full working order, and we had risked our lives because it was going to broadcast *Enter the Dragon* with Bruce Lee. This was Chechnya, after all: first things first. Fighters from different groups gathered at Musa's friend's house to see Bruce Lee kick ass. That night the bearded freedom fighters watched the movie and discussed what would happen if we had Bruce Lee on our side. Most of them were of the opinion that it would turn the tide of the war to our favor simply because the Russians would be too scared to fight Bruce Lee.

I couldn't help but put my two cents in. "What about Jean-Claude Van Damme?" I asked.

"Be quiet, Abu," Musa told me. "He would make us lose the war."

A couple of days later I was back in Kerchaloy with Musa again, just to cruise around. It was a warm, beautiful day and the sun was shining. Musa stopped at one of the market stalls lining the main road and began talking to a beautiful young woman. She had fascinating light brown eyes, and her scarf only partially covered her auburn hair. I asked him who she was and he said that she was the daughter of one of his friends. I'd avoided any contact with women in Chechnya, despite the fact that everyone was always trying to hook me up. But when I saw this woman I knew that I had to have her. Her name was Ayeesha.

During the next couple of weeks Ayeesha occupied my mind. I wanted to get back to Kerchaloy, but there was still a war going on and we had work to do. We would often roam the countryside or hike up and down the mountains looking for action, and we would sometimes come in contact with other Chechen groups. On one occasion, we met a group that had captured four Russian soldiers. Most of the atrocities on the civilians of Chechnya were perpetrated by the same Russian soldiers, over and over again. They often acted with impunity and the tacit approval of their officers, and over time they would build a reputation within particular communities for barbarity. Yet, strange as it may sound, they seemed to think they were somehow anonymous, that people wouldn't remember the faces of the soldiers who'd raped their daughters or killed their grandfathers. The war had warped them; they thought Chechnya was populated with nameless, faceless nonhumans with no memory and no future—like cattle in a slaughterhouse. They believed that the Chechens would forget their faces as fast as they forgot the faces of their victims. That day, these four soldiers were well known in the area, and a couple of our guys watched as the local commander administered drumhead justice, Russian style.

It was a cold dark day with a light, bone-chilling drizzle. A fresh pit had been dug for the occasion, and one of the Russian soldiers stared into it with a blank look on his face.

"You chose to come to Chechnya, and even if you had no choice in the matter as a soldier in the Russian army, you did have a choice in how you behaved once you arrived here.

"You chose to come here and rape our women and murder our children, even though you are fighting in a war you could have conducted yourselves with some degree of restraint and respect for humanity.

"If the Chechen people entered your land and committed the kind of atrocities that you have committed here you would deal with them with no less than execution. So," he continued, "do any of you question what will happen to you here today?"

None of the four Russian soldiers said a word. Their uniforms were covered with dirt and blood. Each had already been beaten to some degree or another, and the one who'd apparently committed the worst atrocities couldn't see out of his right eye, which was swollen shut. They just stood there and looked for all the world like four eerie, breathing cadavers. The field commander finished his sentence.

"In the name of Allah I sentence you to death on this day in the Republic of Chechnya for your crimes against the Chechen people."

He nodded to a burly bearded Chechen fighter standing off to the side, who casually took the first soldier by the arm and led him between the pit and the other three soldiers. The soldier made no attempt to fight or struggle.

"Get on your knees," the burly fighter told him. When the Russian complied, the Chechen kicked him on his shoulder and the soldier fell over on his side. The fighter straddled him and pulled a large curved knife from a sheath on his belt. He pulled the soldier's head back by his filthy hair and ran the knife back and forth over his neck in a ghastly sawing motion. Bright red blood squirted out as the Russian's throat was severed. His legs kicked a few times, and he grasped one of the Chechen's arms. A noise came from his throat as his last breath escaped through his gaping neck. Then the Chechen simply let the soldier's head flop onto the ground. It was tilted so far back now that it was almost completely severed.

Two of the remaining three soldiers stared straight ahead, seemingly oblivious to what was happening. The third, youngest soldier stared at the scene in front of him with horror as tears rolled down his filthy cheeks. Whether he was already chosen to be next or he drew attention to himself by crying, a different Chechen executioner took him by the arm and led him to the body of the first soldier, whose legs were still kicking.

"On your knees," the Chechen said. This time the Chechen backed up a few steps from the Russian and took an AK-74 from one of his buddies. He pointed it at the chest of the soldier and stared into his eyes.

"Please," the Russian whispered, "I don't want to die here today."

The expression on the Chechen's face didn't change. "And my wife and son didn't want to be blown to pieces by Russian bombs," he replied. The soldier started to cry again and muttered something that sounded like a prayer. Before he was finished, the Chechen fighter pulled the trigger on his AK-74.

The Russian's torso split open with the long burst of automatic fire. As the first rounds hit, his face twisted into an expression of agony and he fell over forward. He wasn't thrown back violently or dramatically, as in a Hollywood movie; he simply slumped over and fell on his face. The Chechen then stood over the soldier and put a few more rounds into his back.

The other two soldiers still stared straight ahead. Two of their comrades had just been executed in front of them, yet they just stood there. I couldn't help but wonder what would cause a person to give up all willingness to survive. Although I had no sympathy for them or desire to help them, I wanted to yell, "Do something, you stupid fuckers."

A third Chechen took the next Russian. He didn't grab the soldier by his arm but simply pushed him from behind. The soldier walked himself to the spot where he knew he would die and got on his knees without being told to. I wondered what was going through the Russian's mind. Was he wondering how this Chechen would kill him?

The third Chechen stood in front of the soldier and just stared at him for a moment. He didn't seem to savor the moment; it wouldn't bring back whatever or whomever he'd lost. The Russian actually raised his head and stared back, expressionless. The Chechen pulled a Tokarev 9mm pistol from his waistband. When the Russian saw it he lowered his head and stared at the ground. The Chechen walked to his side and put the pistol to his temple.

"Do you want to say anything?"

"*Nyet.*"

Without further ado, the Chechen pulled the trigger. The soldier simply slumped over and lay motionless in the mud. Blood flowed from the fresh hole in his head for a moment, mixing with the Chechen earth.

The last soldier still hadn't moved, but silent tears ran down his face. The burly Chechen walked over to him, but instead of taking him by his arm, as he had done with the first soldier, he grabbed the Russian by the throat and slammed him to the ground. The soldier didn't fight, but his eyes went wide with fear. Perhaps he expected a gentler execution, like those his comrades had received, but the Chechen didn't waste any time and started sawing away at the Russian's neck. This one kicked harder than the first soldier, and he made the same noise as the air in his lungs rushed out of his gaping neck. His legs continued to twitch for a good thirty seconds or so, and then he was still.

I got along with everyone in our small group, but tensions began to develop between us and Musa, who always seemed to be absent. We lacked direction and were getting bored. To occupy ourselves we started to roam in the forest. After a while, Ruslan, AsSalaambeck, and I got closer and closer to the Russians down the valley. When Musa found out about this he tried to maintain some semblance of command by giving us ridiculous missions. One such mission was to hunt down the Russian gunship helicopters that roamed around the nearby mountains. Musa knew we were ill equipped for such a mission and figured we'd run around chasing our tails. We had other thoughts and set off down the mountain.

As usual, I had my AK-74 and a couple of disposable Mukha rockets. Ruslan and AsSalaambeck were carrying PKM light machine guns and looked like characters straight out of a Hollywood movie. They both had on black jeans with camouflage jackets, a Chechen favorite. Their PKMs didn't have a box on the underside to carry the ammo belt, so they'd crisscrossed the cartridge belts over their chests like Rambo.

When we came out of the valley we saw two hills, the last of the foothills before the plains. From the top of the hill on the left was an incredible view of the cities of Kerchaloy and Tutsanute. A Russian armored brigade was stationed in a very large stand of trees on the outskirts of Kerchaloy, about three kilometers away, surrounded by agricultural fields. We heard the wicked high-pitched scream of gas-turbine engines coming from a number of T-80 tanks. The sound was distinct, quite different from the low, deep rumble of T-72s. T-80s always sent chills down my spine.

That the T-80s were positioned this close to the front piqued my curiosity. The Russians usually kept them at the rear until they were ready for an offensive move. If they were getting ready for a push, our position back up the mountain was going to get hit hard. We were already so far outside the mission parameters that Musa had set for us that I figured we might as well get a little closer and gather whatever intelligence we could to help us prepare for the offensive. We watched the T-80s as they practiced maneuvers down in the fields—they were using smoke screens and moving around. They appeared to be practicing advances from upwind of the smoke screens so that the screen would cover their approach.

I saw through my binoculars that some of the T-80s had drifted off from the main group, probably so the crew could find a nice shady area to sit on top of their tank and relax or smoke some hash. Although Musa would have been angry about such a plan, Ruslan and I talked about the possibility of taking out a stray tank crew. Both Ruslan and I could drive T-72s, and we figured we'd try to drive one of the T-80s if we could hit the tankers silently. We wouldn't be able to get it back up the mountain because we'd mined the road, but we could hide it in the bushes for use in an ambush.

The hilltop wasn't flat; it had a lot of trees and embankments and looked like it had once been a farm. The other side of the hill was beyond one of the embankments, so I told Ruslan and AsSalaambeck to stay put as I went to the other side of the hill to take a look around. I was being cautious but didn't see any need to crawl, because we appeared to be the only ones on the hill. I approached the small embankment bent over and peered over the top. I didn't see anything, so I straightened up and looked around with the binoculars. A few seconds later I felt the air move as something whizzed past my head, followed by the sound of a report. I hit the ground. When I poked my head back up a hail of automatic fire sprayed the embankment in front of me. It sounded like a PKM machine gun. I motioned to the other two to cover me, and I quickly crawled back over to where they were. We waited there, ready to engage whoever came over the embankment, but no one came. We assumed it was most likely a squad that wasn't enthusiastic about chasing some rebels up into the hills. They would probably call in a strike, so we had to get out of there quickly.

We started to traverse the side of the hill that led down to the valley because the tree cover and deep flood-carved ruts would provide a little protection if a rain of death fell before we could make some distance. But instead of destroying the whole area and looking for the bodies later, the Russians were in a playful mood that day; within five minutes two Ka-50 Charney Akula "Black Shark" helicopters appeared on the scene.

They immediately began to circle in a search pattern. We took cover and waited a few minutes, but they kept circling just over our position a couple of hundred feet off the ground. We knew that they wouldn't risk their asses by staying in one spot unless it was for a good reason. Most likely they figured we were only a few guys, and they had standing orders to catch any rebels alive if they could. At that moment a Spetsnaz hunter team was probably double-timing it up the hill we'd just left. As we moved along the slope under cover, the Black Sharks stayed with us, either by coincidence or because they were actually tracking us. We knew that if they stayed with us the hunters would run us down in no time. We had two Mukha disposable rockets with us—not much good against Black Sharks, but we had to get them off our asses so that we could shake any hunters who were on their way. Since the Sharks were so low I figured that the Mukhas might actually do something. The Sharks were circling in a wide pattern by now, going right over our heads. As one was passed over our side of the circle the other was about five hundred meters away. If we could knock out the one, maybe we could move out of the circle before the other could fire on us.

I quickly explained my idea to my two comrades, which was really unnecessary because I could see on their faces that they would be happy just shooting at the Sharks with the PKMs they were each carrying. Chechens don't feel fear the same way other people do, which is not to say that they are fearless supermen. Nevertheless, shooting an armored attack helicopter with Mukha rockets and a 7.62 x 54 general-purpose machine gun doesn't worry them in the least. So on that sunny breezy day, on the slope of a beautiful hill overlooking an even more beautiful valley, with nothing but God and our little disposable rockets, we decided to get it on with two of the most advanced helicopters in the world. I positioned Ruslan so that he was straddling one of the deeper ruts, hoping that this might keep the back blast generated by firing the rocket at such a high angle from burning his ass off. Not having much time, Ruslan waited for the best available shot and took it. It couldn't have been any better; he'd fired from almost directly beneath the chopper. The deep rut dissipated most of the back blast, but it was enough to knock Ruslan over. The rocket made a quick, straight flight and probably armed just before it struck the center of the tail boom. The tail sheared off in a screech of metal. The Shark pitched up violently, then corkscrewed straight into the ground with an enormous crash a hundred meters away. We immediately took off at a dead run, tearing diagonally down the slope toward the valley floor.

The second Shark surprised us. He made one pass over his downed partner, then simply left. Maybe he thought we had Stingers; whatever the reason, it bought us some time. We weren't out of the woods yet; it was a long way back to the base, over rough terrain. If the hunters were behind us they might be able to track us down before we could get some backup.

The mountainous terrain in front of us consisted of little valleys and ravines that ran down toward the plains like fingers. After double-timing for about a mile, we started to wonder if this was the way we had come earlier in the day. We soon realized that we were in another one of these little fingers. We were headed in the right general direction but didn't know how far to the west this finger would take us, which might cause us to skirt around our base and miss it. So we decided to start walking east, humping over the tops of the fingers until we came to the road that would run us back up to our village. It was walking over these ridges that we saw the Russians.

They had established a little firebase on one of the ridges. It looked like no more than a platoon, but they had a couple of BTRs and a BMP with them. On the way down we must have just missed them, but their presence explained the small muddy road that we'd crossed earlier in the day. It also explained all the illumination-flare chutes and burnt casings lying all over the place, as well as why that section of forest that was completely shredded. At night the standard operating procedure for Russians was to hide in their bunkers and, at the slightest sound, open up with everything they have for at least ten minutes. They sent flares up one after another like a kid needing the comfort of his night-light.

Eventually I was able to get back down to Kerchaloy to see Ayeesha again. AsSalaambeck and one of the younger guys from the group went with me, and we walked through Russian lines as usual. The three of us talked to Ayeesha for a while. Islam does not prohibit a man from taking more than one wife, and after some thought I told the younger guy to ask her if she wanted to marry me.

"Do I want to marry him?" She considered it, smiling. "Doesn't he mean the other way around?" But she knew it wasn't the other way around. It was a big honor for a woman to marry a fighter in Chechnya. "I suppose," she said, "but he will have to wait for three months."

I listened to this and shook my head.

"He could be dead in three months," the younger guy said. "It must be sooner."

"Maybe in one month then."

Again I shook my head.

"He could be dead in one month also."

"Three weeks and no less!" she said, blushing.

The younger guy looked at me, and I held up one finger.

"One week?" Ayeesha asked in amazement. "Men court women for years sometimes! He expects me to marry him in one week?"

When we said good-bye that day I promised that I would be back in one week to marry her. That's the way things go in war. No one knows if they will see tomorrow, and nothing can be planned too far in advance. I was very happy. The four-hour walk back to Juglarge went by in no time, and I thought about Ayeesha all the way.

Musa knew that he couldn't stop the guys from following me, so he tried to give us meaningless missions to keep us occupied and out of trouble. But every time we left the house we headed straight for the Russian base down the valley, like kids who've found a beehive.

We'd learned a lot about the Russian position in the course of our little reconnaissance missions. We knew where most of their bunkers were and what routes their patrols took in and out of their perimeter. The outer perimeter was more of a utilization of terrain than a formal position. The second perimeter was a series of forward listening posts that they only manned at night. The third was a large open field with some bunkers, which they illuminated all night long with flare after flare.

We discovered the forward listening posts completely by accident. One day three of us set up in a stand of trees and extremely tangled underbrush just on the edge of the field so that we could monitor the activity in the bunkers. As I was sitting in the bushes I noticed a spot that looked like someone had lain down there several times, judging from the smashed-down grass. That night we hid in some bushes nearby, and sure enough, just after sundown two Russian soldiers clumsily made their way from the bunkers on the far side of the field to the spot in the bushes.

We toyed with the idea of taking out the guys who manned the listening posts. At first we wanted to booby-trap their area. Then we decided to get up close and personal; after all, the Russians did most of their killing with bombs. That turned into a plan to go after the guys in one of the bunkers over on the far side of the field, which finally led to a plan to take off our shirts, roll around in the mud, and kill them with only our knives.

We conducted the operation a few nights later. We stripped off our uniform tops and gear and placed them next to the trail along with our AKs. I winced when the cold mud covered my upper body. "Did anybody think about how we're going to wash this shit off when we're finished?" I asked no one in particular. The three others also smeared mud on themselves.

The listening posts to our left were far enough away that we weren't concerned with them. We heard the *thump* of the illumination flares as they were fired over the field every five minutes or so. The flares rocked back and forth under their tiny parachutes as they drifted slowly to the ground, which cast a spooky flickering light over everything. It was next to impossible to be spotted under this light unless you were actually moving in an upright position, and we were counting on the false sense of security that it gave the Russian soldiers. And the fact that only lunatics would try to come across this open field at night.

Our target was the farthest bunker on the right edge of the field. It was so far away from the other bunkers that the Russians used a vehicle to relieve the soldiers there. The bunker was covered with a tent and had a small trench system. No more than seven men were stationed there at any given time. They had a machine gun inside the bunker and a grenade launcher outside. Two or three Russians were stationed in the trenches at night; the rest presumably stayed inside the bunker to get high and drink vodka. Once night fell on Russian firebases, every bunker became a bastion of psychotic paranoia that even the base commanders wouldn't dare go near; this made our approach more difficult and eliminated the possibility of reinforcement if things got loud.

The plan was pretty straightforward. We were going to crawl across the field along the far right side and use the trenches that branched out from the bunker to sneak up on the two or three soldiers there. We weren't going bare chested just for fun—we didn't want to wear any gear whatsoever so that we could silently slide through the grass field and then into the trenches. After taking care of the guys outside we would slip into the bunker and take care of the rest inside. We figured we could sprint the two hundred meters or so back across the field and disappear into the forest before the base was able to react. One of us would stay back at the edge of the field to cover our exit in case the listening posts to the left started to shoot. All of this could just as easily been accomplished with guns, but this seemed like the right way to do things. The Russians had all the heavy weapons of a modern army, so it seemed appropriate for them to meet their fates at the hands of men armed only with knives.

I was calmer than I thought I would have been as we slid single file through the grass across the field. We were moving very slowly, very deliberately. When we heard the *thump* of an illumination flare we would simply freeze in place and put our faces down in the grass until the light faded away, then we would continue. The temperature was probably in the low forties and the sharp edges of the grass were unpleasant to slide over, but I barely noticed the discomfort. At this pace it took us more than an hour to get to the far edge of the field, where we saw one of the soldiers moving around just outside the bunker. He spoke occasionally to someone, so we assumed a second soldier was sitting down inside the trench line, but other than that we couldn't see anyone else. Once we reached the trench, Ruslan slithered down into the far end and I continued crawling around to the back, toward the Russian who was concealed. The third guy followed Ruslan. After that, things moved so quickly that it was difficult to piece together what happened.

Ruslan slid along the bottom until he was within reaching distance of the standing Russian. The soldier would pace back and forth occasionally, and when he paced back toward Ruslan, Ruslan grabbed his legs. Ruslan plunged his knife into the soldier's neck before he hit the floor. The other soldier jumped up at the sound and started in that direction. I was still lying at the edge of the trench, so I just reached out and drove my knife into the back of his neck when he passed by. I slid into the trench on top of him and finished the job, the only sounds being a few muted cries before I severed his vocal cords. I looked up and saw the shadow of Ruslan and the other guy running hunched over toward me.

I turned and also started running, toward the entrance to the bunker. Without looking to see if the others were with me or not, I burst through the blanket that hung over the entrance. One soldier was standing in the middle of the small room with his back to me. Without even noticing how many others were in the room, I charged him and drove my knife up into his kidneys. Another soldier was lying on a blanket on a raised surface carved out of the dirt wall of the bunker. His eyes were as wide as silver dollars, and before he could even raise his hands I stuck the knife straight into his chest. Ruslan and our third man had came through the entrance right after me and were slashing and stabbing another two Russians who were lying down.

After all the immediate threats had been neutralized I turned back to the Russian whom I'd stabbed in the chest. In the light cast by an old kerosene lamp and a few candles, the soldier was lying there twisting and moaning and clutching at his chest. An older guy with a scruffy face, he reeked of sweat, cigarettes, and vodka. I pulled his head back, looked into his eyes, and cut his throat. Ruslan and the other guy finished the soldier I'd stabbed in the kidneys. We looked at each other for a second. There were plenty of good weapons for us to take, but none of us really thought about that. We wanted to get out of there as quickly as possible.

The three of us moved quickly from the entrance of the bunker and down the trench without saying a word. It didn't appear that anyone had heard us, so we decided to crawl back to the other side of the field. We moved much faster on the way back because we were less concerned about being spotted.

"Good hunting?" the fourth guy asked as we approached.

"Very nice," Ruslan replied. We put our tops back on, grabbed our AKs, and headed back up the mountain.

The big morning arrived. After Salaatul Fajr I was too excited to go back to sleep with the rest of the guys, so I heated some water on the fire outside, trimmed my mustache, and shaved my head. As the day progressed and the crew started to wake up, it looked like we wouldn't be finding a ride down to Kerchaloy. Musa had promised that his personal jeep would take me, but we found out that it had broken the day before. I was too anxious to wait for a ride on another day, so I decided to make the four-hour walk. As usual, Ruslan and AsSalaambeck planned to tag along with me. We even looked forward to maybe taking out a Russian or two on the way to my wedding.

The day was cold and overcast, and the fog that shrouded the hilltops, would provide an advantage to us when we had to walk through the Russian lines to Kerchaloy. But we'd already crossed their lines to see Bruce Lee movies. For all the Russians' military might, we still moved about largely unmolested.

As I finished cleaning up the door flew open and one of the local civilians ran in. He spoke in Chechen so quickly that I couldn't understand him, and he was so excited he looked as though he was going to pass out. Whatever he said made the crew scramble immediately to gear up. Without waiting to find out what was happening I rushed to get my gear on. The only thing I had time to ask was whether or not I should grab my Mukha rockets. "Grab everything," said Ruslan. "Our time has come." Since I was half naked when the guy burst in, I was barely able to grab the last of my gear and make it out the door before being left behind. I ran up the muddy hill with my boots untied and my mag vest unfastened on the sides. We were taking a route to the main road that we'd agreed to in the event of an attack.

Just trying to make it to the top of the hill without losing my gear or falling behind the group kept me from thinking about what awaited us on the main road. The head of the line had reached the road and there wasn't any contact yet, so I figured that the Russians were still approaching. Musa gave a quick briefing when the remainder of the group reached the main road. One of the women from the village had been getting water from the well just outside our perimeter when she'd seen a squad of Spetsnaz. She'd run back to the village before the Spetsnaz troops could get her, and she'd told the man who'd then run into our house. At this point, no more than ten minutes had passed. So it was the usual gig: make contact and take them out before they took us out.

Unfortunately, we had very little information. How many Spetsnaz were there? The woman had described a squad—*zvoed* in Russian—but did she literally mean a squad, or could there be more? Her choice of the word *zvoed* made me lean toward ten or twelve, since most Chechens, including women, have some basic understanding of Russian military structure. From the description of their uniforms we knew that they were Spetsnaz, but there was no way to know if they were hitting us with some kind of raid or if they were running point for a larger force behind them. We doubted that they had any armor with them as we hadn't heard any detonations from the antitank mines in the road, but perhaps there were Mi-24 "Hind" or Ka-50 "Shark" helicopter gunships waiting down the valley. Something wasn't right.

Regardless of what we were up against, we were ready to make contact and kick ass. After all, we were Nokche Bores, Chechen Wolves, and just as a real pack of wolves may hunt with caution, when their den is threatened they will attack whatever is posing the threat with no hesitation. This village was our den and the children of the village were our pups, and so long as a single one of us was still breathing, we had vowed, not one Russian soldier would set foot in our village. There were only about seven of us that morning, but we were ready to hold the road against a brigade if we had to.

As usual, Musa didn't have much of a plan. We simply started to advance down the road. The Russians hadn't entered the village yet, which indicated that they might have retreated when they'd lost their element of surprise, or that they had pulled back to set up an ambush. I had an awful, nagging feeling that it was the latter.

The fog had become so thick by now that our visibility was less than twenty feet. There was a small clearing to our left, and the forest beyond it was at the top of a very steep hill that dropped into the valley, so it was unlikely that the Russians were anywhere on our left flank. On our right, the forest advanced all the way to the road. Down the road and to the left there was a small shack that the farmers used occasionally, and a stand of trees lay behind the shack. Musa ordered everyone to fan out on our right flank into a picket line and advance. I had a bad feeling about the shack ahead of us and motioned for my men to follow me down the left side of the road, but they hesitated to listen to me because Musa was around. To make things worse, the squad bunched up just inside the tree line instead of forming a picket line. After weeks of bitching about intervals, here they were about to walk into an ambush all bunched up.

Boots still untied, I moved to the left side of the road. Musa looked at me and motioned for me to get back to the right, but I just ignored him. Everybody paused for a second and I started to take my Mukha off my back, but it was caught in my gear. We started to advance again and I didn't want to be behind the group, so I left the Mukha on my back, set my AKM in the low ready position, and picked up my pace to get in front of the others. I was getting pretty sure about the shack and the trees behind it, and I wanted to at least give the guys time to react, or else Musa was going to get everybody killed. The closer I got to the shack the more I wanted to get the Mukha off my back. If I saw any signs of an ambush I would just blow up the shack and use the diversion to haul ass around to the left side of the trees behind the shack. Once there, I could hit the ambush from the left flank while the others made a head-on approach.

I motioned for Musa to stop for a minute. He ignored me, so I signaled that maybe there were Russians in the shack ahead. He just looked at me the way he always did when I tried to tell him something and kept going. By this time I desperately wanted my Mukha and was about to cut the strap when I saw movement inside the shack. It was dark and the heavy fog made it difficult to see, but I saw the outline of a barrel move behind one of the window openings. I wanted to yell *Ambush* to the other guys, but didn't know if the Russians had seen them yet. For that matter, I didn't know if they had seen me, either. I ran to a tree that was about 10 meters in front of the shack and looked over at the group. They were a few meters behind me and just inside the trees on the right side of the road. Having no time and no other choice, I pushed down the selector on my AKM from semi to full auto and stepped out from behind the tree. I took one step forward and started to pull the trigger but never made it.

Two simultaneous explosions ripped through the air. Out of the corner of both eyes I saw bright flashes of light and puffs of smoke. The explosions dazed me for a second, everything went into slow motion, and I ducked down as a reflex. I looked back up at the shack, expecting to see something, but didn't. Still clutching my AKM, I started to pivot to move back behind the tree, but when I tried to take a step my right leg gave out and I fell over on my back. There was an incredible burning in my shin, a pain so intense I couldn't breathe. I looked down at my leg and was shocked to see my foot at a right angle to my leg. The lower half of my fatigues were ripped with big holes, and bright red blood squirted out from them. I tried to use my left leg to push myself behind the tree but couldn't move a single inch because just the slight movement almost caused me to pass out from the pain. In a panic I strained to look around to see what the hell was going on. I couldn't see the other guys, and I'd opened my mouth to yell when movement from the shack caught my eye. I looked up to see an RPK squad automatic weapon open up on me. I swung my AKM and mashed the trigger down. Two of the rounds from the RPK ripped through my thigh on the right leg. Another almost tore off my ankle on the left leg. I didn't care where my rounds were going but had enough thought left to fire in bursts and not blow my whole mag at once. The RPK stopped for a second. I was unable to move even an inch and figured that this was it. I started to scream *Allah-u-Akbar* at the top of my lungs. At this time the other guys started firing on the shack. Ruslan opened up with his PKM, and someone hit the shack with a Mukha.

I was close enough to the shack to get hit with flying debris from the explosion of the Mukha. After that, I lost track of what was happening. The pain was so intense that I didn't even care about the fight and couldn't have defended myself if I'd tried. I thought for sure that I was dead so I started chanting, *La illaha ilalallah.* One of the guys appeared next to me. He looked at my legs and then back at my face. It was one of the only times that I'd seen a Chechen with a look of worry on his face. A few more of the guys appeared next to me. We heard a few more isolated shots, but the battle ended as fast as it had started.

I remember one of the older guys of the group cutting my pants off. They tried to bandage my legs, but there were so many holes that we didn't have enough gauze. The older guy pulled out a syringe and a vial of morphine and tried to give me an injection, but I had lost so much blood that my veins were flat. I was lying in the mud and I started to become very cold, shaking uncontrollably. A few times everyone tried to move me, but each time I began screaming with such agony that it must have hurt to even watch. It was about half an hour before one of the guys came back with a Lada Niva, a four-by-four about the size of a Suzuki Samauri, that he had borrowed from one of the neighbors.

Getting me into the jeep just about killed me. My right leg was shredded from the knee down, and the bones had clearly been shattered. When they picked me up I could hear the bones crunching as the leg shifted. I half-sat, half-lay on top of a bunch of gear in the back. We drove to the next village up the mountain and switched to another borrowed vehicle, this time an Awazik. I guess the guys decided that the closest field hospital was in Tutsanute, but to get there we had to drive through the Russian lines.

This meant driving for about an hour and a half through some of the roughest mountain roads possible. This might have actually helped, because just as I would start to lose consciousness we would hit another big rut in the road and the pain would snap me out of it, so much so that I remained conscious all the way to the hospital. The driver and I were alone since the other guys had to stay back at the village to prepare for another possible attack. It was actually kind of comical: every so often the driver would look back at me lying flat on the back seat and call out: *Umair?* Are you dead?

"*Shas niet, paka smatree,*" I'd reply. Not yet, but wait and see.

We had to drive through Kerchaloy to get to the field hospital in Tutsanute. Kerchaloy was were Ayeesha lived, and this was supposed to have been our wedding day. As we entered Kerchaloy I noticed a very familiar Kamaz six-wheeled military truck. I yelled for the driver to stop. Sure enough, standing there on the side of the road was Ibn-ul Khattab, the now infamous commander of Arab mujahideen in Chechnya. I had split from his group sometime earlier, but he knew that I was operating in this region and had even given me some supplies that I had requested for an operation. The driver went over to him and told him to look in the back of the jeep. When he did, I felt an incredible sense of pride. I tried to muster the biggest smile I could.

"Look," I told him in English, "Allah has rewarded me." And this is what I truly felt.

"You are among the ranks of those wounded on the path," he replied. "God willing, your wounds will shine on the day of judgment." He looked at my leg, which was nothing new to him. He told me to wiggle my toes, and at the time I still could. He seemed to think that the wounds weren't all that serious. If only he'd been right.

As we drove on I poked my head up and saw that we were approaching Kerchaloy's central square, where Ayeesha worked at one of the little market stalls. By this time I was starting to feel really bad. The pain was incredible and I had lost so much blood that it was amazing I was still alive. But a promise is a promise, and I'd given my word that we would be married this day. When I saw the stretch of stalls where Ayeesha worked I told the driver to stop. He didn't know anything about me getting married and was probably worried about hurrying up and getting to the hospital, so he ignored me at first. I told him that he had to stop because it was important; Ayeesha was here. In Russian *aiysh* means apples, and he misunderstood me.

He stopped the jeep, turned to me, and said "*Khoches aiysh?*"

"*Da,*" I said, thinking that we were on the same page. The driver got out and walked over to the stalls of produce.

"Can you help me?" he asked the women standing there. "I have a fighter in the car who is dying and he wants apples. I don't have any money, but I'm sure God will reward you if you give a dying fighter some apples."

As usual, a small crowd gathered around the jeep to see the wounded fighter. The driver proudly told everyone that the man lying there bleeding was an American volunteer. Ayeesha was actually a few stalls down from where we were parked when she saw the crowd. Someone called to her to come see the bleeding American in the jeep. Later she told me that her first thought was *Wow, what a coincidence, I'm marrying an American today.* But when she came over and saw her soon-to-be lying on a blood-covered seat she almost passed out.

I motioned for her to get in the jeep. She hesitated. But I must have looked too pathetic, or maybe just too cool to refuse, so she got in the jeep and we went on our way. I will never forget her first touch. Even though it was just to keep my leg from bouncing around as it had done the whole trip until that point, and even though it was on my bloody, mangled leg, there was something indescribable about her touch. It was almost as if it made all the pain go away. That touch would surely later save my life.

The driver honked the horn when we arrived at the hospital, which was actually a school. The hospital staff who had removed my appendix when I was up in the mountains in the village of Benoi had moved to this location. Someone came out, and the driver shouted that he had a wounded fighter. They ran back inside, and the rest of the staff rushed out with a stretcher. The rest of it will always stay with me. A medical worker looked at me in the back of the jeep, turned to everyone else, and shouted, "It's Abu. The crazy American is back again."

They lifted me onto the stretcher and bounced me up the steps of the building, which was chaotic with the activity of a field hospital. I was brought into a makeshift triage room. I'd managed to stay conscious until this point, but I floated in and out of consciousness as my old friend Umar, the Chechen minister of health, started to probe the holes in my leg with his massive fingers. I couldn't fight it any more, and I vaguely remember an IV going into my arm before I finally drifted out for good. I awoke later and saw that I was being carried along the hall, naked from the waist down. Two men held the contraption that had been put on the end of my leg while three more people carried me.

The contraption was a large metal frame that acted as a crude form of traction. While I was unconscious the doctors had drilled through my right ankle with a hardware-store hand drill and had stuck a piece of nonsurgical-grade metal wire through the hole. They'd used nuts and bolts to fasten this pin to an adapter, which was then connected to some torn-up sheets. Once I was in bed, the sheets went over the pulley and off the edge of the bed and some bricks were attached to the end. I screamed a bit more as the doctors maneuvered my leg into place and adjusted the weight of the bricks hanging on the sheets. I think I ended up passing out again. My first clear memory after all of that was lying there with my leg in place. The lovely but imposing Leila was standing there with all the other nurses from my first operation up in the mountains. Someone had put a pair of pajama bottoms on me and bandaged up the rest of my wounds. From that point on, they always had a funny look on their faces when they sat in the room with me. Strange as it may sound, and even though they were nurses, I think that despite their Muslim modesty they'd all seen my dick when they were prepping me for surgery. Nevertheless, they were a caring group of women. It felt good to wake up to familiar faces, and they sat with me for a while to tell jokes and listen to the stories of what had happened since my last stay with them.

The doctor came in a bit later and sat down with me. Before he could even open his mouth I asked him the question he surely knew was coming: How long before I can go back to the front? Looking back I don't know if he really thought that the injuries weren't that serious or if he was just trying to keep me from getting depressed, but he told me that I should be back to the fighting in about three months. My left leg had only taken one round but it had been directly on the ankle, and my right leg was broken in multiple places, with about nine holes from shrapnel and bullets. Two of these were the size of silver dollars and went through my entire calf. One of the rounds had tunneled under the femoral artery and out the other side. Needless to say, if the round had hit the artery I would have bled to death. A piece of shrapnel had caused the most crucial damage by severing my peroneal nerve, and this would alter the course of my life forever.

After the doctor left, Zelemkhan showed up. He was part of Musa's group, and I'd previously recuperated from a minor illness at his house, just a few blocks from the hospital. I asked him where Ayeesha was. He explained that she'd gone home and that two of the guys from our group were there now. It appeared that she was having second thoughts about the marriage. The whole ordeal may have been too traumatic for her. Maybe she was worried about marrying someone who might end up permanently disabled or even die. Zelemkhan told me that the guys were at her house to find out. About an hour later, as Zelemkhan and I were talking, one of the guys poked his head in the door and smiled. "I have a gift for you, Abu," he said. "I'm sure this will make you feel much better." Behind him was Ayeesha, one of the most truly beautiful women I've ever seen. I'd been unable to forget her for a single second from the first time I'd seen her at the market stall. Now, as she stood in the doorway of the hospital room, I could almost forget everything that had happened to me. It was as though we were just a couple of ordinary kids who had met at a park and the Russian army was far more than two kilometers away.

Ayeesha was sixteen years old. She held herself in a very mature way, but at times her playfulness would betray her true age. It was this playfulness, combined with her tender caring, that would keep me alive through our ordeals to come. She sat by me for the rest of the evening and we talked. Later, Zelemkhan's family came by to see me. The first thing Zelemkhan's mother said as she walked in the room was, "See, Abu? I told you not to go!" They had brought me my favorite Chechen food, a kind of pasta shell with ground beef in it. Since Ayeesha lived in Kerchaloy, Zelemkhan's family told me she would stay at their house until we knew where I would be going.

The next day I awoke feeling the way I looked, like someone whose body had been pierced multiple times by hot lead. I'd thought that the painful part was over the previous day, but I was wrong. Ayeesha showed up early, and shortly after that the doctors came in with a tray of instruments, accompanied by some big Chechens. I assumed they were just the usual curious Chechens who wanted to see the American.

Then the doctor spoke. "I'm sorry that we have to do this Abu, but if we don't you'll lose your leg."

I still didn't understand what was about to happen. And even if they had described the pain that was coming I still wouldn't have understood, because no one can understand the indescribable levels of pain a person can endure except by experiencing them.

The doctor took a very large plastic syringe off the tray. It was about the size of those used for giving injections to horses. But instead of a needle on the end there was a piece of plastic tubing about an inch in diameter and ten inches long. As the orderlies held on to my arms and legs, the doctor filled the syringe with saline to irrigate my wounds. Then he rammed the tube into one of the silver-dollar-sized holes in my calf. I let out a bloodcurdling howl of pure agony, like an animal being tortured. It was physically impossible for me to hold back my screams. By the time the doctor had finished with both holes and then played with all the other smaller holes, the orderlies were sweating from the exertion of holding me down. I was totally, utterly exhausted. The pain was so overwhelming that when it was finished all I could do was lie there and whimper. Ayeesha must have thought that I was crazy because I kept whispering in English, "Please God, give me refuge from the pain."

A Chechen woman and a couple of the guys from our unit were standing out in the hallway while I got my treatment. I knew some Russian, but Musa had sent for the woman to translate as the two men made a formal presentation. They came in as I was still whimpering and the woman asked me in English if I was well enough to talk. I mustered something that sounded like a yes. After my comrades greeted me affectionately, they straightened up and took a more official tone, and the woman translated. "We came here on behalf of Commander Musa. Even though you are a volunteer, Musa would like to distinguish your actions in the village of Juglarge. Because of your special military tactics and taking the initiative to be first while we were trying to engage the enemy, you saved the life of not only Musa but the others as well. We have nothing to offer you in the way of medals and the like, but endure your wounds with honor and rest easy knowing that you have earned your place amongst the Nokche Bores.

A man who fights for something he believes in doesn't need praise for what he does or to be rewarded with medals and citations. The satisfaction of doing what you believe is enough. Nevertheless, I felt an incredible sense of pride swell up inside me. The Chechens are an incredibly strong people with courage unlike anything I've ever seen, before or since. From that day on I considered myself a Chechen, my blood mixing with their soil earned me the right.

◆

The next days went by in a blur of tears, exhaustion, and pleasure. By day the doctors would torture me until I would howl at the top of my lungs in agony, and by night Ayeesha would comfort me with her young body. There were four other patients in the hospital room with me, and after they all fell asleep she would sneak in. I couldn't move because my leg was in traction, but we still managed.

The doctors told me that I would be there for at least a month, perhaps more, but I knew I'd go crazy before then, and after twelve days I forced them to release me. I was in no condition to travel far, so I went to Zelemkhan's house to recuperate and took daily trips back to the hospital. By this time everyone acknowledged that Ayeesha and I were married, but we made it official at Zelemkhan's house with a peculiar rite. A Chechen elder came and performed a simple ceremony that Ayeesha wasn't even in the room for, and that concluded our wedding.

One evening after a treatment at the hospital, Ayeesha and I weren't able to find a ride back to Zelemkhan's house, so we decided to walk back. We were at the edge of a field whose far side, maybe two kilometers away, had a tree line with a Russian armored brigade. I wasn't very mobile with my crutches but had an AK-74 on my back. We'd seen the tanks firing at Tutsanute and into the hills beyond on other evenings. I had been in Chechnya long enough to not question why they didn't attack Tutsanute. Nothing here made any sense. But on that evening a Russian BTR approached from across the field. Although we weren't far from the hospital, we were exposed out there in the open, and I was gripped with a sense of real fear. It is one thing to fight Russians when you're strong and can use both of your legs, but another thing entirely when you can't move. There was a drainage ditch on the other side of the road, so I hobbled over to it and lowered myself in. I told Ayeesha to get down with me but she just stared at me.

"What are you doing?" she asked.

"Just get down," I told her, cowering.

"Did I marry an old woman or a fighter?" she said as she walked toward the ditch. But instead of climbing in with me she snatched my AK from my hands and pointed it at the approaching BTR.

"Get down!" I said.

She just stood there, and pointed the AK at the BTR. The Russian soldiers riding on top noticed her, and one of them leaned into an open hatch on top of the vehicle. The BTR stopped, and one soldier swung the heavy machine gun in our direction. Ayeesha didn't flinch or move an inch. The commander of the BTR stuck his head out of an open hatch to see what was going on. When he saw that it was a woman holding an AK-74 he looked almost amused and popped his head back inside. One of the soldiers on top flashed the peace sign, and the BTR rolled off. It was another weird incident in Chechnya that left me wondering why I'd lived through it.

Despite an occasional humanitarian display by individual soldiers, the Russian army was still grinding away and smashing Chechnya out of existence, village by village. One morning someone told Zelemkhan's family that the Russians were encircling Tutsanute. In a few days, perhaps hours, the soldiers would close off all exits, and then the insanity would begin with "mop-up" operations, where soldiers would look for "terrorists" while accidentally killing and raping everything in sight. The soldiers would cart off furniture from civilian houses on their BTRs and BMPs as the OMON looked for fighters, booby traps, and rebel collaborators. Zelemkhan's house would be one of their first stops, no doubt. The Russians would probably kill the entire family because their son was a fighter, and because they had helped me. I would be taken to a Russian base for a slow and painful death, and Ayeesha would be raped and killed.

I told Zelemkhan and his family that Ayeesha and I needed to leave immediately for everyone's sake, but the Chechen code of hospitality requires otherwise; we were their guests, and to allow the Russian army to force us to leave would be, in Chechen culture, extremely coarse. I was worrying about the problem when who of all people showed up but Salaah, one of the wanderers. This wasn't the first time he'd appeared when I needed help. He wondered what I was still doing there; didn't I know that the Russians were about to seal off Tutsanute?

With Salaah's help I was able to overcome Zelemkhan's family and get out of Tutsanute with Ayeesha. We said good-bye to Zelemkhan's family, thanked them for their hospitality, and left against their protests.

As we reached the main road I saw a sight that has forever stayed with me. The road was lined with the people of Tutsanute. Old men, and even old women were standing on the road. People held Chechen flags over their heads and waved them at the Russians, who were poised at the edge of the fields that surrounded Tutsanute. The road to Kerchaloy was still open but would be closed soon enough.

Along the fields on the south side of the town, Chechen fighters were hurriedly digging defensive positions in the almost frozen muddy earth. Mobs of people were burning tires and singing Chechen folk songs. I'd felt pretty unsettled that day, but when I saw the courage of the people of Chechnya my fear ebbed away, and I suddenly felt like a coward for wanting to escape to Kerchaloy. I had come to defend the Chechens, regardless of the consequences. I approached a group of fighters standing on the side of the road and asked if they could dig me a foxhole in the middle of the field.

"But how are you going to move when the Russians start to advance?" one of the fighters asked, pointing at my leg.

"I don't want to move," I replied. "I want to be *shaheed*."

"I'm sure that Allah will accept you soon enough. We'll deal with the Russians for today; you take care of your woman."

It was good advice, of course, and Salaah found someone to give us a ride toward Kerchaloy. They dropped us off on a road that led up into the mountains. As Salaah, Ayeesha, and I slowly made our way up the mountain road we could hear the battle for Tutsanute. I wondered what would happen to all those people, and to Zelemkhan's family.

After some time a dump truck with a small group of fighters stopped and gave us a ride farther up the mountain. I had to ride in the bed because my leg wouldn't fit in the cab, and because Ayeesha wouldn't leave my side. The truck dropped us off at a crossroad that led to Cecin, and we slowly made our way down the muddy road. I fell several times. Salaah would pick me up and we would continue on until I fell again. We carried on like this for hours, and by the end of the day, my leg was becoming extremely painful. All the movement had opened some of the wounds, and blood seeped from the holes in the plaster cast. Despite these difficulties, we made it to Cecin by evening and went to a house where Uthman was staying. I thought that we'd stay there for the night, but Salaah wanted to get to Khattab's camp in Dargho as soon as possible. Uthman found a jeep and we drove to a village near Dargho. I was reeling from pain by then and must have looked pale, because Salaah became concerned and went to search for a place where we could get out of the cold for the night. A local family offered us shelter and even prepared a large meal.

The next day we went to Dargho to look for Khattab so that he could arrange for us to get out of Chechnya. But Khattab had retaken Vedeno from the Russians and had made Vedeno his base. Once we got to Vedeno, we found out that Khattab was wounded. At first he didn't want to help me get out of Chechnya unless I left Ayeesha behind, but I couldn't do that. Finally he relented and agreed to arrange transportation so that I could get medical treatment in Azerbaijan, which would be no easy feat. Getting mujahideen into Chechnya was becoming difficult, and getting wounded fighters out was worse. Khattab told us to wait there in Vedeno until the end of December, nearly a month later.

We traveled first to Zandak, where I saw a group of fresh mujahideen climbing onto a truck bound for Khattab's camp. The scene was reminiscent of those in Vietnam War movies when new recruits arrive as wounded soldiers are leaving. The new guys smiled when they saw me. "*Allah-u-Akbar!*" they yelled.

"Where is the houri?" referring to the maiden of paradise one of them shouted at me.

"She is waiting for you in Grozny," I shouted back.

"*Allah-u-Akbar!*" the mujahideen called out again.

Then Abu Zubair, from Ulbi's group, came up the road with another Arab. I'd grown close to him during our time together and was happy to see him, though it would be our last meeting. He introduced me to his brother, who had just arrived with the new mujahideen. We talked for a while and Abu Zubair asked me if I was still going to take him up on an offer to visit his family, a Bedouin tribe in Saudi Arabia.

Meanwhile, his brother needed a gun. I couldn't take my AK-74 and mag vest with me to Azerbaijan, so I gave them to Abu Zubair's brother, Abu Hafs. Although he was thrilled to receive such gifts and I was happy to give them to him, fate had a weird twist in store for Abu Hafs.

Some days later, the Chechens made a daring raid into Dagestan, wiping out an entire Russian motorized rifle regiment. Abu Zubair and Abu Hafs took a Russian soldier as prisoner, but as they marched the soldier away he grabbed the AK from Abu Hafs and killed him with his own gun. Abu Zubair killed the Russian, but the next day he was hit in the stomach during a heavy firefight with Russian commandos. The Russians were hot on their trail, and Abu Zubair told the others to leave him behind. They leaned him against a tree, and each mujahid gave him an extra magazine or a grenade and a kiss on the head as they made their escape. About ten minutes after leaving Abu Zubair behind, they heard the beginning of a firefight that they lasted for quite a while. Every day I ask Abu Zubair to save a place for me in paradise.

While in Zandak, I was also able to say good-bye to Salaambeck and AsSalaambeck. Both had been wounded since I'd last seen them, Salaambeck quite seriously. They had taken part in a major battle in the town of Gudermes. Salaambeck was fighting from a house when a Russian tank crew saw him. Witnesses said that the tank fired into the house more than ten times, leveling the building completely. Salaambeck had shrapnel wounds in his hands, head, and back, and lost a large chunk from his calf, but he survived. Luqman, who had watched Muhammad Zaky die, was also killed in the battle for Gudermes. A wall collapsed when a tank rammed the house he was in, and he was decapitated. Uthman, who had helped us get to Vedeno, died in Gudermes as well.

Khattab arranged transportation across the border, and late one afternoon two Dagestani mujahideen brought a Lada Niva to take us. I'd given Abu Hafs all of my weapons, with the exception of two grenades. One was strapped to my chest with an Ace bandage. If we were caught, I could just reach up and pull the pin out. It might seem extreme, but a slow painful death after watching Russian soldiers rape Ayeesha would have been unbearable. I was going to give Ayeesha one of the grenades but thought better of it; her stepbrother had been killed at a checkpoint, and it wasn't inconceivable that she might try to conform to the Chechen custom of vengeance by blowing us up at one of the checkpoints ahead.

We traveled north of Zandak, then east to a border crossing of a deep and nearly empty irrigation canal surrounded by muddy fields. The Lada Niva almost got stuck several times as we tried to cross the mud, and our luck finally ran out when we tried to climb the bank of the canal. Just as we got near the top we started to get bogged down and were eventually stuck. One of the Dagestanis said that he would walk to the nearest village in Dagestan to find a tractor that could pull us out. The other guy stayed in the jeep with Ayeesha and me.

We'd been sitting there for about an hour when all of a sudden the ground started to vibrate, shaking the little Lada Niva underneath us. Then we heard the low rumble of a Russian helicopter gunship. The Dagestani jumped out to look for it while I told Ayeesha to get out and run to some nearby bushes, but she refused. There was no question about whether I would be able to get out of the jeep in time, so I just sat there. As the noise got louder the Dagestani did what Ayeesha wouldn't. I'll never forget the expression on his face at that moment on that day—it seemed to say, "Sorry, what do you expect me to do?" A moment later we looked over and saw two helicopters cruising along the border, not more than fifty feet off the deck. Our jeep was sitting in the open, and there was no way that the helicopters couldn't see our tracks running across the field. As the choppers came close one of the door gunners looked right at us. He could see where we'd come from, where we were going, and who we were. Ayeesha slid her hand up into my shirt and put her finger through the pin of the grenade. She laid her head on my shoulder and whispered, "*La illaha ilalallah.*" I was too tired and in too much pain to be scared anymore and simply leaned my head against hers. The door gunner stared at us as the gunships passed by, and then they receded and were out of sight as quickly as they'd come.

As the sun began to set we saw a tractor making its way across the field. The other Dagestani had found somebody to help us, but once the jeep was pulled free the engine wouldn't start, so the tractor towed us back to a Dagestani village. Our driver went off to find alternate transportation and came back with an empty minibus, then drove us to the main road to Makhachkala, the capital of Dagestan. From there we had to use a public minibus to travel into the city. The Dagestani who had driven us from Chechnya stayed with the jeep, but the other one traveled with us on the bus.

The situation was less than ideal. I was obviously a wounded Chechen fighter, and Ayeesha wore a veil that signified that she was definitely Chechen. This wasn't a problem as far as the Dagestanis were concerned, because they were mostly sympathetic toward Chechens. However, it was going to be hard to avoid soldiers and cops while riding on public transportation, and at one of the bus stops a Dagestani police officer got on the bus. He gave us a second look but didn't say anything. At the next stop an extremely drunk middle-aged man staggered onto the bus. He decided that of all the places he could sit on the bus, he'd sit in front of us. Of course he immediately turned his attention to us and began to make so much noise that the cop who had gotten on at the previous stop started to stare at us. Our Dagestani guy tried to whisper something in the drunk's ear, but this just made him louder. What came next was surprising. The Dagestani rang the bell for the next stop and when the bus halted, he grabbed the drunk by his jacket and threw him out the back door. Good way to keep a low profile, I thought. I was sure that the cop was going to make trouble for us, but to my additional surprise he just laughed at the Dagestani. Our companion also had a big beard like mine and I guess the cop just assumed that we were religious fanatics who were offended by the drunk.

We got off at a bus stop and took a taxi to an apartment block. There an English-speaking man told us that we would stay with him for a few days until we could get fake passports so that we could cross the border into Azerbaijan. We ended up staying there about a week; a couple of days after the New Year of 1996, a man came for us and said that everything was ready. They moved us through a series of safe houses on our way to the border. At one of the many checkpoints along the road I saw that our passports weren't exactly fake but borrowed. Our Dagestani drivers had been passing me off at the checkpoints as a sixteen-year-old dark-skinned Dagestani kid named Maghomed, and Ayeesha's passport wasn't much better. It was just another example of the weirdness that characterized my whole stay in the Caucasus. Nothing seemed real there; it was some sort of parallel universe where everything logical was illogical and vice versa. When I saw the passport I laughed so hard I almost began to cry. I could only imagine the conversations that had taken place between our Dagestani driver and the checkpoint soldiers as they looked into our car and then at the passports.

"Let me get this straight," the soldier would probably tell our driver. "That pale white man with a foot-long red beard who has a bloodstained cast on his leg is in actuality a dark-skinned sixteen-year-old named Maghomed, not a wounded mujahid?"

"Yes," our driver would answer. "The picture on his passport was taken a long time ago."

"Oh, well, *that explains everything.* Please pardon my mistake. You may pass."

Whatever the case, we eventually made it to the border.

Just as on the journey into Chechnya in what seemed like an eternity ago, the Dagestanis never told us any of the plans. This time, we would cross at a very large checkpoint where several cars were waiting. The guide sitting next to our driver got out and jogged up to one of the buildings at the checkpoint. After a few minutes he came back and motioned to us. Ayeesha and I got out of the car. He pointed to a small dirt path that led behind the wall of the checkpoint, where there was a hole in the barbed-wire fence. Although it was nighttime, it still didn't seem like we could just blatantly sneak around the checkpoint.

I looked at our guide.

"Go," he said.

"But—"

"Go. Go!"

We followed the muddy path behind the buildings at the border crossing. The soldiers at the checkpoint obviously threw all their garbage over the wall, because the path was littered with beer bottles and cans. I tried to be as quiet as possible, but my crutches were getting stuck in the mud every few feet, and the beer bottles clanked as we walked over them. I thought to myself, This is insane! We can't possibly make it through here! I kept waiting for a Russian soldier to stick his head over the wall and yell "Will you guys keep it down back there? We're trying to watch TV." Then I saw something that made my nuts shrivel up.

Two Russian soldiers with AKs slung around their necks stood at the end of the path. Now I'm going to have to blow us all up, I thought. Ayeesha said nothing and stayed by my side. The soldiers looked over at us. One of them said, "Who are you? What are you doing?" The other one tapped his shoulder and pointed at something. They both looked at a man who was walking toward them from the Azeri side. He had a sharp leather coat and an expensive fur cap and wore a big diamond ring on one of his fingers. He ignored the two Russians and looked at us.

"*Nokche chu?*" he asked in Chechen. Are you Chechens?

"*Huh,*" Ayeesha replied. Yes.

"*Howala,*" the Chechen mafioso said, motioning us forward. One of the Russian soldiers started to say something, but the Chechen waved him off the way you would a small child. He put his hand on my shoulder as we walked past the two soldiers and started chatting. So, how's the weather? Did you send postcards from your trip? Meet anyone unusual? I learned later that he wasn't part of our crossing plan. Our Dagestani guides had assumed that there weren't any soldiers behind the checkpoint. The Chechen mafioso had just happened to be there and had used his considerable clout to get us past the two Russian soldiers. Thank God for the Chechen Mafia.

Once we crossed into Azerbaijan, everything went smoothly, and we arrived in Baku late that night. We no longer needed the grenades, so I took the detonators out and asked Ayeesha to bury them at the side of the road. Our guides took us to a hospital in Baku where the whole fifth floor was dedicated to wounded mujahideen. The next morning I met Shamil, one of the heads of the Chechen Mafia in Azerbaijan. Shamil was tall and well groomed and wore an expensive leather coat like the guy who had helped us across the border, and I never saw him without his two extremely enormous Chechen bodyguards. He made everything happen in Baku and took care of all the wounded fighters.

Ayeesha and I stayed in the hospital for over a month. We had our own room, but spent our days in a common area yelling and cheering at cheesy Hollywood action movies with a room full of bearded rebel soldiers all missing at least one body part. Bruce Lee was always a favorite, but Van Damme was always booed, and the Chechens would shout what they would do to him if he came to visit the war. *Braveheart* was our favorite movie, and we watched it at least once every couple of days. One Chechen fighter who had lost his arms would always jump up and demonstrate to all of us how he would swing a sword like Mel Gibson if he still had arms. "Look, I'm so fast you can't see my hands," he would say as he swung his stumps around. Then another guy would jump up and hop up and down on one leg, telling us how he would run around on the battlefield like Mel Gibson if he still had both legs.

The medical care there was better than in Chechnya, but the doctor in charge, a giant man named Genghis, told me that I needed an operation on my leg. He explained that my peroneal nerve had been severed, and that if I were to get any use from my leg it would have to be reattached. They couldn't perform the operation there, so I made arrangements to travel to Jordan for the operation. I wanted Ayeesha to go with me but she didn't have a passport. Plus, as we found out, she was pregnant, so she stayed in Baku with Shamil and his wife.

Once I got to Jordan I was taken to the best hospital in Amman and was scheduled for surgery with a military surgeon. He thought I'd be able to walk again if he could reconnect the nerve, so I went under for a five-hour operation. The surgeon took nerves from other places in my leg and tried to make the connections, but nerves grow only about a centimeter a week, and I needed fifty-six centimeters before I could regain the use of my foot.

I went back to Baku after recuperating. Although walking was slow and painful, I wanted to go back to Chechnya to fight again. I made arrangements to return to America to visit Sumaya, round up financial support, and get the supplies I'd need for the next trip to Chechnya.

The Arabs in San Diego who had originally gotten me to Chechnya in 1995 were trying to distance themselves from me. Since I needed to put together my own program in order to return to Chechnya, in 1996 I returned to the States to make some arrangements.

My first stop was Phoenix. Things hadn't been going well with my wife and I since she had left Pakistan. While I was in Phoenix dealing with this issue, I ran into an old friend. One day after Friday prayer at the mosque an Arab guy walked up to me and asked me if I remembered him. At first I didn't recognize his face, but when he said his name I immediately knew who he was. Shortly after I'd become a Muslim while in the custody of the CYA, or California Youth Authority, a group of Muslims from Los Angeles had came to visit us in jail. One of them was named Hisham. I'd taken a liking to him, and we had written each other until I had gotten out, but hadn't seen or heard from him since.

Hisham had moved to Phoenix and was doing very well financially because he owned two gas stations. I told him all about my experiences since we had last seen each other. He expressed a strong concern for the situation in Chechnya, and said that he would like to help. Over the next couple of weeks I formulated a plan for getting myself back into Chechnya and Hisham donated a large sum of money to make this happen.

During this time I traveled to San Diego to purchase some equipment. While in San Diego I ran into Abbas. My wife Sumaya had stayed with his family in Pakistan, and he told me a strange story about why he'd never followed me on my first trip to Chechnya. But now he had an American passport and swore that he would go. I didn't have a very good feeling about him anymore, but the jihad was supposed to come before all else, so I ignored this feeling and told him that I could get him to Chechnya. He said that he had an Afghan friend who also wanted to go, and that he could get enough money to pay for their airfare.

Within a month I was ready to get back to Chechnya. While in Phoenix I had my leg looked at by a doctor. It was healed by now, but the nerve graft that had been performed in Jordan still wasn't having any effect and my foot was still useless. I went to an orthotic company that made braces for people with foot drop, and together we created a brace that suited my needs. I brought a pair of Danner boots to the orthotic guys and they built a hinged, spring-loaded arm out of aircraft aluminum for my right boot. It was large and clunky, but it allowed me to walk without too much of a limp.

I returned to Azerbaijan in mid-June. Abbas and his friend agreed to follow after a week, so I left a large portion of the equipment with him. Things had come full circle. I had gone to Azerbaijan in 1995 carrying other peoples' stuff and had relied on their plans and contacts. Now other people would be traveling to Azerbaijan carrying my stuff and relying on my plans and contacts.

I put the rest of my plan together back in Azerbaijan. In addition to Abbas and his friend, I'd gathered six or seven Azeris who wanted to join the jihad in Chechnya. I planned to purchase weapons for our group in Azerbaijan, enter Chechnya through the mountains as an armed fighting unit, and then link up with other mujahideen once inside Chechnya. Until this time, small groups of two or three mujahideen could enter Chechnya through Dagestan only by bribing the checkpoint soldiers. This was extremely risky at best. Several Arab mujahideen were sitting in Dagestani jails because just one Russian officer at one of the countless checkpoints had decided that he didn't want to play that day. To me, it made more sense to go armed through the mountains and at least have a fighting chance if anything unexpected should arise.

I made arrangements for the weapons through Shamil, the Chechen mafioso. I'd give him cash and some electronic equipment for five AK-74s, two PKMs, and an RPG. I would also provide uniforms, web gear, and helmets for the guys making the trip with me. One of the Azeris knew a woman in Baku who could sew, so I designed a magazine vest; the ones she sewed actually turned out better than I'd expected. They were made from a heavy-weight olive-drab canvas and had four double-stack AK-74 magazine pockets with Chinese-type fasteners and two pockets for grenades. There was a simple crisscross strap on the back.

Although Shamil never really took my plan seriously, he still played along with it and even promised that he could provide a guide who knew the area we'd be going through. Azerbaijan doesn't have a border with Chechnya, so our plan was to exit Azerbaijan through the northwest corner, skirt along the border of Dagestan for a short distance, then turn north into Chechnya. It would be a tough hike, but I figured that it wouldn't take more than two weeks. We could easily carry enough food for this, and even if Shamil's guide didn't come, we could navigate with maps and a GPS. The local Azeri guy who'd helped with the mag vests also turned out to be helpful with the planning of the trip. He introduced me to another guy who hunted in the region we planned to cross through, who provided invaluable information about the borders and gave us a detailed map of the area.

The hardest part of our trip would be from Baku to our jumping-off point in the northwest because there were so many checkpoints in between. Most traffic involving Chechen matters traveled on the north and south roads between Baku and the Dagestan border. The soldiers manning the checkpoints there were more susceptible to bribes and would turn a blind eye because they were somewhat sympathetic about the situation in Chechnya. But on the roads we'd be traveling, there was a good chance we'd be mistaken for criminals

The solution to this problem came through another local Azeri. Rukshan was a friend in the Azeri military. He was interested in doing his part to help Chechnya, but there was little he could do while he was in the service. One day while talking to Rukshan about my plans for getting into Chechnya, I asked him how the police treated the military at the checkpoints. He told me that cops didn't hassle the military. It was all about power, and the military simply outgunned the cops, so theoretically a military truck would be able to pass through the checkpoints unmolested. Rukshan was just a simple conscript soldier, but we both had a mutual friend who was an officer. I asked Rukshan to approach the guy and he said he would.

It turned out that the officer was quite eager to help. He could get us not only a truck and driver but also transport orders, just in case any difficulties arose with the checkpoint cops. We also decided that instead of trying to hide the mujahideen and the weapons inside of the truck, we would go as Azeri soldiers until we reached the jumping-off point. Then we would go covertly over the border. Everything was set and I was looking forward to a successful trip—but then all of that changed.

I talked to Abbas on the phone a couple of days before he was to leave, and the conversation didn't go well. He was frightened and kept expressing concerns about bringing the boxes with him from San Diego. I reassured him that I'd taken care of everything on my end and that it would be a piece of cake. But he kept asking question after question. I had to cut him off over and over again to keep him from revealing our plans over the phone. No matter how much reassurance I'd give him, he still wanted to ask more questions. Finally I told him that if he couldn't handle it he should forget the whole thing. In the end he agreed to come, but I wasn't comfortable with the way he was acting.

A couple of days later I was at the airport with one of Shamil's guys. Shamil had all the connections in Baku, and this matter was no exception. Shamil's guy told me to wait and came back with an Azeri customs agent a few minutes later. The agent shook my hand in a genuinely friendly manner. He must have known that I spoke Russian but he wanted to impress me with his broken English. "No problem!" he said, "You friends welcome here!"

We walked out onto the tarmac. The customs agent left us together and went off to talk to some soldiers who were milling around, waiting for the airplane to arrive. While we were standing there, a British Airways employee was inspecting the underside of a nearby plane. When he noticed me, with my combat boots and a red beard way down to my chest, and another guy dressed like a Russian mafioso standing in an airport secure zone next to his airplane, he became extremely agitated. As the customs agent started to walk away from the soldiers the British Airways employee started yelling at him in English. Who were these two people and why were they standing around his airplane? The customs agent waved his hand at the irate man and sarcastically told him in Russian, "They are the president and vice president of Chechnya. Show some respect."

Shamil's guy burst into laughter. I thought it was pretty funny myself and was even more amused at the expression on the British Airways employee's face. He obviously didn't understand what the customs agent had said, but could he tell from the Chechen's laughter that it was something bad. As we walked past him to move farther out onto the tarmac I put on my best Russian accent. "Don't wuurry. We are here to catch the donkeys that are running loose on the runway. Donkeys werry bad for incoming airplane."

A few minutes later the Lufthansa flight carrying Abbas and the Afghan arrived. The plane taxied up the runway and stopped next to a bus where a group of Azeri soldiers were waiting to herd everyone off the plane. As the truck with the stairs on top of it rolled up to the door of the plane, the soldiers formed a human corridor leading from the base of the stairs to the waiting bus. The Chechen and I stood behind one of the soldiers at the base of the stairs and waited for Abbas and his friend.

About half of the passengers had exited before I saw Abbas come out of the plane. For such a big guy he had a pathetic, sheepish expression on his face as he started down the stairs. Halfway down, he noticed me standing behind the soldiers. As he neared the bottom of the stairs, I motioned him to come with me. The soldiers were standing shoulder to shoulder, and when he stepped off the last step I had to reach through the two soldiers in front of me and pull Abbas between them. Shamil's guy reached through and did the same thing for his Afghan friend. We walked across the tarmac with the customs agent as all the other passengers herded onto the bus that would take them to the terminal. Some of the passengers stared at us curiously. Once inside, we retrieved the boxes that Abbas and the Afghan had brought with them, and the agent whisked us through customs without any problems.

Our next stop was Shamil's flat in downtown Baku. Part of the deal that I'd put together with Shamil was that he would also provide the two guys with an apartment while we waited to finalize our plans. Everything seemed to be going as planned. Shamil gave me the directions to an apartment that he had set aside for a few days. I took Abbas and his friend there and got them settled in for the night. Before leaving to go back to my apartment, I asked these two only that they stay inside and not go out wandering around.

When I returned the next morning, nobody was at the apartment. At first this worried me. I went to Shamil's to see if maybe one of his guys had taken the two out or something, but Shamil wasn't in and none of his men had heard of any such plans. A couple of hours later I returned to the apartment, and this time Abbas answered the door. I asked him where they had been and why they hadn't stayed inside as I'd directed. I was more than a little shocked when they tried to cop an attitude and told me that I wasn't their boss. From that point on, everything went downhill.

The next day the two took off again for a local mosque to ask complete strangers how they could get into Chechnya. When I found this out I blew up. I went to their apartment and asked them what the hell it was that they thought they were doing. I had spent a lot of time and money putting together a very solid plan for all of us, and within days of getting to Azerbaijan they were acting like they knew everything. The more they talked, the more I could see that I'd totally misjudged Abbas from the beginning. Everything came to a boil when he pointed out that according to Islam, when a group of mujahideen travel they must choose someone from the group to be the leader for the journey. I translated this to the Azeri who had been helping me plan the trip, who said that there wasn't even a question about that: it was my trip and that duty fell upon me. But much to our surprise, Abbas and his friend had already decided that Abbas was going to be our leader.

This totally blew my mind. These two had never been in a war or had any kind of military experience. They understood nothing about what was going on here or in Chechnya. Yet, they still had the nerve to start telling me what to do. I told them that this wasn't even a subject worth arguing. If they thought they knew so much, they were free to do whatever they wanted to, but they could do it without me.

The next day I went to Shamil's office to tell him about the change of plans. When I got there, Abbas and his friend were just leaving. The slimy pricks couldn't even look me in the face as they passed. In Shamil's office, I motioned toward the door and asked what all that was about. What he told me nearly sent me into a rage. It seemed that Abbas had informed Shamil that he would be going to Chechnya without me. But that wasn't the bad part: Shamil was giving him and his friend two of my AKs. These were weapons I'd paid for, and Shamil obviously had no business turning them over to anyone except myself, but there was no point in arguing with Shamil. I said, "okay, just give me the rest of the weapons and we'll call it even." Then Shamil's Mafia side came out.

"I have handed over the weapons and kept my end of the deal," he said. "I am finished talking about it."

Shamil had double-crossed me, and there wasn't much that I could do about it. He'd probably been planning something like this for a while and had simply used Abbas to make it happen.

At this point I had no weapons for the Azeri mujahideen and was running low on money. I decided to go to the compound where Khattab's guys lived, if only to get their advice. I laid out my plan to Abu Zubair, Khattab's right-hand man in Baku. (He was not the same Abu Zubair of Ulbi's group mentioned previously.) I was surprised by his response. He told me that it was risky, that I had been watching too many Hollywood movies. I pointed out that their method of getting fighters into Chechnya wasn't much better. It cost thousands of dollars to send just a couple of mujahideen into Chechnya, and lately more guys were getting arrested than were getting through. When told that my method included a two-week walk through the mountains, the Arabs in Khattab's group informed me in all seriousness that this was impossible, that no one could walk for two weeks straight. This mentality is characteristic of Arabs; their minds fix on one thing only, and once something is thus decided, there can be no other way.

Abu Zubair told me that if I wanted to cooperate with him and Khattab, they could come up with a good plan for us. I told him that I'd think about this, but in the meantime I had other problems. The Azeri who had been helping me put the trip together had disappeared with most of the equipment. He wouldn't return my calls, and after a couple of weeks his family said that he no longer lived at the number I had for him. I found out from some local Azeri gangster acquaintances that he was known in Baku for scamming people, and my acquaintances even helped me track the guy down. For what it's worth, they were upset with him because he gave a bad name to good criminals.

His apartment was in a shady area of Baku that was known for its drug addicts and criminal activity. The police wouldn't enter the area, so we weren't terribly discreet about having a "talk" with the guy. He had already sold most of the equipment for our trip, so after a nice talk with him I took everything he hadn't sold.

Since my plans were pretty much shot to hell, I didn't have any other choice than to work with Khattab's guys. My leg still wasn't doing well, and they wanted me to go to a hospital in Saudi Arabia that was run by and for mujahideen. So I decided to send Ayeesha back to Chechnya and promised that I would come back for her soon. I moved into a compound house with Khattab's guys and waited for them to make arrangements for my trip to Saudi Arabia.

The compound comprised two houses next to each other with a wooden fence in between. One house was for all the mujahideen coming and going to Chechnya; the other was for Abu Zubair and Khattab's other "special" people. I stayed in the former house. There was always a mixture of healthy, young mujahideen who were excited to get into Chechnya and battle-scarred veterans who were on their way home. The atmosphere was always cheery, like nonstop party. We all stayed up until dawn every night drinking tea and coffee and playing football or other silly games in the courtyard of the house. Then we would make the morning prayer and go to sleep until the noon prayer.

The mujahideen were always playing practical jokes on one another. One morning I heard kids in the street playing with firecrackers, so I bought some from them. I couldn't help but giggle as I went back to the house. I grabbed one of the Arabs who was awake and told him the plan. He climbed up to the awning over the porch and began lighting the firecrackers and throwing them over the edge. They were much larger than American firecrackers and sounded like gunshots, especially if you might be coming out of a deep sleep.

"*Ya shabaab!*" I yelled at the top of my lungs. "*Russ jundi huna!*" Hey guys, the Russian commandos are here! Meanwhile, I was inside, kneeling at the front windows pretending to be taking cover.

"*Allah-u-Akbar*" the guys mumbled as they scrambled out of their sleeping bags.

"Where are they?" they asked.

"What's happening? What are we going to do?" a young Qatari asked.

"They're attacking the other house first!" I said. "Stay here and I'll try to look over the fence." I quickly went out the door, and halfway to the fence I threw myself down. "I'm hit! I'm hit!" I yelled. Before we could finish our prank, the guy who was lighting the firecrackers went into a fit of laughter and nearly fell off the awning. Everyone in the house got up slowly. Their eyes were wide. They didn't really know what to think.

"You're not Abu Mujahid, you are Abu Mushakil," one of them said as they all stumbled back to their sleeping bags. I wasn't the father of a fighter; I was the father of trouble.

Though most of my equipment was gone, I still had my rappelling gear. There was a very tall tree in the front yard, so one day I decided to set up my stuff and do some rappelling for fun. Since you could reach the tree from the awning of the porch, I rigged some rope from one of the higher branches. At first all of the Arabs thought it was funny and began calling me Batman in Arabic, but when one of them tried it, the jokes ended. Once Arabs decide they like something, they won't stop doing it. For the next three days they were swinging out of the tree from noon till dawn. I had only one rappelling harness, and to keep them from fighting over it I had to make more from some nylon webbing.

One of the Arabs was a prominent Islamic scholar from Saudi Arabia. Abu Umar was a fairly young guy, maybe in his late twenties, but everyone treated him with respect because of his position. He had a long beard, and although he was very reserved and didn't joke around like the rest of us, he was a kind man. He watched us without any interest as we rappelled from the tree for three days, but late one night I saw something in his eyes that indicated otherwise.

"*Ya sheikh,*" I said to him. "Would you like to try this?"

"I'm not very interested in these kind of things," he said.

"Of course your knowledge of Islam is far greater than mine, but didn't Allah say that we should prepare ourselves for war?"

"Of course," he said.

"Well, rappelling is a very important skill to have in a war. Just consider those *American* commandos."

He stroked his beard, deep in thought. I'd thrown in the American commando thing just to rattle him, knowing that Arabs never want to be outdone by Americans.

"I suppose . . . I suppose you are right," said the sheikh. "I will try this."

I helped Abu Umar into the rappelling harness, but at first he didn't want to go through with it. He was a very modest person and felt uncomfortable with the way the harness made his genitals bulge out of his *shawal kamece*. He overcame his apprehension, however, and followed me onto the roof and then up the tree. It took a while to explain rappelling to him, but I eventually had him on the edge of a branch, ready to go. His first rappel was a comical affair as all of the other guys cheered him on. It was late at night and the guys were really making a ruckus. Every so often Abu Zubair would stick his head over the fence to angrily yell at us to shut up. Finally, he said that if we did-n't hold it down we would be in big trouble.

When the sheikh was finished I climbed back down the tree and helped him out of the rope. I was about to undo his harness when he stopped me and said, "Maybe I should try this one more time. To be sure I do it correctly." One more time turned into about thirty more times.

A large circular metal plate about the size of a manhole cover sat on the roof near where we climbed the tree. It was there for no apparent reason, and all of the guys just went around it. On Abu Umar's last trip up the roof he somehow bumped this metal plate. It tumbled off the roof and landed on the concrete courtyard with a boom that was as loud as any bomb in Chechnya. Everyone looked at one another like kids who'd just broken a window while playing stickball. Some guys scattered into the house and dove under their sleeping bags, while others ran and hid under some bushes near the fence. Within seconds the courtyard was empty and the sheikh was left on the roof all by himself. We all heard a crash as Abu Zubair threw open the door from the other house and marched toward the fence.

"I swear by Allah I will hurt someone over this!" he shouted as he stormed out. But when he stuck his head over the fence he saw an empty courtyard and Abu Umar the holy man standing on the roof in his rappelling harness. Abu Zubair's jaw hit the ground with a thud. He was speechless. They just stared at each other for a minute.

"Excuse me, Sheikh," said Abu Zubair, "do you know where the rest are?"

"Allah-u-allam," he replied. Only God knows.

Abu Zubair stared for a second, then disappeared behind the fence. As soon he shut the door to the other house, everyone began roaring with laughter.

Although I had many good times at the house, and was learning Russian from the Azeris and some Arabic from the others, I was getting frustrated about the long wait for my trip to Saudi Arabia. My Azeri visa was about to expire and I needed to do something quick. Abu Zubair promised that he was working on arrangements for me to get out, but it was starting to look like I was getting hosed. Around this time I met one of Usama Bin Laden's associates named Abu Amin, whom I would see later in London. When my visa eventually expired and there still wasn't any word from Abu Zubair, Abu Amin gave me an "extension," but it would still be tricky getting out of Azerbaijan. Although Abu Zubair promised that his guys would make sure I got out okay, as time went on I found out that they were just toying with me. I was running out of options, and finally, out of frustration, I left the compound of the mujahideen and went back to my old apartment. Ayeesha came back out of Chechnya at this time and we lived together. She was very pregnant by now and would be ready to deliver soon.

Then things really started to fall apart. My suspicion was that Khattab's group had felt threatened when I'd tried to organize a Chechen tour. There were only a couple of other Arab players in Baku who sent people in, so they pretty much had a monopoly on things. I couldn't understand why they would care or feel threatened. After all, we were all supposed to be working for the same cause.

During this time I ran into some old acquaintances. I'd actually sat next to them when I'd flown from Amman to Baku, after my surgery. They were putting their own group together and had gathered together nearly thirty Arabs, Turks, and Azeris. They were very different from Khattab's guys, and when I told them about my ideas they wanted me to help them. I was going to go back to the States one more time to buy some supplies for them, but I missed my flight in Moscow and had to return to Baku. It seemed that fate had caused me to miss my flight from Moscow, because that's when things really started to get weird in Baku.

Abu Hamza, one of the shady Arab players in Baku, had caught wind of the mujahideen group that my two new Arab buddies were putting together. He tried to disrupt them subtly at first, but it didn't have much affect. Instead of taking my route, they decided that they would try to get to Chechnya through the Georgian border, in the back of a truck. But someone informed on them and they were caught before they even left Azerbaijan. I believed that Abu Hamza was behind this because I'd caught flak from him while I was trying to put my group together.

Not content to leave well enough alone, I started to poke around and discovered some very disturbing things about Abu Hamza. He had been involved in the mysterious disappearance of three shipping containers of humanitarian supplies that Kiffah had sent from the United States. As it turned out, the Azeri authorities had taken one container and Abu Hamza and another Arab had taken the other two. I tried to tell Kiffah about this, but he didn't seem to care. I was starting to see that there was a shady side to just about everyone and everything. I tried to push Abu Hamza about the issue. I implied that I knew what was going on and would do something if he didn't knock the shit off. His reply was very interesting.

I got the peculiar sense that something was about to happen when the car pulled up. I already had a bad feeling about the Arabs who were running scams in Baku. When they asked me to come see them late at night and offered a driver on top of it, they only confirmed my suspicions. Of course, nothing was forcing me to go, but I figured what the hell, whatever was going to happen might as well happen when I'm ready.

If the car that pulled up outside my apartment block had had an Arab behind the wheel, I might not have been so sure of what was about to go down. Arabs didn't have the balls for this kind of stuff; they always hired out. But as it came to a stop I saw that a local Azeri guy was driving. And he definitely wasn't one of the usual Azeris the Arabs hired. He was a very large, muscular guy with a clean-shaven face and a large mustache, and he wore an expensive leather coat, which was the uniform for most of the gangsters of Baku. As I opened the car door and sat down in the front seat, the smell of leather and cheap cologne overwhelmed me.

"Oh, it's you," I said. "I saw you at Abu Hamza's place the other day. How are you doing?"

"Good, thank you," he said as he started to drive off.

I was lying. I had never seen this guy before, and I hadn't been at Abu Hamza's place the other day. I almost started to chuckle out loud. Did the Arabs think this little of me? I wondered. I rated only one unprofessional Azeri gangster to deal with me?

After driving in the direction of Abu Hamza's house, the Azeri started taking side roads. I knew Baku well by now, and we were heading toward a bad part of the city. I didn't ask the driver where we were going, or give him any reason to suspect that I knew we weren't still headed to Abu Hamza's. I had a feeling that in their arrogance, the Arabs had severely underestimated me. They'd probably told the Azeri how easy it would be to kill me. That was fine with me. I didn't want to do anything to change his thinking.

The driver didn't try to make small talk, which I thought was a mistake. He wasn't nervous, but I think he was enjoying the tough-guy role too much. As we drove on I recognized the neighborhood; I'd purchased a few AKs from someone nearby. It was good to be in a familiar area, but I also knew that this was an exclusively Azeri neighborhood. I'd entertained the possibility that maybe we were going to see Abu Hamza at another location, but now I was sure that that wasn't the case.

When we turned onto a small side street, I figured that we were getting close to our destination. I doubted he would try anything by himself; therefore some other guys would probably be waiting for us when we stopped. The driver had been silly enough to come pick me up by myself, so I could have made a move at any time since we'd left my apartment. But I was curious to see where we were going and to get some idea of who was involved.

My hands were folded and resting calmly in my lap. The bulge in my waistband pressed against my forearm. I had to control myself to keep from laughing out loud. For some reason I couldn't stop thinking about an old line—"Is that a gun in your pants or are you just happy to see me?" And I couldn't help thinking about a response. "I'm just very happy to see you, Mr. Bad Guy Driver. So happy that I even have a friend I would like you to meet."

A few months earlier I'd had the opportunity to buy an unusual gun called the CZ75, a 9mm pistol made in the Czech Republic. The unusual feature was that it was fully automatic. Most people think that all modern pistols are automatic, but they're really semiautomatic, or autoloading. Only a few gun makers sell a truly automatic pistol, and this was one of them.

The handgun in my waistband was definitely comforting, but a gun is only as good as the person using it, and I had to do something before we stopped. I never intended to kill the Azeri. I figured that I would just have him drive somewhere for a nice little chat followed by a good old-fashioned pistol whipping to send a message to the Arabs. But I guess fate had something else in store for him.

I probably waited too long. Before I knew it we'd stopped by a big steel gate in front of a house. I pulled the gun from my waistband just as the driver was putting the car into park. As I swung it up to his head and started to tell him to drive, he caught me off guard. With lightning speed he grabbed the gun and my hands. He had massive, rough hands that completely enveloped my hands and the gun. Maybe I was the one who had done the underestimating. Oh shit, I thought, this is definitely not good. With surprising ease the big Azeri started turning the barrel of the gun back toward me. My hands were trapped under his, so it was almost impossible to do anything. To make matters worse, he slipped one of his fingers over my trigger finger.

My mind was racing: Oh shit, I can't die this way, this fucker is going to kill me and my own finger is going to pull the trigger. My brain started making split-second calculations. You are going to die in seconds if you don't do this, and this, and so on. Almost unconsciously, instinctively, I swiveled in my seat and kicked him in the face with my right foot, which had the big metal brace and a combat boot. Two metal arms ran up each side of my foot, from the sole of the boot to a band around my calf. One of the metal arms smashed into the man's face.

To my surprise the first blow didn't loosen his grip on my hands, but when I kicked again he had to release one of his hands to cover his face. An even crazier thought went through my mind: You poor bastard, I thought. You just killed yourself. As he moved his hand, I was able to rip the gun free from his grip. I pulled it back to keep him from grabbing it again. Then I saw an image that has been with me every time I have closed my eyes since that moment. As blood dripped down his face, his eyes made contact with mine. The instant I pulled the gun away from him he knew that he was dead. I was actually staring at death itself. I don't think that words can adequately describe the look in his eyes; he was already dead. Fight, you stupid fucker! I was shouting inside my head. Don't let it take you!

He had been trying to kill me only a second earlier, but I knew it wasn't personal, and now I felt an incredible sense of compassion for him.

I think his soul was already gone before I almost unconsciously depressed the trigger of the automatic pistol. The bullets entered his neck, then rose up the side of his head as the gun reared from the burst of automatic fire. I watched in what seemed like slow motion as the window behind him first turned red from the spray of blood and then shattered. His head rocked back and came to a rest at an odd angle, and his body slumped against the driver's door. My ears rang and the smell of copper and gunpowder filled my nostrils. Then, except for the ringing in my ears, everything was silent.

Before I could take in everything I caught a movement out of the corner of my right eye. Two men came out of a small metal door next to the large gate. They must have been his accomplices. I reached over the dead driver and opened his door. I tried to shove him out so that I could get into the driver's seat, but I couldn't budge him. Before I could figure out why he wasn't moving, a series of pops went off and the passenger window exploded inward.

Shit, now I'm really screwed, I thought. If I try to crawl over the body to get through the driver's door, then I'll get shot in the back before I can even get out. Instead, I swiveled to the right and dumped the rest of my magazine toward the two guys without knowing which one of them was shooting at me. A car is the last place you want to receive return fire, so I was opening the passenger door before the last round left the gun.

Whoever was shooting at me didn't know how to handle return fire very well and ran back to the little metal door. I jumped out of the car and ran toward the rear to put some cover between us. Before I rounded the back end I already had a fresh magazine out of my coat pocket and was dropping the chamber.

Part Two

Youth

SOMEONE ONCE WROTE that a part of you dies every time you go into combat. My father was probably a man of ideals and strong convictions when he enlisted in the U.S. Marines for duty in Vietnam. After a tour he was stationed at Kaneohe Marine Corps base outside Kailua, Oahu. There he met my mother, who worked at the PX. She was the adopted daughter of Air Force Colonel Bob Bradley. They got married, and I was born on February 13, 1974, at Queens Medical Center in Honolulu. Maybe my life would have been different if I'd been born in Ohio to a couple named John and Susan, but no one gets to pick their family.

After finishing his enlistment, my father followed my mother into the hippie world. He grew his beard down to his chest, and she had the whole tie-dye-and-beads thing going on. The two merry hippies and their baby left Hawaii for Florida, then Indiana, but the Midwest was too dull for them, and we settled in southern California. My parents decided to build a boat, and my earliest memories are of being a dirty little kid with long blond hair and puka-shell beads running around a boatyard in San Diego. They built a very nice forty-foot trimaran and called it the Aukai II; Aukai means "from the ocean" or "of the ocean" in Hawaiian. Years later I would acquire the Arabic name "Aqil." I'm sure they had a very nice life planned for us, but it never worked out. Maybe my father had some issues related to Vietnam—I definitely know the feeling—or maybe my mother was just too much, or maybe they had conflicting personalities. For whatever reasons, they split up when I was four years old.

My father went to live on the boat and my mother took me to Ocean Beach in San Diego County, between Point Loma and Mission Beach. It's a beach town with a pier and a jetty, but O.B. didn't have "beach community" residents. Most of the people back then were Hell's Angels, burnt-out hippies, or homeless.

Although I don't really know much about my mother, it seems that she wasn't a bad person before moving to O.B. She got in a lot of trouble when she was growing up and even spent some time in the California Youth Authority. As fate would have it, I would serve my own time there, too. She was very health-conscious and wouldn't even let me drink soda when I was little. But O.B. seemed to change all of that. We lived in a dirty little house half a block from the beach. If you followed the beach for about five blocks you came to the main drag, called Newport Street, which ran down to the pier. There was a parking lot with a low concrete wall that separated the asphalt from the sand at the base of the pier, and this was called "the wall." All the homeless trash and bikers used to sit on the wall to drink beer and while their lives away. My mother was drawn to that wall as though it held some kind of spell over her, and she started to drink beer and stay out till all hours with the wall crowd.

I'll always remember a few of the figures from the wall. Two of them were Hell's Angels. They wore Hell's Angels motorcycle jackets and had big beards. One of them seemed very gentle; he always had some kind of little toy, like a balsa-wood airplane, to give to me. I spent a lot of time hanging out on the wall with the people there or playing on the beach behind them. Although I wouldn't expose my son to life at the wall, I can't say that I regret it, and I even learned a lot of practical lessons about life there.

One of the Hell's Angels gave me a small pocketknife. I was playing with a friend in the alley behind our house when he saw some big kids throwing rocks at his dog through the fence. There were three of them and two of us, and although they were bigger, my friend wanted to fight with them. I decided that I would use my pocketknife to even up the odds. It was almost like a security blanket because it came from one of the Hell's Angels; who would want to mess with that? But when the time came I hesitated. One of the big kids grabbed it from my hand and cut my face. When I told the biker what happened to my face, he gave me a lecture about how you should never pull a weapon unless you're fully prepared to use it, which also means accepting the consequences.

During those years I also learned about walking softly and carrying a big stick. I used to get teased a lot in school about my name, and to make things worse I was quiet and shy. One kid in particular tended to start the harassment and all the other kids took his cue. So I decided to make an example of

him, and I didn't want some silly playground fight that could be broken up
before I could get my licks in. One day after school I followed him home, and
when I was ready I attacked him. He was a year older, but like cowards and
bullies the world over he didn't even fight back when confronted. When I got
him on the ground I kicked out his front teeth. I got in trouble later that
evening when my mother found out, but all my problems stopped the next
day at school when the kids made the connection between the bully's busted-
up face and my big grin.

Although O.B. offered many valuable lessons, my mother's crowd had a
lifestyle that was destructive, not only for themselves but for the people
around them. During this period my mother took us back to Hawaii a couple
of times, and all the while she was getting sucked deeper into drugs and alcohol. Not only was she using drugs, but she had somehow become involved in
selling them as well. She used to drag me along on trips to Mexico; we even
had a house down there for a while. I vividly remember the days when my
mother used to send me home after a day of hanging out at the wall. I would
walk a couple of blocks and then cut up a side street and make my way back
to see her. I'd sit behind some bushes and watch as the cars pulled up. Then
she would walk up and make a sale.

I must have been about seven when she started to disappear for two and
three days at time. I mostly remember eating cold SpaghettiOs, falling asleep
with all the lights on and the TV blaring to keep myself from getting scared.
As if this wasn't enough, she started to go out with a guy named Greg, and
the domestic violence started. My mother wasn't soft by any means, and on
more than one occasion she broke Greg's nose or blackened his eyes with the
gold and brass bangles on her wrists. Looking back, I guess God provided me
with a well-rounded troubled childhood theme.

My father didn't come around very often. I resented him for leaving me
in this situation, but now I see that the American system is designed to dis-
criminate against men in family issues, and I can understand his predicament
a little better. I remember an occasion when he came to visit me and we wanted to go somewhere. My mother wouldn't let him take me, and they started
to fight. She pulled a knife on him and put me in the middle as a shield, but
when the cops came they arrested him. I even told them that she was the one
being violent. But no matter—that's the American way.

One day we packed in a hurry and boarded a flight to Hawaii. My mother said that it was for good this time, and that we wouldn't be coming back. Years later, I heard more of the story from different people, and it appears that she'd screwed somebody over a drug deal and had fled to Hawaii.

Life went on normally there—normal for our standards—but her drinking increased to the point where it's difficult for me to remember her ever being sober. I used to beg her to not drink because when she was drunk she was a real bitch. We lived in her mother's studio in Kailua, on Oahu. Colonel Bradley had built the studio as an attachment to their house on Kainue Drive, which was a long horseshoe-shaped street. The street was divided by a wide, grassy strip planted with coconut trees all the way down. Behind the houses on our side of the street a steep bank led to a canal, which ran down to the ocean. At the end of the street was a huge swamp. If you looked past the swamp you could see the Koolau Mountain Range, which divides the island into unequal halves. Outside my mother's crazy life, it was a vast improvement over the dirty alleys of Ocean Beach. I used to spend all day running barefoot up and down the bank of the canal with my friends, and we made forts along the dirt trails that webbed the forested areas of the swamp. In our childish imaginations, the swamp always had a dark aura. We told all the usual stories that children associate with places like that—bodies and murders and such—but there was more to the swamp than spooky stories; it seemed to have a truly dark nature.

There's no way for me to be sure after all these years. Maybe the people in San Diego put out the word, or maybe she just screwed people wherever she went. Either way, someone had it out for my mother, and the end was nearing. She'd been dealing with some shady locals from the North Shore area who were definitely not the kind of people that a stateside haole chick should mess with. One of them was named Dean. He was a head case and he liked to take down scores, mostly banks. I never understood what she was doing with Dean and his gang, but one of the rival local groups decided to mix it up with my mother, so they got her alone and beat her up pretty bad. When her friends found out, they asked if I would help them trick some of the guys into coming into an abandoned house. They told me that they just wanted to have a talk with those bad guys who'd beat up Mommy. I figured otherwise, but I didn't really care. I was part of that lifestyle too by now. Somehow I lured these guys into the house, where my mother's friends were already waiting. A few more were in the bushes outside. I think that was the first time I heard the guttural, animalistic sounds of men engaged in an actual life-and-death struggle.

One night in July 1982, my mother was drinking in the front yard with a couple of local Samoans from the Waimea area. They were giant guys with long hair. From the second I'd seen these two pull up in the front yard I'd sensed that something was terribly wrong. Their behavior was odd, and while my mother drank beer after beer, they just sipped at a single bottle each. I tried to tell my mother that I didn't feel well and that I wanted her to take care of me inside, but she ignored me. I stayed outside as long as I could, thinking that my presence would prevent whatever these two bad guys were planning for her. After a couple of hours the Samoans told my mother that they should all go to the store for more beer. I said that I wanted to go too, but my mother told me to go inside and go to bed. I tried to throw a fit, but it didn't work. She didn't care. As she got into the car one of the guys walked back over to me. His face was almost compassionate.

"Listen, little bruddah," he said in the pidgin accent of the locals. "Everyting gon' be all right fo you. Someday you gon' see why people do da tings they do. I see you eyes. Dem is da kind loco eyes only da kind people who kick ass got. You gon' be one bad bruddah."

He turned around and got in the car, and they drove off.

That was the last time that I ever saw my mother. That night in the swamp, probably only a few hundred meters from where I sat and waited for her in our house, Geraldine Faye Bradley had a date with the angel of death as the two Samoans strangled the life out of her. Knowing my mother, she probably put up one hell of a fight. In the end she wound up floating in the water, her once lovely and slender hands picked apart by the little crabs I used catch under the bridge with a dip net. I have always believed that her last conscious thought was of me, that as her muted cries and short gasps of breath escaped her lips, she could think only about what would happen to her little "beastie." I can't help but think she'd appreciate the irony that her murderer's advice would give me the strength I needed to carry me through all that life could throw at me.

Those words will stay with me for the rest of my life. Although I would experience fear and terror many times, from that point forward, emotions like fear only strengthened me.

◆

The next morning I awoke to an empty house. This wasn't unusual, but that day it felt different. I rode my bike to a friend's house on the other side of the swamp, and most likely passed within feet of my mother's body. When I arrived I asked if they'd seen her, and of course the answer was no. I went home, and at noon I started to ask the neighbors if they'd seen my mother. Even though her absence wasn't unusual, everyone seemed to feel that something was wrong. That evening the neighbors called my mother's friend. She wasn't exactly a close friend and I didn't like her, on top of it. The woman put a bunch of my stuff in her car and said that I would go with her until everyone could figure out what was going on. I told everyone that I didn't want to go with her, but they put me in the car anyway. As she turned the key to start the engine, I picked up something hard and hit her in the face, then took off down the street to the house of a kid I knew and started banging on the door. They let me in and helped sort things out. In the end I was able to stay at my friend's house.

Three days went by without a word. I didn't have a clue as to what praying really was, but I prayed for my mother to be all right. I made all the usual promises that if God would bring my mother home alive I would devote myself to Him and so on. On the evening of the third night we recognized the swamp at the end of Kainue Drive on the evening news. Two kids fishing in the swamp had found a body. Everyone in the room knew, but no one said anything. A short time later a detective from the Kailua Police Department knocked on the door.

After he'd introduced himself, my friend's mother and I went into a bedroom with him. This part of a cop's job really sucks. I'm sure he was prepared for the hysterics and screams of denial that a kid of my age would normally go through after hearing that his mother had died, but I just sat there. He must have felt terrible looking at this cute little boy with blond hair and blue eyes. I don't think my face even changed expression.

I can remember that night as if it were only a few minutes ago. The cop asked a few questions and then left. I looked at my friend's mother and walked outside. My best friend, Brandon, was sitting on his mother's boyfriend's truck with his sister and the boyfriend. They couldn't look at me, didn't know what to say. I sat down next to them and stared up at the sky. An incredible weight pressed down on my entire body, and as I sat there I wanted to pass out. Lori, Brandon's sister, touched me on the shoulder and told me that it was okay if I wanted to cry. I went inside with her and lay down on the couch with my head in her lap. I cried until my head hurt and my eyes were practically swollen shut. It must have been more than an hour before I was able to stop. The next time I would cry again over my mother's death was eighteen years later, as I write this.

For some reason, no one was able to get in touch with my father in San Diego. Someone contacted his family in Indiana, and my uncle flew out the next day. I think my uncle wanted to take me back to Indiana, but my father showed up a couple of days after that. We spent a few days together, just going to the beach and playing around. It seemed like the best way to get over what had happened.

My uncle left a few days later, and so did my father. He left me with my best friend's mother. She was a nice woman, and between her, my friend, and his sister I was able to get through my mother's death. I don't remember how long I stayed with them, but it was for quite a while. Eventually my father came back to Hawaii and got a place there and I started living with him again.

But once again, the environment was far from ideal. He'd gotten married to a psychotic crystal-meth addict named Gail. I've run across some truly odd people in life, but she takes the cake hands down. That situation didn't last even a year before she forced my father to send me back to his parents in Indiana.

I lived with my grandparents for the next couple of years before they got tired of me and sent me back to my father, who by that time had moved back to San Diego. The situation with Gail hadn't gotten any better because she was using crystal-meth more than ever. By the time I was fifteen I was involved in gangs and was carrying a .357 Magnum to school in San Diego. When I was sixteen, Gail finally forced my father to kick me out. I slept at friends' houses as much as I could, but that didn't always work so sometimes I'd steal cars to have a place to sleep. Stealing cars led to robbing liquor stores, and eventually I was arrested. I was only charged with auto theft and was sentenced to a juvenile camp in the mountains of San Diego for eight months.

I've never been able to sit in one place for long, so I escaped across the border to Mexico. Eventually I was caught again in San Diego and was resentenced to Campo for another eight months. This lasted for all of a month before I was running through the mountains and over the border again.

The next time I was caught I was sentenced to another camp, this time in Arizona. The Arizona Boys Ranch was all about helping troubled youths, and upon my arrival with a few other guys from San Diego, the staff immediately gave us a severe beating. They thought they could terrorize bad kids into going straight. This might have worked with kids from Arizona, but for hardened gang bangers from San Diego it was nothing less than provocation. After a few months the situation got so out of hand that it culminated in a full riot between the kids and the staff at one of their mountain camps. We used shovels and pickaxes to defend ourselves against what turned into a severe beating. I decided to call it quits one day and pull my usual escape routine.

If the detainees were good little boys, the staff would take us to Payson on Sundays. Before the riot I'd met a girl at a rodeo in town. On our next trip there, she helped me escape. I was caught with her a week later; she didn't get in any trouble, but I definitely did. The staff at the camp separated me from everybody else and forced me to dig a twelve-by-twelve-by-twelve hole in the ground, from sunup to sundown. By the end of the first day my hands were a bloody mess, but I stuck it out and never once opened my mouth. I dug holes for an entire month, after which the staff put me back in a normal routine. I played along until I could make another move and then escaped again with a friend, but this time I didn't fuck around. We stole a Ford Bronco and headed for San Diego. I wouldn't see the girl from Payson for another couple of years, but we eventually linked up again, as I mentioned previously.

Once in San Diego I hooked up with all of my old friends and we started acting crazy. We got into a shootout while robbing a house, and a few days later someone ratted me out. The San Diego police kicked in the door one night while I was sleeping, and I was quite impressed when I saw thirteen police cars outside. "All for me?" I asked. "You shouldn't have." But the courts didn't think I was funny and sentenced me to eight years in the California Youth Authority. CYA was the most feared place in the juvenile system. It was basically a prison system for minors, but it housed people up to the age of twenty-five. The facilities in the CYA system were organized according to the offenders' ages and the seriousness of their crimes.

I was only seventeen and my offense was relatively minor, but I started off on the wrong foot. The guys from the Aryan Brotherhood had a problem with me because I wouldn't join their group. It was only a matter of time before they would try to do something to me, so I initiated a preemptive strike with the Asian gangs. One morning while the cell block was lining up for breakfast I attacked one of the Aryans, and the Asians joined in on the rest. This caused the blacks to attack the Mexicans, and so on. In all the confusion, the guards were never able to prove anything, but one of the supervisors saw to it that I was shipped off to the CYA's maximum-security facility. You had to be at least eighteen years old to be sent there and all of the twenty-five-year-olds were housed there. So at the age of seventeen years I walked into what was called "Gladiator School."

Prisoners in America divide themselves up into racial groups. The blacks are with the blacks and whites with the whites and so on. No one goes outside of this self-imposed segregation. If you are white, you are expected to join the Aryan Brotherhood, and there aren't any exceptions. But since I've always had a problem with being a follower, I decided to buck the system. When the Aryans approached me for the first time, they assumed that I was one of them. When I informed them that they could go to hell, they were a little surprised. The surprise turned into hatred, and for the next two years they tried to kill me. It would have been a lot easier and less painful to join them, but I wouldn't have been able to look at myself in the mirror.

Over the next two years they jumped me and even tried to stab me, but I just kept doing my own thing. About a year and a half into this ordeal something happened that would alter the course of my life.

It was an ordinary day like any other behind bars. In the morning I had my G.E.D. class. Like a lot of classes in the prison school, the students were here just to get out of their cells and hang out with their friends. No one was really making an attempt to get their general equivalency diploma, and to make things worse, the teacher wasn't much different from the people in his class. The students would exchange drugs for favors like getting their buddies transferred into or out of the class. I thought it was odd that the inmates had more access to drugs than the teacher, who lived in the "free" world.

One day, there was a new guy in the class. I'd seen him before in the prison and had found out that he was a lifer. In an environment where anyone can try to kill you, lifers have no disincentives. He was a quiet black guy who wore a funny little white skullcap and held himself in a certain way. One day he sat at the desk in front of me. I noticed that he was reading a large, strange-looking book. When he got up to use the bathroom I glanced at the book with an unusual urge to see what was inside, but I hesitated. I can't describe why I felt that way; it just seemed that I shouldn't touch the book. After he came back from the bathroom I continued to try to peer over his shoulder to get a look at the book. I don't know if he felt my curiosity or just caught me looking over his shoulder, but after a while he turned around and started to talk to me. The first thing he said was, "Where are you from?" This made me defensive because I thought he was asking about my gang affiliations.

"I don't do that anymore," I said.

"No, where are you from, outside the prison?"

After we talked for a while, I asked him about his book. He told me that it was the Qur'an, and that I could touch it if I washed my hands. This was obviously unusual, but I was impressed by his respect for this book. We continued to talk and he introduced himself as Kesacee.

The next day Kesacee brought me some small books and pamphlets about Islam. The small book was called *Qur'anic Verses*. It was just a small paperback book with selected *ayat*, or verses, from the Qur'an. I took the books back to my cell and found that the *ayat* were practical, interesting, and logical. But beyond these observations I had no desire to look any further into Islam.

I was sitting in the day room the next Saturday watching *Soul Train*, my weekly treat, when one of the guards called me up to the control-room window. He had an odd look on his face.

"Hey, Collins," he said. "That Muslim chaplain guy wants you up at the chapel."

"Huh?" I said. "What does he want?"

"How the hell should I know? Here's your pass—go and find out."

We had only one hour out of our cells on Saturday mornings and if I went to see what this was about I would miss *Soul Train*, but I figured what the hell, something new always helps.

I walked up to the chapel were the Muslims had their Saturday class. As I walked in, about fifty black guys turned around and stared at me. This wasn't a big deal for me; after all, I was the guy who had a price on his head for not joining the White Power group. Kesacee stood up, walked over to me, and we sat down together. He briefly explained that he had told the Imam to call for me today. I listened to the class, and what they had to say immediately impressed me. They subjects they spoke about were thought-provoking.

During that week I continued to talk to Kesacee in class. The following Saturday I was called to the chapel for the Islamic class again. I was looking forward to the class but didn't have any plans to become a Muslim anytime soon. One of the other things that impressed me about the Muslims was that they never proselytized. The religion seemed to pretty much speak for itself.

But as I sat there and listened on that Saturday, I had a sense that I wanted to convert. Just before the class finished I told Kesacee. He seemed quite pleased and went to tell the Imam. The Imam asked me to come up in front of everybody. I wasn't exactly sure what becoming a Muslim entailed, but I was pleased when I found out how simple it was. The Imam explained the basic tenets of Islam and told me to repeat after him: *"Ashadu Allah illaha ilalallah, wa ashadu ana Muhammador rasulallah."* I bear witness that there is no God except God, and I bear witness that Muhammad is His messenger. That brief statement would change the rest of my life.

Part Three

The fully-automatic CZ75 handgun.

Shamil Basaiyev, the Chechen commander who led a raid on the Russian city of Buddenovsk.

Field Commander Ibn-ul Khattab, a Saudi-born jihadi who fought in Chechnya. At press time, Russian news agencies reported that the Russian Federal Securities Service (FSB) infiltrated his inner circle and assassinated him.

A shaheed in the frozen foothills of Chechnya.

Performing wudhuu in the Argun River gorge in Chechnya.

A mushroom cloud from one of the many 2,000+ pound bombs dropped on the Chechen and Russian civilians of Grozny. BELOW *Evidence of Russian atrocities in April 1995 against civilians in a Chechen town called Semashki.*

LEFT *Dilapidated stalls of a market in Grozny, where two hundred civilians were killed by a Russian bomb or SCUD missile. Most of the market operators and shoppers were women.*
RIGHT *An orchard on the outskirts of Grozny, where the author and a handful of Chechen rebels took a stand against an armored division of the Russian army.* BELOW *"Grad" type missile launchers in Chechnya. The Russian army would monitor radio and satellite phone transmissions, triangulate coordinates, and launch strikes. They would also hit civilian targets.*

The devastation of an abandoned factory building on the outskirts of Grozny. The author was across the street when the bomb or bombs struck the building.

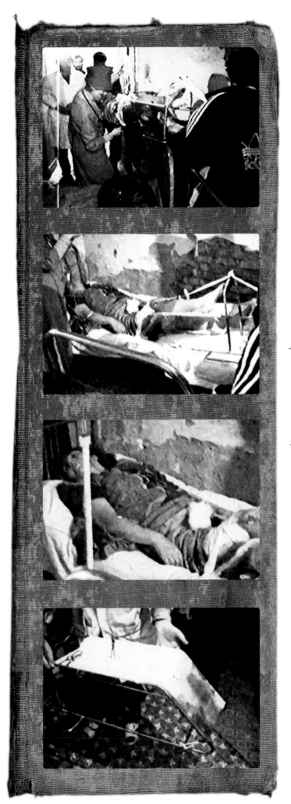

Scenes from a Chechen field hospital. This woman was injured as a result of a Russian army barrage. Such attacks were frequently leveled at civilians in populated areas to cause terror, and many of the victims were ethnic Russians.

The author, foreground gives a tour of the position on the outskirts of Grozny.

Chechen mujahideen. The mujahid on the right wears a Spetsnaz paratrooper uniform.

The author among comrades-at-arms.

ABOVE *A group photo of mujahideen in their teens and early twenties. Included are AsSalaambeck (standing, third from left) and Ruslan (standing, second from right).* LEFT *Mujahideen praying on the road to Zandak, a town in eastern Chechnya.* BELOW *The author (left) with a comrade. A third party altered the photograph due to fear of FBI reprisal.*

Chechen "terrorists" trying to escape Chechnya.

The refugee situation during the winter of 1999-2000 on the border of Chechnya and Georgia.

A Chechen child on the Georgian border who suffered the loss of an eye as a result of the fighting.

A caravan of mujahjideen traveling to Grozny and certain death.

How the CIA Betrayed Me

1996-99

ALL THESE YEARS LATER I still am unsure as to exactly why I did what I did. Many factors led up to it. The fact that Khattab's group had screwed me was definitely one of them, but not in an obvious way. I had many options at the time if I'd simply felt scorned and had wanted revenge; I could have easily sold them out to the Russians, or I could have collected the $7 million that the Russians were offering for Khattab's head. I could have played the Azeri intelligence against them. But I didn't.

To me, the fact that Khattab's group betrayed me was just more evidence of why the Islamic world is in the state that it is, and why the world's one billion Muslims can't prevent the slaughter of Chechnya's children. As long as the Arabs control the way the jihad was handled, it will never progress or accomplish anything. I was as loyal to the jihad then as I am now—and God willing always will be—but I felt that big changes needed to be made. With this in mind, one sunny afternoon in the city of Baku, I walked into the American embassy.

Up until that point I had never even seen an American embassy. The first thing that struck me was the size of the line of people outside. There must have been at least fifty people standing there, waiting to get in. I walked up to the armored glass window of the guardhouse door. I must not have fit the image of Mr. Typical American, because the Azeri guard behind the window looked at me as though he were royalty and I were a peon.

"Sto te khoches?" he asked me in Russian. By this time, I was able to speak and understand Russian passably well, although I had difficulty with the Cyrillic alphabet.

"Ya khachu spraciet Americansky consular," I replied.

He continued his contemptuous questioning. Do you have an appointment? What's your business? After a couple of minutes I stuck my American passport up to the window.

"Just let me in," I said in English. "I need to see the consul."

The Azeri guard suddenly had a sheepish look on his face.

"Why didn't you tell me that you were an American?" he asked.

"You didn't ask," I said.

He issued me a visitor's pass and I proceeded through the compound to the main building. I still didn't have a clue as to what I was going to say or do. I walked up to another armored window for the first of many run-ins with the "little people with big jobs" mentality.

"Um, hi," I said in a friendly tone.

"What do you need?" The man behind the window replied.

I tried to explain to him without coming right out and saying it that I wanted to talk to somebody who handled intelligence issues.

"You are going to have to be more specific for me to be able to help." Whatever I would say, he would repeat this, over and over, in a shitty little tone. I remained patient and tried to explain things in such in a way that even a kid would have gotten the hint.

"You are going to have to be more specific for me to help" was all I kept getting.

Finally I ran out of patience and said, "Can I talk to a fucking CIA agent? I fought with the mujahideen in Chechnya, you little prick."

I can still remember the look on his face.

"Wait here" was all he said. A few minutes later a woman in her thirties came out of the side door next to the windows.

"We don't actually have any CIA personnel here," she said, "but I'm a political officer, and you might want to talk with me."

Since I'd never never done this before, it seemed fine to me. In retrospect, she may have been CIA. I started by telling her a little bit about who I was and where I had been.

"What exactly is it that you want?" she asked. I told her that honestly I wasn't sure; it just seemed like I should talk to someone in the intelligence community. I guess I told her enough to spark an interest, because she told me to come back the next day, when she would give me some idea of what to do. Of course I didn't know if guys with handcuffs might be waiting the next day, but I figured this was how the game was played. In hindsight, I should have called the shots that day, not her.

I showed up the next day. I wasn't nervous, but was unsure of what was going to happen. This time she was much friendlier when she greeted me. "I spoke to my superiors and somebody from Washington is on their way to see you," she said.

"Just like that?" I asked.

"Just like that." She asked me to come back in three days, and of course I agreed. I can't even really say that I lost much sleep during the next three days. I figured that my intentions were honorable and that God would take care of me as always, and this is how I took my first steps into the world of espionage and real-life spooks.

Three days later, I went back to the embassy, but this time when I handed over my passport the guard checked a special list and saw my name. He got on the telephone, and a minute later a big American with an I.D. badge appeared and asked me to follow him. We entered the main building through a different door than the consulate section this time. We passed an armed American at the bottom of some steps and went up. The area at the top of the steps was obviously some kind of operations room. At the far end was a door with a little conference room inside. The big American walked me in and said that someone would be with me in a minute. A short time later a man appeared. He looked like he was in his early forties and had red hair and a red mustache.

He introduced himself—I don't remember his name—and sat down. The first thing I noticed about him was that he was very straightforward. I got the impression that he believed in what he was telling me, and this initial impression was probably what convinced me to go through with it. If he'd been one of the clowns I would have to deal with later, I never would have returned after that meeting.

I told him my whole story from beginning to end, much as I've written it here. Because I had good intentions, I didn't think to leave anything out. I'd use this approach with them over the next few years, and eventually I would come to regret it. I learned later that you can never deal truthfully with people whose intentions and agenda are dubious, and that employees of the United States government rarely reciprocate goodwill.

The questions he returned to over and over again were, Why had I come to the embassy? And what was it I wanted? I told him the same thing I say even now: I don't really know. I don't think they ever believed me on this point. Since many of their policies are so contrary to what I believe, they couldn't just accept the fact that I felt it was the right thing to do, especially because I was unable to fully define it. Looking back, I can't say that I really regret working for them—I benefited from it in many ways—but I definitely would have never considered it if I'd known how much the organization contradicted the principles I believed in.

The man listened to what I could offer. To most any other country, what I had in mind would have worked out very well. But to make it anywhere in the U.S. government, you have to be absolutely unable to formulate thoughts that have anything to do with logic, common sense, or originality. He told me that what I was thinking probably wasn't very realistic but said he would talk it over with Washington. From his reaction, you might gather that I had concocted something out of a James Bond movie, but that would be far from true.

One of the major factors that had brought me to the embassy in the first place was an incident in Cairo, Egypt. On April 18, 1996, some of the guys from al-Gama'at al-Islamiyya killed eighteen civilians in front of a hotel. They'd thought the people were Israelis. It would be the deadliest act of terrorism in Egypt until November 17, 1997 when al-Gama'at al-Islamiyya would kill sixty tourists outside the pyramids in Luxor. I was outraged and felt betrayed, because as I was fighting the Russian army and shedding my blood in the defense of Islam, a bunch of cowards in Egypt were killing old ladies and kids in the name of jihad. I thought that the people in intelligence could use me to save innocent lives and that I could protect my religion at the same time.

At the end of our meeting, the man told me to come back in a couple of days when they had a better idea of what was going to happen. I asked about getting Ayeesha back to the States, but he had no interest in helping me with that problem. Before I left he asked if I was okay for money. I had no money at all, so he pulled three hundred dollars in U.S. currency out of his wallet and gave it to me. Whether he was reimbursed or not, I appreciated the gesture, and that night I had the first good meal I'd had in a long time. Our next meeting was brief. He said that for whatever the reason, the CIA couldn't deal with me. This surprised me. He continued by saying that if I wanted to pursue my plan I needed to travel back to the States, where the FBI would pick it up.

"The FBI?" I asked. "What the hell do they have to do with this?"

He just shrugged and said, "That's the way it has to be."

We'd talked earlier about how I'd violated probation to come fight the Russians; this was immediately a source of concern for me. Would they be waiting to arrest me at the airport? He assured me that traveling back to the States was purely up to me, and he gave his word that the FBI would not be arresting me on my return. He told me to think about it and said that if I wanted to pursue it, I should come back to the guardhouse in a few days. There would be something waiting for me there in an envelope.

There weren't many options; either do it or don't do it. As usual, I trusted my instincts and left it in God's hands. A few days later I walked up to the guardhouse. This time the Azeri guard opened the door as he saw me coming.

He handed me an envelope and said, "Just sign here as proof that you received this." He started to open his mouth, probably to ask a nosy question, but I turned and walked out before he could say anything. I slipped the envelope into my pocket and walked at a brisk pace away from the embassy. The last thing I wanted was to be spotted by the Chechen Mafia or the Russian FSB as I was leaving the American embassy with an envelope in my hand. I was relatively new to this game, but I tried to use all the counterintelligence training I'd received in Afghanistan. This was for keeps, and I wasn't about to be taken out before I even got started.

I didn't open the envelope until I got back to my apartment. Three things were inside the envelope: a folded piece of paper, a Lufthansa airline ticket, and seven one-hundred-dollar bills. In two weeks I would be flying coach class to LAX. I unfolded the white piece of paper. The message was very precise and to the point. In typed letters it said, Your contact upon arriving at LAX is Special Agent Tom S. Ishiguro. He will be waiting for you *after* you clear customs. Under no circumstances are you to reveal this to the customs agents or anyone else. The backup contact is Special Agent So-and-so. Then it listed their cellular-phone and pager numbers. Three days before I had to leave, Ayeesha gave birth to our daughter, Nusaiba.

"Sir, can you step over here for a second?" the customs agent said. A minute later another officer approached me, his hand resting on the butt of his pistol.

"Come with me," he said in his most intimidating voice. He escorted me over to the secondary area, where a third customs officer with an out-of-date perm and pursed lips was waiting for me behind a stainless steel inspection table.

"Put your bags on the table, sir," she said.

"Ooh, I like a woman who knows what she wants," I said.

"Shut up and put your shit on the table."

I put my bags down.

"Where are you coming from?"

"Where everyone else who was on my flight came from," I said.

She glared. "Where did your journey originate from?"

"Azerbaijan."

From there the whole situation became downright ridiculous. Why was I there? How did I get there? Who'd sent me there? How did I get the money to get there? I stuck to my story that I was in Azerbaijan doing humanitarian relief for Chechnya. Then the woman's questions became absurd.

"What the fuck is your problem?" I said. "Whatever profile I fit doesn't really matter because I don't have anything on me and I'm not doing anything illegal. Whatever I did in Azerbaijan or anywhere else for that matter is neither here nor there as long as it's not going on as I enter the U.S."

This didn't go over very well. She started in with the meaningless threats.

"If you wanna play, we can play," she told me. "You can walk out of here in handcuffs!"

"Oh really?" I said. After everything I'd been through, handcuffs seemed negligible. I couldn't help myself and held up my hands as I started to laugh. "Here they are, cuff away."

"I have all day," she snapped. "Stay here until you're ready to cooperate."

I sat down on the stainless steel table and noticed a middle-aged Japanese guy in a suit and tie who was trying to look inconspicuous. I wondered if it was my FBI contact, Tom Ishiguro. I waited to make eye contact with him, so when he finally looked my way I smiled and nodded very carefully. He looked away quickly with an odd expression on his face. I wondered what must have gone through his mind when I made him.

I was actually in a pleasant mood when the customs lady finally came back. She seemed even more annoyed to find me sitting there on her shiny table, smiling and enjoying myself.

"Are you ready to cooperate?" she asked.

"Nope. I'm like you. I have all day."

This really got her riled up. She waved her hand at a couple of other customs agents, one in uniform, one in plainclothes with a gun on his belt. The plainclothes agent was a short, stocky redhead with a goatee and a sour look on his face. They came over behind me and the one in plainclothes grabbed my arm.

"Get your fucking hands off me," I said through gritted teeth.

"Or what?" he taunted.

"I exhibited no signs of physical violence. You don't need to escalate this to a physical level. But if you don't take your hands off me we'll get as violent as you want to."

He looked over at the uniformed officer, who nodded. The red-haired prick released my arm.

"You need to come with us," the uniformed agent said.

They led me over to one of the holding cells. The woman waited outside as the two guys walked me into the room. The uniformed agent told me to sit on the bench against the wall and start taking my clothes off. I thought of a smart-ass comeback but by this point was too angry to start joking. Once I'd stripped down to my boxers the red-headed prick told me to stand up and turn around with my hands on the wall. When I put my hands on the wall he grabbed my wrist.

"If you move I'm going to take you down," he said.

"You know what?" I shot back. "Fuck you and your mother, you little fascist bastard. Who the fuck do you think you are? Whatever profile I fit that caused me to get this treatment can't possibly be as bad as the profile you meet. And you guys are still leaving out the most important part here: What in the hell am I guilty of?"

"This isn't personal," the uniformed officer said as he began to pat me down through my boxers. "We're just doing our jobs."

After they were finished with their pathetic games and I had gotten my clothes back on I looked over at the redhead. "Let me see you on the streets someday and see what happens. Outside you aren't any different than me, and I guarantee you that you won't so much as look at me."

I retrieved my bags from the inspection table and headed for the door. As I left the customs area I looked around but didn't see the Japanese guy who'd been lurking inside. I walked to a bank of pay phones and called the number that was printed on the piece of paper next to Special Agent Ishiguro's name. He answered the phone after a couple of rings.

"Where did you go?" he asked.

"I'm right here at the pay phones as you walk out of the doors."

A few minutes later the guy that I had figured for Ishiguro came over to me. He shook my hand.

"I'm sorry that I couldn't do anything back in there. What was her problem, anyway?" he said.

"Beats the hell out of me. I figured you'd know."

"We don't work with customs," he replied.

We walked out to the street and another guy in a suit came up to us. Ishiguro introduced us and I recognized his name from the paper too. I kind of expected a Ford Crown Victoria with dark windows to pull up and we would all get in rapidly, so I was a little disappointed when Ishiguro said that he was parked in the garage and that we could walk to his car.

The special agents told me that we would be going to a hotel for a few days for debriefing. I expected a run-down motel in Los Angeles packed with FBI agents in their shirtsleeves with old coffee cups littering the room, but my disappointment turned to pleasant surprise when I found out that we would be staying at the Marriot Residence Inn and that I would have a whole one bedroom-apartment, complete with an upstairs loft, to myself.

They left me to get settled in and cleaned up but said that they would be back in a couple of hours and we would all go out to dinner. That night Ishiguro, the other guy from the San Diego office, and a female agent from the L.A. office took me out to dinner. We talked during dinner, but they saved their detailed questions for the debriefing. I don't really know how I should've felt having dinner with three FBI agents, but I was rather comfortable around them, and the two guys seemed comfortable around me. The only one who seemed slightly awkward was the female agent. I assumed that this was because it is one thing to interrogate bank robbers and criminals but another thing to sit down and have dinner with an Islamic rebel coming over from the war zones.

I didn't sleep much that night. The next morning I woke up at six o'clock and called Ishiguro's suite. He answered the phone in a grumpy half-asleep voice. I asked him if he was ready to get started for the day. The early bird gets

the worm, right? He said "No" and promptly hung up. Later that morning, around nine o'clock, he and the other two agents came to my suite to start the debriefing. They all found it amusing that I had woken up Ishiguro at six in the morning.

In the debriefing, I just told my story as I remembered it, detail after detail. They would occasionally stop me to ask a question or request that I elaborate further on something. They had a map of Chechnya with them, and they wanted to know about all of the places I had been to and where certain events had taken place. They seemed to have a particular interest in Ibn-ul Khattab.

After three days Ishiguro finally gave me some idea of what they had in mind for me. He told me that they would like for me to work out of the San Diego office, doing counterterrorism. Because terrorism had, in part, motivated me into approaching the U.S. government in the first place, this seemed all right. At the time my wife Sumaya and baby daughter were still living in Phoenix. Ishiguro told me to go back to them for a couple of weeks while the FBI got all the paperwork going; then I would come out to San Diego. But this would present the first of many operational mistakes the FBI would make.

The FBI put me on a plane, and fifty minutes later I was in Phoenix. As I hugged my wife who was waiting for me at the gate, I had a strange feeling about what I had just done in Los Angeles. If I'd known at the time that for the next three years my life would be one big giant tangled mess of lies that would eventually destroy my marriage and everything else, I might have fallen to my knees right there and begged God for mercy.

I called Ishiguro a couple of days later, and he told me that he would fly out the next day and that we would talk about what I could do for them. He also told me that Bureau rules said that he had to have another agent present with him. He said that he had a good friend in the Phoenix office who he trusted and that this would be the other agent present. I am sure that any old agent out of the Phoenix office would have done fine, but once again fate would intervene.

The next day I went to the Metro Center mall in Phoenix and walked to the food-court area where Ishiguro had said they would be waiting for me. As I approached the area I didn't see Ishiguro anywhere, but I noticed a guy with his arm in a sling sitting by himself at one of the tables off to the side. He was well dressed with rugged good looks and short-cropped hair and seemed to be in his thirties. He looked up at me, and something about the way he regarded me made me walk over to him.

"Are you Tom's friend?" I asked.

"Yes. Tom is going to be a few minutes late. Have a seat."

He introduced himself as Andres Sanchez but said to call him Andy. We started talking, and by the time Tom showed up we had completely forgotten about him. Tom told me that everything was fine and moving along but that it was going to take a week or two longer than he expected to get everything in order. He said that I should just stay put and that Andy would be my contact if I needed anything while in Phoenix. Before leaving, Andy and I exchanged numbers and Tom said that he would contact me.

A week later, Ishiguro called and said that he would be coming out in a couple of days and that we needed to buy a car. They were smart enough to buy me a 1989 Mazda 929 off a shady dealer on Scottsdale Boulevard. It was old enough to not arouse suspicion with people like my wife but reliable enough to keep me working. The dealer actually tried to scam me by "forgetting" to send the registration papers, and Ishiguro had to call the guy after two weeks. He told the guy that he didn't have time to deal with shady businessmen but he had a friend down at the DMV investigative division who did. The very next day the guy called me and told me to come down because he had all the papers ready.

Andy and I talked regularly over the next couple of weeks and found that we had a lot in common. Andy was a former army Ranger who'd moved on to become an Apache attack-helicopter pilot; and he'd been a company commander by the time Desert Storm rolled around. After joining the FBI he decided to work counterterrorism. Maybe it was because he was ex-military or maybe he just had things thought out a little better, but for whatever reason I liked Andy's approach to counterterrorism better than Tom's.

The day finally arrived when Tom called me to say it was time to come to San Diego. I'd assumed from the beginning that my wife and daughter would be included, just from an operational standpoint; I would obviously still be who I had always been to everyone in the Islamic community, so why would I move to San Diego and leave my wife and child in Phoenix? Tom informed me that my family would not be included in the move, which indicated to me that he had a poor understanding of the Islamic community in America. I agreed to come to San Diego with some reluctance, but I felt like I was making a major mistake, and so was the Bureau. In the meanwhile, I had to come up with a cock-and-bull story to explain to Sumaya why I would be living in San Diego and she would be living in Phoenix.

I drove to San Diego in the Mazda purchased by the FBI, but Tom hadn't made any living arrangements, so at first, they put me up in a hotel. The plan was that I was to find an apartment and the FBI would pay for it. Tom started to get more involved after I'd been in San Diego a few days; I was dragging my feet more than anything and came up with all sorts of excuses about why it was difficult to find an apartment. I told Tom that I didn't have a job, so how would anyone let me move into an apartment? He came back with a cover story that I worked for a Toyota dealer, and he even had a phone number for my manager.

After a couple of weeks I moved into a town house in El Cajon. Tom was a nice enough guy, but he didn't seem to get the whole counterterrorism thing and how hard it was going to be for me to maintain a decent cover out here alone in San Diego. We were now what is termed "activated" or "operational," and used secret meeting places and code names.

Tom's first goal was for me to get back in contact with the guys I'd always dealt with in California, starting with some of the Afghans. This seemed odd to me because these guys weren't players in much of anything anymore, and if that was the way the FBI wanted to use me, Phoenix had more important Islamic figures. The second goal was to get back into the mosque, which also seemed odd. *Everyone* knew that the mosques discouraged any sort of talk about participation in jihad-type activities. If you wanted to infiltrate radical U.S. Islamic figures you had to get into their homes and their inner circle of friends. Furthermore, infiltrating them would be easier if I had my wife and family with me in San Diego instead of having to explain why they were living in Arizona.

One day I drove back to Arizona without telling Tom. Once I got there, I called Andy. He met with me right away, and I told him about the operational and family problems in San Diego. Andy said that he'd thought the same thing since the beginning but that the Bureau has certain formalities and procedures. I'm not an expert in these procedures, but Andy explained that he couldn't say anything to try to influence me because it was already Tom's show. However, now that I'd initiated some sort of complaint, he could bring it to the bosses. He seemed sure that he could get things changed.

A couple of days later Andy and I had a meeting with another agent, Leonard B. Cosgrove. Len, as we called him, also turned out to be an ex-Ranger. He was fresh out of the military and had decided to specialize in counterterrorism because of Andy. We didn't know it at the time, but this would be the first of many such meetings for what would become one hell of a trio. Andy told me that his boss, Jonathan Canter, had proposed that I move back to Phoenix and that Washington had given its approval. All that was left was get my stuff out of San Diego. I saw Tom Ishiguro only once more after that, and he didn't seem pleased with me.

Things progressed very well over the next few months; I took a polygraph examination and passed. We changed my operational code name and my monthly pay was increased. I had started in San Diego at $1,000 a month but would eventually end up making over $2,500 a month plus all expenses before parting ways with the FBI. As it has been explained to me, my participation was voluntary, I was free to leave at any time, and I was being paid a "fee for services." Although I would not then, nor now, divulge information that would impede a current or prior investigation, our arrangement suited me because I would be able to prevent terrorism, protect my religion, and get paid for it. Although our relationship later soured, I've tried to cooperate with the FBI on any case where I thought I might be able to help, and I plan to continue offering my help.

Andy compiled a list of radical figures in Arizona (some of whom I already knew); he wanted me to become acquainted with them. I developed a very solid reputation as someone who was able to get close to almost anyone and maintain a solid cover. I never needed help when things started to go downhill, and I was probably the only person in this capacity whom they allowed to work armed.

I continued to have problems with my leg through 1997. One day I met someone who'd been in an accident and had chosen to have his leg amputated. When he showed me how fast he could run with his prosthetic I considered the option, because my leg was slowing me down. At first Sumaya and everyone else didn't take me seriously, but when they finally realized that I was serious they thought I'd gone crazy. Andy was the only person who understood my reasoning, and he promised that if I wanted to have an amputation, the FBI would pay for it. The first doctor I spoke to told me that I was crazy, and that I'd never find a doctor who'd be willing to do it. Andy used his resources and gave me the name of a doctor whom he considered to be one of the best in Arizona. This doctor agreed to perform the amputation if a specialist gave his approval, and soon after that we scheduled my surgery.

The night before the surgery was one of the most difficult nights of my life. My wife didn't try to talk me out of the surgery, but neither did she understand why I wanted it. As my leg was, I would always walk with a limp and I certainly would never run again. My intention was to return to the jihad, and this would be too difficult with the current situation. There were also drawbacks to being an amputee, but I knew I'd be able to walk and run again with a good prosthetic.

I was shaking with fear the next morning on the operating table as they prepped me for surgery. The setting brought me back to all my experiences in Chechnya—the appendectomy, the agonizing irrigation procedures. The O.R. nurse saw me shivering there and thought that I was cold, so she put an extra blanket on me. I told her I was scared shitless, but when the doctor came in and asked if I was ready, I said yes. It's difficult to explain how it felt to lie there waiting to be put under, knowing that when I woke up my leg would be gone. I considered chickening out for a moment, but as always, I just couldn't do it.

I woke up in the recovery room. I always come out of surgeries hard, but this time was the worst. My throat was so dry I couldn't swallow, and I felt the most intense pain coming from my right leg. When I came to the orderlies moved me to my room. It was a long trip and every bump in the hospital floor was like a knife stabbing into my leg to the bone. My wife was by my side. A short while later Andy and Len showed up. The appearance of two clean-cut guys in suits seemed odd to Sumaya, but she didn't say anything. Andy and Len's presence gave me strength, and we talked about my getting back to work soon.

The next day the physical therapists came to my room to get me up and moving. They only wanted me to do some exercises in the bed, but I told them that I wanted to get up and walk around. After following me around for a half an hour as I hopped up and down the hallway with crutches, they told me that I needed to get back in bed.

Two weeks after my amputation I was on a flight bound for Istanbul. A group of Chechens had gotten Ayeesha a fake passport, and we'd agreed to meet there so I could bring her to America. Intercontinental travel with a fresh amputation isn't such a good idea. There was no way to elevate my leg during the flight, and the pain from the swelling was intense.

I hadn't seen Ayeesha in about eight months, since Nusaiba was born. We stayed in a hotel in Istanbul run by a couple of Chechen mafiosi. The plan was to take Ayeesha to the American embassy and get her a visa as my wife. Sumaya and I were married according to Islamic custom, but not legally, so there was no reason to believe that I wouldn't be able to bring Ayeesha to America. However, I should have expected that the U.S. government would give us problems.

After arguing with a Turkish employee for half an hour I was finally able to tell an embassy employee about Ayeesha and Nusaiba. He told me that he couldn't do anything without some kind of marriage papers. When I explained that Chechen elders had married us in the village of Kerchaloy in the middle of a war and that we had no such papers, he told us that we could get married in Turkey. But he knew full well that in order for us to get married in Turkey, we would have to get permission from our respective governments. This was no problem on the U.S. side, but who would do that for Ayeesha? The United States didn't recognize the Chechen government, and the Russian government was unlikely to help us in any way.

Nevertheless, we approached the Russians. The Chechens who ran the hotel told me that they'd made special arrangements with someone at the Russian embassy. They were lying, of course, and when we asked for him at the embassy he acted like he didn't know anything about it. We tried to explain that we just needed him to sign a simple piece of paper so that I could marry Ayeesha in Turkey and take her back to America, but he didn't care. Ayeesha told him that someone had told us that he would do something to help.

"You two are with those Chechen rebels and you expect me to help you?" he said. He started to laugh. "You're lucky I don't take your fake passport away and have you arrested."

I went back to the American embassy a few times to see whether there were any loopholes, but the officials there weren't even remotely interested in helping us. I also went to the Chechens and asked why they had lied to me. As always, they had some kind of excuse. I stayed with Ayeesha for a month and a half in Istanbul, but I was unable to find any sort of solution and eventually exhausted my resources. I was having problems with my leg and needed to get back to the States. The Chechens told me that a group of Chechen refugees were headed back to Chechnya and that it would better if Ayeesha traveled with them because of her fake passport. At the time I believed we could still find a way to bring her back to the States someday and promised that I wouldn't abandon her. I took a flight home that night and Ayeesha left for Chechnya the next day. If I'd known that it would be the last time I ever saw her or my daughter I would have hijacked an airplane to try to get her to America.

Back in the States, I received a fax from Ibn-ul Khattab. He criticized me and accused me of abandoning Ayeesha.

In Arizona, I got down to the business of walking again. The trip to Istanbul had set me back considerably, but I was still determined to be up and running. After a few weeks of fits and starts and trouble with prosthetics companies, I ` was fitted with a prosthetic and learned how to run and walk without a limp.

My work with Andy, Len, and the FBI continued to move along. Our operation started to expand past Phoenix out into Los Angeles, San Diego, and even Chicago. While in Phoenix I caught wind that a ranking member of the Palestinian Authority would come to town, and I arranged to be his driver when he got there. Things even progressed past counterterrorism and into the plain old criminal realm. I was able to generate enough information on a dangerous group of armed robbers to prevent a violent hit. What we did in the counterterrorism field was far too important to risk blowing my cover over some local law enforcement issue, but we were always able to cooperate with local police departments in ways that never jeopardized me.

I don't know if we can make this claim, but I think we were among the first to bridge the gap between different law enforcement agencies, altering the way they view their respective fields. In the past, crimes took place with the full knowledge of one agency because they didn't want to jeopardize an investigation by telling another agency. Now that was changing. Islamic radicals were connected to shady Arabs. Shady Arabs were connected to fraud and drug trafficking. Fraud and drug trafficking led of course, to Americans. So an investigation that started out with radicals could lead to a big bust down the road by the DEA, the ATF, the Treasury Department, or local law police officers, and would ensnare characters that were completely unrelated to the original radical person in question.

In December 1997 my wife gave birth to our son, Saifudeen, or "Sword of the Religion" in Arabic. When he was coming out, he was so big that he got stuck on his mother's pelvic bone. By the time the nurse worked him free they realized that the umbilical cord had been wrapped around his neck and that he wasn't breathing. As the nurse frantically called for the doctor my heart felt as if it had stopped, and I thought I was going to pass out. I couldn't bear the thought of my son not making it. After some frantic moments the doctors had him breathing, and once they felt that he was safe I held him in my arms and made the *azan*, or call to prayer, in his right ear. From that moment on he would be the closest thing to me on this earth.

In early 1998 I had more complications with my leg and had to go in for another operation. It was a rather rough surgery, and I spent three days in the hospital, but when I came out of the recovery room, Sumaya, Andy, and Len were there for me, like before. This time when they walked into the room my wife didn't show any curiosity. I had so much weird shit going on in my life— all concealed from her, of course—that she never asked who these men were or how I knew them.

It took me a couple of months to get over the surgery, but we forged on. Everything was moving so fast that in hindsight, I think that we were getting too creative for a Bureau that had been so static for so long. As far as I can tell, the beginning of the end was an operation on which Andy and I spent a lot of time and resources. Some wealthy Arabs in Los Angeles approached me about starting a kind of training camp in the mountains of Arizona. The plan was to have the Arabs come to Arizona to train while a team of special agents in covert positions ran surveillance and a tactical team stood by to intervene should anything go wrong.

Andy, another agent, and I took a Cessna up and scouted the mountains north of Phoenix for a suitable location. We found a valley outside of Bumble Bee that was accessible only by four-wheel drive. It was far enough out of the way to avoid any accidental contact with locals, and this was important because this part of Arizona is militia territory. No one wanted to see what would happen if a group of redneck militia guys ran into a group of Arabs training with firearms in the mountains.

The preparations were meticulous. We scouted nearly every square yard of the valley and measured distances between landmarks. We rented two Chevy Suburbans from a local dealer and outfitted one with audio surveillance gear. I was to activate a small switch on the side of the driver's seat when conversations took place in the vehicle. To avoid a lot of paperwork and legal headaches, we would use only my personal firearms during the training. These were a few semiautomatic AK-47s and a couple of handguns. All of the guns were legal and approved by the FBI; if they had been fully automatic or if we had planned to use prohibited devices, it would have triggered all sorts of bureaucratic procedures. As it was, the circumstances surrounding the training and the weapons we planned to use were as legal as any rifle range in a Boy Scout camp.

Everything was set two days before the operation. We had full approval from Washington. I took possession of the Suburban with the audio equipment, packed for the trip, and even helped myself to a sneak peek at the audio-surveillance gear the FBI techs had installed. But the day before the Arabs were due to arrive in Phoenix Andy called to tell me we had to meet immediately at a hotel. Andy and Len were there along with their boss, Jonathan Canter. They told me that Janet Reno, the attorney general, had pulled the plug on the operation. I was furious.

"Call the bitch up and let me talk to her," I said to Andy. They told me that although this would be amusing, of course it wasn't possible. I asked what her reasons were, but they wouldn't tell me. Perhaps Reno was gunshy after Waco and Ruby Ridge. Maybe she thought we weren't attracting the right targets, or the operation whiffed of entrapment, or we were eating up too many resources, or she was afraid of headlines that might read FBI TRAINS TERRORISTS! Whatever the reasons, I can't help but think that it was a fateful, disastrous decision, and it wouldn't be the last. With time and patience we could have attracted many, if not most of the terrorists to one place, under surveillance, with leads to everyone they knew inside the United States, with all their telephone calls traced, all their e-mails decoded, all their financial transactions calculated. Instead of spinning our wheels by infiltrating pacifists in all the mosques of North America or detaining hardworking Pakistani store clerks for months on INS violations, the investigation would have revealed the lines and nodes of the terrorist network like a chance ray of sunlight on a spider web. It wouldn't be our only chance to gather intelligence on those who wish to do us harm, and sadly, it wouldn't be the last time the Washington worthies would make such a colossal mistake. The next missed opportunity would be on an international level.

Now that the operation was down the tubes, I had to worry about damage control and get out of the deal while still maintaining good relations with the Arabs. I played up the Arabs' habit of being bossy know-it-alls to fabricate a disagreement over how the camp should be run and then invented a family emergency that would take me out of town for a week. To smooth over the problems they'd created, the FBI put me on a plane to the Midwest with my daughter and lots of spending money. Asiya and I spent the next week visiting family.

After the camp incident everything started to take a weird turn. I'd expected to work with the CIA from the beginning, and looking back it seems inevitable, but this is the point when the Agency started to get involved. Andy became curious about Abu Amin and the other Pakistanis I'd met in Khattab's compound in Baku; he wanted me to start contacting them through the Internet. The FBI had taught me a little about computers, but I hadn't really pursued it all that much. The first computer they'd bought for me was an old 486, but now Andy gave me some money to buy a new one.

That's when Harry, a CIA computer tech, came into the picture. They knew that the London-based Pakistanis communicated only via encrypted e-mails, so Andy told me that Harry would come to install a program that would enable me to talk to them. It wasn't anything "classified" or "top secret"; rather, it was a free program available over the Internet. However, you had to have a working knowledge of computers to get it up and running, and since it was an encryption device, Harry would install it so that the Agency would have a means to listen in.

I was concerned about having someone from the Agency come to my house. The sight of a Brylcreemed 1950s-era IBM engineer would be a little strange if one of my underworld contacts happened to pass by, but Andy told me not worry. The folks at the Agency said that Harry was a bit of a slob and that he wouldn't attract any attention. When Harry showed up at my front door, he definitely didn't bring a CIA computer tech to mind. He was a tall gangly guy in his late forties with a mustache and a scruffy face, dressed in faded blue jeans and cowboy boots. Harry seemed pleasant enough, but I wondered about his computer skills; he looked more like a truck driver than a computer geek. When he sat down in front of my new computer, however, all my doubts vanished. He started making the computer do all sorts of funny things and spoke in technical terms that completely lost me. I tried to get some idea of what the CIA was up to by talking to Harry as he installed the encryption program, but what he said left me more confused than before.

A little later, Andy asked me to establish a relationship with the Pakistanis in London in the months ahead, which I did. I don't remember what led up to it, but during this time Andy told me that the CIA wanted to run an operation into Chechnya; it appeared that the Agency was interested in the Pakistanis because of their involvement in Chechnya, and that the interest ultimately led back to Ibn-ul Khattab. The picture was becoming clearer now that they were telling me the Agency was thinking about Chechnya, but it was difficult for me to gauge their motives and interests: the oil of the Caucasus region? Islamic separatists? the state of the Russian Federation? the preparedness of the Russian Army? terrorism in Chechnya?

Before I knew it, I was sitting in a Phoenix hotel room with Andy, Len, and an older woman named Tracy. She was a CIA case officer, and we were gathered there to see how we could cooperate and start operating overseas. I took a special polygraph exam, not the usual routine one, to satisfy the agency about some question or other they had about my involvement with the Russian FSB while I was still in Azerbaijan. They were satisfied with the results of the exam, and an operational plan slowly started to materialize.

The idea was to mount an operation in which I would go back into Chechnya and attach myself to Khattab's group. I didn't feel very good about this because I didn't view Khattab as a bad guy. When I'd gone to work for the United States, I'd made it clear that I wasn't turning against the jihad but that I was against terrorism. Khattab wasn't a terrorist, so the CIA's intentions seemed off the mark. But I kept this to myself throughout the entire discussion. I still needed to get Ayeesha, and if the CIA was willing to send me to Chechnya I would figure out what to do with Khattab when I got there.

Planning the operation was excruciating. Everyone argued about all sorts of minute details. Every time we made progress we would get set back just as far by some pencil pusher with questions about what to do if this happens or what to do if that happens, but by mid-1998 we had something of a plan. Andy and Len would travel with me as far as London, and then I would set out for Chechnya on my own. Andy and I went shopping at a police store for my trip, and since everything would be on the Bureau's dollar we got all sorts of gear I couldn't ordinarily afford. This included an $800 top-of-the-line piece of bulletproof and stab-resistant body armor. Getting stabbed would be as big a threat as getting shot. I also went to San Diego and had a custom-made magazine vest put together by a company that made tactical gear for the navy SEALS.

Finally the day came when we were supposed to go. I had all of my gear packed and waiting by the front door when Andy pulled up in Jonathan Canter's GMC Jimmy. It was an emotional good-bye. I don't think Saifudeen was even walking yet, but we'd become extremely close. Inside I didn't want to go, but something drove me to it. I didn't want to do anything to leave this beautiful boy fatherless, but life and death aren't up to me, and I felt that I would return safely if it was meant to be.

Everything went sour even before we got to the airport. Andy got a call telling him that approval had been suspended, again, probably as a result of the attorney general, and that we had to go into a holding-pattern. I knew the holding-pattern game. We'd become officially operational as soon as we'd left my house, and as a result I couldn't return home until we went officially de-operational. So instead of going to the airport we headed to a hotel in Phoenix.

Although I was allowed to call my wife I wasn't allowed to tell her where I was. For all she knew I was halfway to Chechnya, but I was actually just halfway across town. Every day was the same. Andy would come over in the morning and we would wait for a green light. At lunchtime we wound entertain ourselves by seeing who could order the biggest, most elaborate room-service meal on the Bureau's account. In the afternoon, Andy would go back to the office to argue about the situation with everyone and anyone who'd listen, and then we'd wait for the next day.

The Bureau got tired of paying for our lunches after a week, and we then went deoperational. I was able to go home, but now I had to come up with a story to explain why I'd been gone for a week but had never left the country; on top of that, I might be leaving again at any time. The web of lies grew.

Andy called two days later and told me that we were on again. He'd fought it all the way to the top. Instead of letting them put the whole operation on hold until they could pull the plug, he'd forced them to give us partial approval. This time when Len came to pick me up, we actually made it to the airport, and then we actually made it onto a plane. The plan was for Len and me to travel as far as Virginia, where we'd wait until the next day, when Andy would join us. At that point we'd take things day by day. We chose

Virginia so that we'd be close to Langley, where we'd bug the shit out of the CIA until they made something happen.

When Len and I got to Dulles International we rented a Mustang and drove to Tysons Corner, Virginia. The next day, the Fourth of July, Andy came out and that night Tracy, from the CIA, invited us to have dinner at Harry's sister's house. Though I guess people are people, it was as though I'd walked into some bizarro world as I ate grilled hamburgers and hot dogs with two CIA agents, two FBI agents, a sister of one of the CIA agents, and her husband, a local sheriff's deputy. The war in Kosova was heating up and Tracy tried to say that since the region was volatile it could potentially affect the entire world. Therefore the situation warranted CIA intervention. Harry disagreed, saying that the whole region was a toilet bowl that had always been in conflict and that it never had much affect on anything, so the CIA should leave the region alone. Harry would later catch flak about these comments. At the time I had no idea that in a few weeks I would be in Kosova wearing a Kosova Liberation Army uniform.

We spent the next few days as we had in Phoenix, only now we were at a Hyatt, which gave us more room-service entertainment options. Over this time I had countless meetings with FBI and CIA bigwigs. Finally it was decided that we needed a meeting with the top brass at the Agency and that Andy, Len, and I would go to the headquarters in Langley for this. But that idea was scrapped at the last minute, and we had the meeting in a top-floor suite of the hotel instead.

It turned out that one of the Agency's biggest concerns was the issue of whether or not I would be involved in any sort of combat once I entered Chechnya. But here was the kicker: they weren't concerned about whether I was going to get hurt; rather, they wanted to satisfy an asinine policy that prohibited assets from participating in military operations. That is, the Agency wanted me to cozy up with an aggressive frontline rebel commander in my capacity as a mujahid, but I was prohibited from actually going to the front lines or acting in the capacity of a mujahid.

Brilliant! Genius! I asked them how I was supposed to negotiate this, but about the only thing they knew was that they wanted intelligence about Ibn-ul Khattab. In what was becoming a common theme, I would have to come up with the game plan or there wouldn't be any show at all.

I wouldn't be fooling anybody if I tried to avoid action, but by this time I didn't really care and was ready to tell the CIA just about anything they wanted to hear if it would get me to Chechnya. So I told them that I promised to behave myself, cross my heart and hope to die. No, I insisted, I wasn't just saying that; the scales had been cast from my eyes and I had seen the wisdom of their policies. I was a reformed man who no longer needed the ways of combat, and who would go and sin no more. They asked what I would do if I was with Khattab and he suddenly mounted an operation—how would I avoid combat without arousing suspicion? I told them that I would suddenly "fall down." After all, I was missing a leg and wouldn't be able to keep up with the others.

Whatever I said must have convinced them, because the next day Tracy came to deliver some fancy CIA toys: a digital camera for taking pictures of "people of interest" and a popular CD-ROM videogame. The agency knew that the targets in the London phase of the operation were very fond of video games. I was instructed to get them to load the game on their computers and then to retrieve the CD-ROM, at any cost. The disc was supposed to record everything on their hard drive while it downloaded the video game. They also gave me a copy of *The World's Most Dangerous Places,* by Robert Young Pelton. It was a sort of chapter-by-chapter tour guide to places like Chechnya with tongue-in-cheek dos and don'ts.

A couple of days later Andy, Len, and I went to see some of the sites in Washington, D.C. We visited the Vietnam Veterans wall and Arlington National Cemetery. We even walked around the outside of the White House. Andy took a picture of me giving the White House the one-finger salute. I might have been going to Chechnya and risking my life for the U.S. government, but that didn't mean that I had to like the guy who lived in the White House, or his attorney general, for that matter.

Our next stop was Baltimore. I forget why, but we stayed there for a few days and had a fairly fun time, because Baltimore wasn't as dull as Virginia. At some point approval for the next leg of our trip came and we packed up our little dog-and-pony show and headed off to London. The London phase of the trip was to be more covert than things had been up until this point. There hadn't been any reason why the three of us couldn't hang out together until now, but from here on out it was strictly by-the-book spook stuff. I caught a flight to London by myself, and Andy and Len followed the next day. Once on the ground, my cover was that I was just a regular mujahid on his way to Chechnya.

Before leaving for England, we had gone over final procedures for covert procedures while in London. Andy already had a cell-phone number activated for use in London, and I was to call that number when I could to arrange meetings. I was also given a number for emergency use only, in case my cover was blown or I needed emergency extraction. I could have used such a number when I would eventually reach Kosova, but it would have been to the wrong people.

The targets were expecting me in London, but they didn't know exactly when I was coming. I made my way from Heathrow Airport to a hotel far away from the touristy areas of London and called Abu Amin, whom I'd first met in Baku, Azerbaijan, two years earlier. He was an associate of Usama Bin Laden's and Abu Zubair's, and was the man who had given me an extension when my visa ran out while I was waiting to go to the hospital for mujahideen in Saudi Arabia. He said that he would be right over, and when he arrived he told me that there was no way they would let me stay in a hotel.

I told Abu Amin that I wanted to go back to Chechnya to sort out the issue with Ayeesha. We discussed routes into Chechnya and possible options about what to do with Ayeesha once I got back into Chechnya. I would have gone home that day with Abu Amin, but he lived with his family, and it would have been inappropriate to stay in their house while his mother and sister were there. Instead he told me that a guy I knew from when we were all back in Baku wanted to see me and that I would stay with him while I was in London. When I asked him who it was, Abu Amin told me that it was a surprise. We drove to a neighborhood about fifteen minutes from Abu Amin's house, to a flat on the second floor of an apartment building. When we rang the bell the guy who answered the door took me by surprise. It was Abdul Malik, a young Arab from Bahrain. He'd been only a teenager when we were in Baku but had already been respected among the mujahideen because he had an extensive Islamic education and had been in *madrasah*, or religious school, since he was a kid. Then, Abdul Malik had been a short, chubby kid with glasses, and during our stay in Baku he hadn't known a word of English, but we'd become good friends nevertheless. Now as he opened the door to the flat he greeted me in almost perfect English. He told me he'd been studying English for as long as he'd been in England, about six months. I was definitely impressed. If I hadn't known him before I wouldn't have believed that he had been studying for only six months.

Abu Amin left, and Abdul Malik and I settled down and spent the rest of the day talking about anything and everything. We went to a mosque that wasn't far from the flat and met a young British kid who was waiting for Abdul Malik. Abdullah was sixteen years old and had become a Muslim after his older sister had converted. He was a tall gangly kid and looked like any other British teenager. Abdul Malik had taken a liking to him and was now teaching him about Islam every day after Abdullah got out of school.

A couple of days later I called the number I had for Andy. He picked up on the first ring. As we started to talk I detected a genuine sense of worry in his voice and was reminded of the vast cultural chasm between the FBI and the mujahideen. Andy asked how I was doing and seemed to think the entire situation was dangerous, as though I were operating in a den of exotic cut-throats. I hadn't thought of it quite that way. I was among old friends and felt comfortable.

He didn't sound too optimistic about the situation on his end. I told him that things were progressing just fine on mine. Andy said that we should meet the following day and that anything positive would help things along. When I showed up at the hotel room Andy had given me, nobody answered. I was about to walk away when I noticed a small piece of paper stuck in the crack of the door. I pulled it out and opened it up. It said to go to the front desk and tell them my name. I went to the concierge, who handed me a sealed envelope. When I got to the street I opened the envelope, which had a hand-written note inside of it instructing me that the meeting place had changed and that I was to proceed immediately to a bookstore on a certain corner. Once I got there I was supposed to go inside to the new-release section and look for Tracy. After we made eye contact I was to follow her outside. She'd have a newspaper in her hand, and if she threw the newspaper in a trash can anytime *before* she hailed a cab I was to break contact and leave the area. If she *didn't* throw the newspaper away before she hailed a cab then I would jump in behind her. The newspaper business was a precaution; other agents would be on the street outside the bookstore when I entered. If I had a tail the other agents would signal Tracy when she exited. She would then signal me to abort by throwing the newspaper in the trash.

I arrived at the bookstore and started to browse the new-release section. I didn't see Tracy and figured the spooks were trying to be slick. They must have watched me enter the store and then given Tracy the all-clear signal to go inside. Just for the hell of it, I ducked behind a large display rack where I had a good view of the front doors but couldn't really be seen and watched Tracy stroll in a moment later. She paused for a moment and casually scanned the store. When she didn't see me she walked over to the new-release section. I watched for a minute as she picked up a few books, all the while looking around for me. I wanted to see what she would do if she couldn't make contact with me. I doubted that she had any communications gear on her, and I assumed that she would look for visual signals from another agent outside the store; I wanted to see who else was in the operational background.

After a minute or two Tracy turned toward the front door and looked at a clean-cut guy standing just outside on the sidewalk. She discreetly raised her hands in a "Where is he?" gesture. The guy outside shook his head, which amused me. I decided to stop playing around before someone started crying or Tracy had me paged and casually moved out from behind the display stand. As I walked toward Tracy she looked vaguely confused. Then she nodded slightly and started walking toward the door, newspaper in hand.

She exited the store and looked over at someone whom I didn't quite catch. I followed at a safe distance. We walked a short distance down the street like this, the newspaper still in her hand. Then she headed for a taxi stand across the street, in front of a park. Without looking to see if I was behind her, she got into the back of the first cab in line. She left the door open, and after a quick look around I jumped in next to her. The driver looked at us in the mirror with a quizzical expression and asked where we were going. We went to another hotel and waited for Andy and Len, who weren't in a very good mood. This is when things really began to get weird.

The Agency, in its infinite wisdom, had decided that in order for me to proceed to the next phase of the operation—entering Chechnya—as a diplomatic nicety they would first have to declare me to their Russian counterparts at the FSB. If you've read this book from page 1, it should be apparent to you that the FSB was thoroughly compromised, with everyone from rogue agents to operatives working for the highest bidder. I'd planned to use the fact that they were compromised in order to get into Chechnya in the first place; if the Agency declared me as an asset I would surely be killed before reaching Khattab.

But the Agency was stuck in some kind of idiotic stupor. Somehow its agents had convinced themselves that not only was the declaration mandatory but it also didn't compromise my safety. Andy and Len argued that it obviously compromised me, and besides, since when did we cooperate with the Russians? The Soviet Union might have dissolved, but Russia was no ally. And did they really think they could tell the FSB about me? Did they really think the FSB was like the California Highway Patrol? Tracy's people, however, just wouldn't listen. I left the hotel that day with nothing resolved. Andy talked to me privately before I left and told me that I didn't have to worry about anything. The Bureau would stand behind me, and if the Agency didn't come back to reality they would scrub the operation.

I went back to Abdul Malik's flat and hung out for a few more days, until the next secret meeting with Andy and the agency clowns. At this time the situation in Kosova was escalating. It was turning out to be another Bosnia all over again. The Serbs had murdered approximately fifteen thousand civilians already, and the only thing between them and a horrible genocide was the Kosova Liberation Army. Abu Amin was organizing a group of mujahideen for an assessment to determine whether or not it was a true jihad, but the very idea of making an assessment eventually led to a falling out between Abu Amin and myself. Certain conditions make a war a jihad, and although I am not a Qur'anic scholar and I don't have the training to tell the difference independently, I viewed Kosova in terms of black and white. If the Serbs were raping and murdering people because they were Muslims it was reason enough for me to try to stop them.

I met with Andy and Tracy's people a couple more times over the next week or so. For a moment it looked as if the Agency had pulled out of its perilous, misinformed prudence. The agents asked me how I would get into Chechnya if not through Russia, as they had planned. I told them again, as I'd told them from the beginning, that it wasn't even an issue and that I would go through Azerbaijan using my personal contacts. I laid out one possible plan for Tracy and her people in the plainest terms possible, but they were dumbfounded by the sheer simplicity; they were accustomed to running operations that involved far too many complications and ate up vast resources. "Give me a little cash for bribes," I told them, "and I'll be in Chechnya in a week, tops, after getting to Azerbaijan."

As I left this meeting it looked as if things were finally going to start rolling. I would fly to Azerbaijan and proceed on the ground. It would be just like I was trying to enter Chechnya on my own. This would also be much safer. Although I still had to run the usual risks of getting into Chechnya, such as encountering a Russian checkpoint agent who wasn't in the mood to play nice or being kidnapped by Mafia types, it would still be safer overall. Once I hit Azerbaijan and started talking to people about getting into Chechnya, word would filter back to Khattab's circle and everything would look more natural.

But the Agency didn't keep its head out of its ass for long. Who the hell knows why they were stuck on declaring me, but Andy and I still argued that the Azeri angle would work. Azerbaijan was just a pathetic little Third World shithole that needed good relations with America. But, as usual, we underestimated the Agency's colossal stupidity. We had another increasingly absurd meeting. I had grown accustomed to seeing the usually mild-tempered Andy in a bad mood, but this time he was actually angry. Len had a pretty sour look on his face too, and I couldn't help but wonder what new bullshit the agency had dreamed up. I didn't have to wonder for long.

If declaring me to the Russians wasn't bad enough, now the idiots had decided that in order to transit—*transit* mind you—through Azerbaijan, they would have to declare me to the Azeris. If declaring me to the Russians would get me killed before I reached Chechnya, declaring me to the Azeris would get me killed before I even left London. If Russia's intelligence service was thoroughly corrupt, it wasn't worth mentioning what the Azeris' intelligence service would be like. The last time I was in Azerbaijan, I'd convinced an Azeri army officer to take me to the border of Dagestan! To fight in Chechnya! What was I supposed to tell him this time? Oh yeah, by the way, I was that CIA guy you were told to look out for?

We had an interesting meeting, to say the least. Although Special Agents Andy and Len had to control their tempers, they still had some pretty strong words for the agency people in the room that day. On the other hand, I was just a lowly undercover operative, or expendable asset, or cannon fodder, or whatever. I told them what I thought and didn't mince words: that they were the biggest bunch of fucking idiots I had ever seen. They made the Arabs look like they had their shit together.

Andy, Len, and I went somewhere to talk by ourselves. I was more than a little surprised when Len told me that he was going back to Phoenix to protest the shit the Agency was pulling. It was no small matter for an FBI agent to walk away from an operation in protest. Andy stayed because he still wanted to see this thing happen somehow, and if he left too the whole thing would be scrubbed. I agreed to stick it out with Andy, knowing that he wouldn't give up until there wasn't any hope left.

Looking back at the whole situation, I have to admit that the only reason I put up with the situation was because of Ayeesha. I'd never believed in the operation in the first place, but it was still a means to an end: I had to get back to Chechnya for Ayeesha's sake. By now I'd also decided that I would tell Khattab about my involvement with the Agency and the Bureau. At this rate he would probably have known even before I told him. There wasn't much I could do if he wanted to execute me for treason, but I felt somehow that he would understand. We were all playing a nasty game and had to do what we thought was right at any given moment, even if it led us to our destruction. Of course, it would literally be my head if I was wrong, but that's all part of the game.

While Andy tried to do his thing, I continued to do mine in London. Abdul Malik and I had long discussions about the best way for Muslims to help the cause. We talked about my role and what I could do. It turned out that Abdul Malik was aligned with Al Qaeda and that he'd been to Usama Bin Laden's camp in Afghanistan since the last time I had seen him in Baku. At the time Bin Laden was known to the intelligence agencies of the world and would soon be wanted by the United States for the embassy bombings. Abdul Malik told me that I could offer Bin Laden many valuable services. Simply being an American allowed me to travel to a wider variety of places and with greater ease than many Arabs could. After an extremely long discussion, Abdul Malik made an incredible offer. He told me that if I wanted, he would call someone I knew in Pakistan who would in turn contact Bin Laden. If Bin Laden agreed, I would go to Afghanistan and meet him.

I was absolutely thrilled with this possibility. I wasn't convinced at the time that Bin Laden was a bad guy, but I would be willing to go there on the Agency's nickel to see what the guy was all about for myself. I called Andy and told him that we had to meet immediately, and we met the next day. Andy had already told Tracy that I had big news, and I could barely contain my excitement as I explained Abdul Malik's offer.

Tracy said that it was nice but doubted that anything like that would ever happen.

What the fuck, I thought. I had an invitation to the big bad bogeyman's pad—quite possibly the first offer of its kind for a Western intelligence agency—and these clowns were acting as though I was that kid Jack who was supposed to go sell the cow and brought home beans instead. I pressed the issue to try to see what the problem was, but all that Tracy would say was that there was no way the United States would approve an American operative going undercover into Bin Laden's camp.

It's impossible to say what might have been—perhaps an obscure footnote to an Al Qaeda operation that never happened. But it wouldn't be the last time I would come into contact with Usama Bin Laden's operatives. The next time would be in the United States.

Despite my grievances, I still held out for the original plan, to go to Chechnya. In the meantime I continued with Abdul Malik and Abu Amin. One day Abu Amin took me to meet a legend in mujahideen circles. His name was Abu Ubaidah and he was from the Saudi royal family but had long since been disowned for fighting in the jihad. He must have weighed 450 pounds, but everyone said that he moved like a cat on the front lines. He was legendary for killing seventeen Russians in one battle during the war in Afghanistan. The part that made him legendary wasn't the number of soldiers he killed but the way he killed them. In a close-quarters battle, he clubbed them to death with the barrel of a big 90mm recoilless rifle. Later he went on to fight in Bosnia against the Serbs as the commander of the infamous Abu Ubaidah group. These guys were like the mujahideen special forces and didn't associate with other mujahid units. They sat around monitoring the radio frequencies of frontline units until they heard the first signs of a battle. Then they would haul ass to engage the Serbs in that area. They were so vicious that supposedly Abu Ubaidah was wanted by The Hague for war crimes.

It was a big deal for this guy to meet with me because he was on the lam, and I considered it an honor. It seemed that Abu Amin wanted me to speak with him about the situation in Kosova. I was starting to get the impression that Abu Amin wanted me in Kosova and not Chechnya. During our meeting he also broke the news to me that the Serbs had ambushed his assessment group. The details were still sketchy but they had been hit pretty hard and one of them was critically wounded with head injuries.

There was also information that the KLA might have sold out the assessment group and led them into the ambush. Abu Ubaidah wanted to get an accurate picture of what was really going on there to determine whether or not he would invest mujahideen resources. I definitely wanted to help Kosova but I still had the issue with Ayeesha to worry about. Abu Amin told me that if I went to Kosova he could arrange for Ayeesha to come to London and I could take care of her there. I told him that this was fine with me but that he needed to be sure he could do it. If I didn't get Ayeesha out of Chechnya the Islamic court was going to divorce her from me for abandoning her. He promised me that he would.

Now I was forced with an impossible decision. I wanted desperately to go and defend Kosova against the Serbs, but I didn't want to do anything to further hurt Ayeesha and my daughter. In the end I trusted Abu Amin's word and put my oath to the Muslims first. If he could get her out of Chechnya without my actually going there, then I had to go to Kosova. Of course there was still the issue of Andy and Tracy, but I had a feeling how that was going to turn out anyway.

Before meeting with Andy again I talked to Abdul Malik about his offer. As is always the case with my life, I had a number of things brewing at the same time and would end up going with the one that finished cooking first or looked the best to me. Abdul Malik told me he'd made the phone call and that the guy had gotten back to him. The word was that Bin Laden had agreed and I was officially invited to come and have a chat with him. I would have taken this course over both Chechnya and Kosova but that depended on the Agency.

Another pointless meeting was arranged. The secret-agent stuff to get to the meetings had fun in the beginning, but now it was just downright lame. They were so meticulous about operational security when it came to our secret circle jerks, but they were willing to declare me to a bunch of crooks at the FSB and even to the Azeris. I told them about the invitation to Bin Laden's camp but the Agency people started to act really funny about this. They told me to get the thought out of my mind because it would never, ever happen. On the Chechen matter we were still stuck on stupid: no go if they didn't declare me to somebody, anybody. I asked Tracy if the problem was that they just couldn't wait to tell someone about me, like a schoolgirl and her new boyfriend. Why not call the Chechens and declare me to them too? No, better yet, why not take out a full-page ad in the *New York Times* and declare me to the whole world? Looking back on the situation, it's funny to think that no one suggested that we just operate in secret. You know, send me in secretly. To conduct espionage.

Andy had also brought another Bureau guy with him, a not-so-special agent working the London office. I recognized him as the person to whom Tracy had turned to when she couldn't find me in the bookstore. I had no idea that the FBI, a domestic law enforcement organization, would involve itself with intelligence gathering in a foreign scope—that is, "spying." He immediately jumped into the fray with a tirade about the Agency and the appropriateness of their declarations. Whereas Andy had been on my side, this prick started to threaten me. Maybe the Bureau thought that I was getting out of line and Andy wasn't reining me in. Andy was having trouble reining himself in and just sat there with his head down as I went at it with the London-office guy.

I often spoke my mind or acted like a smart-ass when dealing with the FBI and CIA, but this was the first time that I actually went into a rage. This guy almost put me over the edge, and I set into him almost to the point of getting physical. He threw a bunch of threats at me about what would happen if I didn't behave, and so on. I told him to shove his threats up his ass and suggested that he declare himself to the FSB and the Azeris and go to Chechnya instead of me.

Andy and I talked privately after the fight. He knew that I'd been increasingly concerned about the situation in Kosova before going operational back in Phoenix, and he understood me too well by now. He said that if I wanted to go to Kosova that I would have to go back to the States to go "deoperational." I had a right as a U.S. citizen to go to Kosova, but the U.S. government wanted to make it clear that if I went there my travel wasn't related in any way to any official government function or funding. I'd agreed to that and would now exercise that right. I told him that this whole operation into Chechnya or Afghanistan was obviously pointless and that I would go to Kosova. We agreed that the Chechen operation wasn't going to happen as long as the idiots at the Agency were involved and that as far as we were concerned the operation was scrubbed. He told me that he didn't blame me, and that I would have to go back to Phoenix first to sign out and collect a cash bonus.

I hung out with Abu Amin and Abdul Malik in London for a few more days to discuss our plans. Abu Amin told me that he knew a Saudi guy in the States named Ghareeb who was a good person and was involved with the jihad. He'd just moved from Oregon to Sierra Vista, Arizona. That's funny, I thought, wondering if he knew that he was living next to Fort Huachuca, the base for the army's military-intelligence school and an FBI training area. Abu Amin talked with Ghareeb about me and said that Ghareeb would come visit when I got back to Phoenix.

One of the things I liked about Abu Amin was that he realized that the mujahideen needed better training and skills. This thinking was a bit different from that of most Arabs, who thought they knew everything there was to know and never put much effort into preparation or training. Abu Amin was extremely impressed with what I'd been doing in Phoenix over the past couple of years, and before leaving London I invited him to come to Phoenix to see what was available in the States. He agreed to visit about a week after I got back.

I went back to Phoenix shortly thereafter. I was happy to be home and had missed Saifudeen especially. Even as a baby he recognized me, smiling when I got off the airplane. That made all the difference in the world, but I wouldn't be home for long and it would be a hectic stay. I had to settle things with Andy, meet Ghareeb, show Abu Amin around the States, and get ready for my trip to Kosova.

Andy had come back a few days before and had gotten all the paperwork ready. When we met he apologized for the bullshit the Agency had pulled and asked me to rethink a visit to Kosova. He said that such a trip wouldn't necessarily end my relationship with the FBI, but that his boss had told him to ask me not to go. My reply was that I'd started working with the FBI to fight terrorism, not bureaucracy, and although it was state-sponsored, what the Serbs were doing in Kosova was terrorism. I didn't really see that we'd done much to fight terrorism since we'd started; instead we'd spent all our time and energy fighting bureaucrats and their idiotic madness. We were always covering up their fiascos and were never allowed to do what was necessary. If the FBI truly believed in counterterrorism, they would send a squad of volunteers to help the KLA fight against the Serbs.

At any rate, I had to sign a paper saying that I was going to Kosova as a private citizen and that I didn't represent the FBI or any other branch of the U.S. government. I also got a $3,000 bonus for going as far as we had on the Chechen operation, and some additional money as a reimbursement for expenses, and the last month's pay. All told, Andy handed me $5,000 in cash that day.

After dealing with Andy I called Ghareeb in Sierra Vista. I told him that I was Abu Amin's friend, and he said he would come up to Phoenix to see me. A couple of days later a car pulled up in my driveway. It was a newer model Ford Taurus with black windows and chrome wheels. As four very Saudi looking Arabs got out of the car, I had no idea what fate and her odd sense of humor had in store for us.

I walked outside to greet them and the shortest one introduced himself as Ghareeb. He introduced one of the others as his brother and the other two as his brother's schoolmates. They came inside and ate food that my wife had prepared. Ghareeb seemed like a very good Muslim who was truly into the jihad. The other guys kind of struck me as a little shaky, so I conducted the conversation mostly with Ghareeb. When it was time to go I invited Ghareeb to stay and told him I'd take him back to Sierra Vista later. Except when I went to Kosova, Ghareeb would be with me pretty much every day from then on for almost a year.

A couple of days later Abu Amin showed up from London, and both he and Ghareeb stayed at my house. Abu Amin was amazed at the amount of firearms and ammunition available to me. It was his first trip to America, and while he'd known that people owned guns in the States, he hadn't imagined that it was quite like this. His first question was, "Can we actually shoot them?" I told him, "Of course." The next day we went to my favorite spot in the desert, where Abu Amin and Ghareeb burned through about a thousand rounds of ammunition.

Abu Amin had come for a purpose, and we discussed plans for a training program in the States for mujahideen living in the United Kingdom. He also had a shopping list of items that weren't available over there that he wanted to purchase while he was here. I took him to army-surplus stores and a gun show in town that weekend, where he bought some items and made a list of others that he wanted.

Abu Amin stayed for a few days. Ghareeb hung around until a couple of days before I was to leave, then went back to Sierra Vista so that I could have some time alone with my family. The plan now was that I would also return to England and then go on to Kosova from there. Abu Amin had left me with some money asking me to bring some of the items he wanted when I came through London. Among other things I carried in my luggage for him was a box with fifteen Kevlar helmets that I had purchased in Phoenix.

At about this time, August 7, 1998, terrorists attacked the U.S. embassies in Nairobi, Kenya, and Dar es Salaam, Tanzania. The bomb blasts destroyed the buildings, killing 223 people and injuring 4,722 more. The prime suspect was Usama Bin Laden, who had left the Sudan for the Taliban regime in Afghanistan. President Clinton's response thirteen days later was a cruise-missile attack on Sudan and the camps where I'd trained in Afghanistan. The cruise missiles hit a major pharmaceutical plant, depriving thousands of people their jobs and vital medicines. We still don't know whether the Clinton administration had bad intelligence or were just peevish at the Sudaneese for harboring Usama Bin Laden. The cruise missiles that hit Afghanistan had to travel over Pakistan, which required permission from the Pakistani government. It appears that Bin Laden sympathizers in the Pakistani Inter-Services Intelligence warned Usama Bin Laden about the attack in advance so he was able to get out in time. I sometimes wonder how many $500,000 missiles they sent to blow up the mud shacks I described earlier, or whether I could have taken care of the matter myself. That is, if the bed-wetters in the Agency could get over having to declare me to the Taliban.

Again I kissed Saifudeen good-bye and was on my way back to whatever fate had waiting for me. In London, Abu Amin gave me what you could loosely call a set of mission objectives for Kosova and we went shopping for the best airfare to Tiranë, Albania, which would be the jumping-off point for Kosova.

KOSOVA AND SURROUNDING AREAS

CROATIA

REPUBLIKA SRPSKA

BOSNIA-
HERZEGOVINA

Srebrenica

SERBIA

Sarajevo

Goražde

MONTENEGRO

Dubrovnik

Podgorica

KOSOVA

Bajram
Curri

Tropojë

Lisene

Adriatic sea

Skopje

MACEDONIA

Tiranë

ITALY

0   50
MILES

ALBANIA

GREECE

MAP DETAIL

Bajram
Curri

Tropojë

KOSOVA

Drim

Lake
Scutari

Lisene

ALBANIA

A couple of days later I was on a SwissAir flight to Tiranë. As the airplane descended I was astonished by what a shithole the place was. Looking at the airport, I was brought back to the time I'd first touched down in Baku, but this place was worse than Baku, much worse. I'd read in Robert Young Pelton's book *The World's Most Dangerous Places* that Albania was the poorest country in the world or at least not more than second or third up the list. The country was still in turmoil from the chaos that had erupted a year earlier. With the government's blessings, a foreign film company had set up a pyramid scheme. The dirt-poor people of Albania had invested their life savings in it, and when the firm took off with the entire country's money, the people turned their rage on the government. They looted every government building, including all of the armories, so almost every Albanian household had an AK-47 and the government couldn't do anything about it.

Tiranë's airport made Baku's look like LAX. At least Baku had some semblance of order, with soldiers directing the people from the plane to the bus that would take them to the terminal. In Tiranë, the soldiers on the tarmac resembled vagrants hanging out in the park more than anything else. More than a few of the passengers from my flight wandered around the tarmac looking confused. I was reminded of the U.S. government's constant meddling when I heard the roar of an airplane. A big, gray four-engine C-130 was roaring down the runway. The Americans were here, and this wouldn't be the last time I woud see them.

I looked around the terminal and saw a guy holding up a sign written in Arabic that said ABU MUJAHID. I almost laughed. That was either Abu Amin's odd sense of humor or an attempt to conceal my identity from other Americans on the flight. Either way, the guy holding the sign was also supposed to be the KLA liaison in Albania. I walked up and greeted him.

"*As salamu alaikum,*" I said.

"*Wa alaikum as salaam,*" he replied with an odd look on his face.

"Do you speak English?"

"Yes. Are you from Abu Amin?"

"Uh-huh."

"I was expecting an Arab."

He seemed pleasantly surprised that I wasn't an Arab. As I would find out later, the initial assessment group hadn't gotten along very well with the KLA, and as a result, this guy didn't look forward to dealing with more Arabs.

As in Baku, he evidently had some pull here in the airport, because he got my bags with all of my gear in them through customs with no problems at all. As we were leaving the airport, a convoy of cars led by an olive-drab Chevy Blazer with a flashing blue light on top started up. The other cars in the convoy had tinted windows, and another olive-drab Blazer brought up the rear. As the first Blazer passed us I saw four Americans. The driver was in U.S.-issued fatigues, and all three passengers were in plainclothes but had weapons. The front-seat passenger had a Benelli Super-90 12-gauge shotgun and the two rear passengers had MP5s on their laps. Just to be an ass, I shoved my video camera out the window and taped them as they drove by. They all gave me sour looks, but they didn't slow down.

The drive into Tiranë from the airport was interesting. The entire countryside was littered with little circular reinforced-concrete bunkers that had a small aperture in the front. They looked to be just big enough for a machine-gun crew, but there appeared to be no apparent logic to their placement or direction. Some faced north and some faced south. Others faced every direction in between. They looked like thousands of R2-D2s running around the countryside. The KLA liaison told me they were a product of the old Communist leader's paranoia and insanity. Enver Hoxa had created his own form of communism, which made East Germany look like an open tourist state. To this day I wonder what exactly he planned to do with all of those bunkers all facing different directions.

Once we hit the city of Tiranë things really got crazy. It wasn't violent per se; I had seen much more dangerous places. It was just insane. There was no order anywhere. People drove their cars anywhere and any way they wanted to. The intersections that did have traffic cops were crazier then those without, because everyone was busy trying to go around the cop standing in the middle of the street. When he would raise his hand for one direction of traffic to stop, they would simply continue on anyway. The streets were filled with a mixture of old Russian cars and brand-new BMWs and Mercedeses driven by teenage boys who still had acne problems. The women were incredible. I hadn't seen women this beautiful since Azerbaijan.

After what seemed like a never-ending game of chicken with other drivers, we finally reached the house the KLA was using in Tiranë. It was like any other house I'd seen from Azerbaijan to Russia, and had the usual high wall with a courtyard on the other side. The KLA liaison honked the horn when we reached the big green steel gates, and someone on the other side opened them. We drove into a courtyard filled with trees and shrubbery. Quite a few guys were sitting around, some on chairs, others on the steps of the porch that led to the house. They resembled all the other mujahideen I'd seen over the years, but they were more Anglo-looking than most Arabs, and had my approximate complexion but with curly hair.

They seemed friendly enough when they came over to greet me. I didn't get any bad vibes from anyone there and sat down and started chatting with everyone. The guy who picked me up at the airport translated. I found out that most of them were leaving Kosova instead of going in. They'd all fought against the Serbs but were leaving now to go live with their families in Europe. I found this somewhat disturbing; why they would abandon the war before it was even close to over? But all in all, they appeared to be decent fellows.

Later that afternoon another KLA member came to the house. The guy who'd picked me up from the airport introduced him as someone important from Kosova. He had just returned from a trip to Turkey to raise funds for the people of Kosova and the KLA. The three of us talked about the situation in Kosova and what I could do to help. Abu Amin must have told them that I was one of his representatives, because they kept asking when he would send help. I asked them what had happened with the first assessment group, and they told me that the Arabs had been extremely rude and had insisted on doing everything their way. Big surprise. When the Arabs finally went to Kosova to talk with the KLA commanders, they pissed someone off, and the ambush developed from that somehow. I asked if the KLA had sold them out. The guys told me that as far as they knew, it didn't happen that way. They weren't sure what had led up to the ambush, but when it did happen the KLA left Abu Amin's group to fend for themselves. This indicated that either the KLA was a bunch of cowards or the assessment group had really rubbed somebody the wrong way.

I didn't really care either way. I wasn't there for the KLA or Abu Amin. I had come to help the people of Kosova and it didn't matter to me who did what as long as they didn't leave me during a fight. The guy who'd picked me up from the airport said that he would try to get me up to Kosova as soon as possible, which turned out to be the next day. I would leave early in the morning with one of the KLA guys in a van for hire, similar to the vans in Pakistan.

The road to Bajram Curri, on the border of Kosova was long and tiring. From there we would go Tropojë, just inside Kosova. At the time there were two ways to get to Bajram Curri. The way we were going was all the way up through Albania until we reached a large river. We would then take a ferry the rest of the way. The other route went around the mountains but was far too dangerous at the time due to groups of armed bandits working the area.

By afternoon the road had started to wind up into the mountains. We traveled for maybe an hour over steep mountain roads, then suddenly saw a massive dam looming in the valley ahead of us. It was as big as any dam I've ever seen, but it had the rough, unfinished concrete-and-steel quality that characterized public projects in post-Communist countries. The structures at the bottom of the dam appeared to have been long since abandoned, and they looked spooky. The road ahead seemed to disappear near the top of the dam, but when we got up there we saw a tunnel—nothing more elaborate than a rough hole thirty feet high and twenty feet wide cut into the rock—that led into the mountain. The driver turned his headlights on as we drove into the tunnel, which didn't have any concrete walls or any visible reinforcements, and we stopped at a traffic jam in the middle of the mountain. There was an endless string of vans and buses in front of us. I was momentarily disturbed by the realization that the tunnel wasn't ventilated, but like most Westerners in the Third World, I just figured that if everyone wasn't dead yet, it couldn't be all that bad.

Over the next half an hour or so our van made a little progress, but the driver eventually killed the engine when it looked like we couldn't go any farther. I thought this was a problem at first; then my companion told me to get my bag because we were going to walk the rest of the way, which turned out to be only a few hundred meters.

When we reached the end, the craziness of the situation really hit me. The tunnel opened up on a small patch of land perhaps fifty yards wide. The top of the dam was to the right, the river stretched out to the left, and strange-looking concrete-and-steel structures poked out of the cliffs on the opposite side of the gorge. The drivers from all the various vehicles parked in the tunnel were milling around, smoking cigarettes, and talking. One of them spoke English, so I asked him what was going on. He told me that this was the ferry landing and that the ferry made the trip from here to Bajram Curri once a day. All the Kosovar refugees came down the river on the ferry so they wouldn't have to risk the bandit-infested mountain route.

A little while later one of the drivers shouted. The ferry started to poke around the bend in the river. I couldn't believe my eyes when it came into full view. It was a boat of medium size that reminded me of the ferry we sometimes took to Ford Island in Pearl Harbor when I was a kid. It had probably been designed for ten to fifteen medium-size cars, but this one had at least thirty vehicles on it, and most of the vehicles were vans and microbuses. There were even a few dump trucks. As if the overload of vehicles wasn't enough, there were people packed onto every available open space.

As the ferry approached the concrete blocks of the landing ramp, all the drivers who had been milling around ran down to the edge of the water and instantly transformed from drivers to riverboat pilots. They gestured wildly and shouted all sorts of conflicting advice to the bridge of the ferry. Then the people who were overflowing off the front ramp of the ferry started in with their own wild gestures and shouts of advice. All told, there must have been fifty people telling the ferry captain how to dock the boat. The metal of the ferry screeched against the concrete of the landing as it smashed into the shore, and everyone screamed at the tops of their lungs, but the ferry captain brought it in just right.

The front ramp dropped with a loud boom and people started swarming off the ferry. The drivers swooped in, and bunches of people formed everywhere as the refugees made deals with van and bus drivers. When the vehicles started coming off the ferry it really got insane. The drivers pulled their vans and buses into the little patch of land, loaded the people and their belongings, and then turned around to go back out through the tunnel. At the same time the vehicles on the ferry were trying to get off and into the tunnel.

The guy who had ridden with me had disappeared, but now I saw him running up behind me. The expression on his face was somewhere between worry and panic. There was a small shack in the corner of the clearing that was occupied by some guys in what could loosely be called uniforms. They must have had a telephone in there, because now the guy who had ridden with me told me that we needed to go back to Tiranë. Oh shit, I thought, what now? Over the objection of my traveling companion, I grabbed one of the drivers who spoke English. The driver explained that someone in Bajram Curri had called and said that the cops up there were cracking down on KLA supporters and that we had to go back to Tiranë.

I asked whether this was a direct order from Tiranë or if he was just chickenshit. He said it wasn't an order but that we had to go back immediately. Now I understood the look on his face. He was spooked and didn't want to continue on. I told the guy who spoke English to tell him, "Fuck that." I wanted-ed to continue. I said that we would deal with whatever was happening up there when we got there, but my traveling companion wasn't having it. Okay, I said through the translator, then tell me where I'm supposed to go and I'll go by myself. But the coward still wasn't interested. He was determined to get back to Tiranë, and I couldn't very well continue without knowing my destination. I told him through the translator that I'd kick his ass for screwing up my trip when we got back to Tiranë.

It was a long ride back. I had to sit in the front seat of a van, sandwiched between the door and some girl, and occasionally turned around to give my chickenshit companion a withering glare. We didn't get back to the house until late that night. When we came in, the guy who had picked me up at the airport and the other guy who had just returned from Turkey looked surprised to see us. They started asking my traveling companion what the hell was going on. He stuttered as he tried to come up with an explanation. In the end it turned out that he had called his brother in Bajram Curri and his brother had said that he saw cops in the area harassing a friend of theirs. He then blew this up into a crackdown on the KLA and made us come all the way back. The next morning the guys told me that for whatever reason they couldn't get me back up to Kosova so I spent the day sitting around the house. However, the previous day's bullshit would cause problems for me that would stretch for years to come. If I hadn't returned to Tiranë I could have avoided what transpired that night.

I was sitting around chatting with some of the guys in the house when there was a loud bang on the steel gates. The bang was followed by shouting. Oh shit, I thought, don't tell me.

But it was. After a few more loud bangs, the steel gate crashed open. About fifteen Albanian cops burst in with AK-47s. They shouted and menaced us with their AKs until everyone was against the exterior wall of the house at gunpoint. Some of the cops held their guns on us as the others ran into the house and pulled out a couple of guys who had been sleeping inside. Two plainclothes cops appeared to be giving the orders.

The hardest thing about these situations is trying to determine whether you stand a chance of getting out with only minor problems or your bed will be a cold ditch before the night is out. It's better to go out fighting if it looks like the latter option will transpire. But you don't want to do anything irreversible if it looks like the former option is likely. I've been in several of these situations, and the fact that I'm writing this book demonstrates that I learned how to walk the line, but that doesn't make it any easier.

One of the plainclothes cops came up behind us as we stood facing the wall and slapped each of us on the backs of our heads before shouting what I interpreted as "Nationality?!" Some offered their papers; others just replied, "Kosova." I had to come up with a game plan before he got to me. As always, I had a knife in my pocket, and I considered making a move when the cop tried to hit me in the back of my head. I could get the knife to his throat, and since he was giving the orders I could probably get the other cops to drop their guns; but if the KLA guys didn't follow suit, it could turn into a massacre.

By the time the plainclothes cop got to me, I had already managed to work my hand inside my pocket. The metal that I had cupped in my right hand was cold. I wanted to move before he was able to hit me. After finishing with the guy next to me, he turned his attention to me. Before he could slap me, I swung my hand toward him. Instead of going for broke and getting my knife out of my pocket, I'd grabbed my Arizona concealed-weapons-permit badge. I flashed it in the cop's face and raised my finger to my lips: *Shush!* I nodded my head toward the others, who were still face-first against the wall, and looked back at the cop with my badge exposed and my finger to my lips. The cop got the cheesiest expression on his face, as though he'd just been let in on a major secret. He winked and pulled me away from the others.

The badge was mounted in a leather holder on a chain and looked like something a detective would carry. It resembled a cop's badge and had the seal of the State of Arizona with the inscription CONCEALED WEAPONS PERMIT along the top, with my permit number directly underneath. The actual permit was on the other side, under a plastic window. The plainclothes cop took it from me and examined it more closely. He probably couldn't read English, but it looked official. He raised his hands and his eyebrows as though to say "What are you?"

"American police," I whispered as I retrieved my passport.

The other plainclothes cop came over. They spoke in low tones. Later, when I found out who had put them up to the raid, it made sense why my corny trick had worked so easily. Americans were already involved that night, and as a result of some miscommunication these cops somehow got the impression that I was one of them. For whatever reason, the cops started rounding all the other guys up. As the last uniformed cop went out the gate I looked at the plainclothes cops and raised my hands. He gestured for me to relax. He asked his partner something in Albanian, and his partner said, "No problem" in English.

"Aha," the first cop said. "No problem." Then they walked out the gates.

So there I was standing in the now-empty courtyard wondering what in the hell I should do next. I figured that it would be best to get out of here before the cops caught on, so I went in the house to get my bags. That's when I realized that the other cops had taken all the bags in the house, including mine. Great I thought, getting to Kosova should be fun now.

I caught a cab on the street and went to a hotel in the center of Tiranë. My bags were gone, but I still had about a thousand dollars in my pocket. The next morning I went to a kiosk with international phone service and called Abu Amin. In code, I told him what had gone down, and he said to stay put for the moment before trying to get out of Albania. I told him that I didn't want to run but to continue on with the plans. He advised against it, since the situation was obviously getting weird, but said I should call tomorrow either way.

It was a nice day, so I decided to just hang out in the central square for a while. As usual, fate would intervene. A short while later a guy walked up to me and asked in English if I was American. I figured what could it hurt now, and said yes. He introduced himself as Raxhab, pronounced "Rajab," and said that he was Albanian. He'd been studying at an international school in Malaysia and had only recently returned to visit family in Tiranë. I was suspicious at first, and even more so when Raxhab said that he'd overheard me at the phone kiosk. But the more he talked, the more I wondered. He didn't seem like a cop or an intelligence agent or somebody to let your guard down around; rather, he was something of an opportunist. I decided that he'd eavesdropped on my phone conversation and was looking for a way to benefit from it.

Whatever his angle I needed all the help I could get so I continued to talk to him, although a bit cautiously. I didn't tell him why exactly I was in Tiranë but explained a bit about what had happened the night before. I grew a little more suspicious when he said that he knew a guy that was with Albanian intelligence, but at this point I really didn't care, so I told him to call the guy.

We arranged for the intelligence guy to meet us there in the central square. A little while later, a Russian Lada with dark windows pulled up, and a guy in a dress shirt carrying a walkie-talkie got out of the passenger side. Not bad, I thought; some pissant desk clerk wouldn't warrant his own driver. Maybe this guy could help out. He walked up to us, and we greeted each other. We spoke through Raxhab for a while, and the subject of my missing bags came up. The intelligence guy asked me a few questions about them and spoke to someone over his walkie-talkie. After a minute or two he smiled and told Raxhab that he had located the bags.

That was easy, I thought, but what would I have to do to get them back? The Albanian intelligence agent said that he wanted to go back to his head-quarters to look into what exactly had happened the night before and that he would meet us in the same spot in a couple of hours.

A couple of hours later he showed up. He told Raxhab that he wanted me to come with him to talk to some other agents. He also told Raxhab to buzz off because he would be providing a translator. This seemed worrisome, but it was all part of the game, so I agreed. Raxhab gave me a phone number where I could reach him later and told me to call him when I was done. He also said that if he didn't hear from me in a few hours he would try to find out what had happened to me.

"I thought you knew this guy!" I told him.

"Not very well,—but even if he was my brother, this is still Albania," he replied.

I got into the back seat of the car while the agent and his driver sat in the front. I was almost indifferent about the whole situation. The fact that I was sitting behind them told me that they didn't have a "leave the gun, take the cannoli" scenario planned out. Or they were stupid. Either way was fine with me. We pulled up to the gates of a three-story building not far from the central square. It had a high wall all the way around it with a uniformed Albanian cop holding an AK-47 standing out front. The cop opened the gates as he saw our car approaching. Inside the courtyard, the building appeared to be some kind of police station. Cops milled around outside, and there was some sort of official seal next to the front doors. This was bad, bad news, I thought. But it was a little late to do anything now.

The intelligence agent got out of the car and motioned for me to follow him inside. As we walked inside I was immediately confronted with an unpleasant odor. The inside of the building was shabbier than the outside and reminded me of many of the buildings in Azerbaijan. We walked down a hallway with offices on either side until we reached a stairway. As the agent started up the stairs, a familiar noise from one of the floors below made my stomach tighten. Someone was howling in pain, and I knew all too well what was causing that pain. The unpleasant odor I'd smelled on entering the building seemed to emanate from whatever hell lay waiting for me downstairs as well. The agent must have heard the noise too, because he paused on the stairs and turned around to look at me. I started to follow him up the stairs without changing the expression on my face. He must have known I'd heard the noise, but I didn't want him to think that it bothered me in the least. I was more than a little relieved that we were headed up the stairs instead of down.

We went to the second floor, which was lined with holding cells on one side and offices along the other. The agent went to the second office and motioned for me to follow. Another man was already waiting for us there, and he was dressed like the intelligence agent. They talked for a minute, and then the guy who had brought me here tapped his watch and motioned with his hands that he would be back in a little while. The other guy told me to sit down. He said in halting English that a translator would come and that we'd talk then. A few minutes later a scrawny, weaselly-looking fellow showed up.

They didn't waste any time in getting down to business. The agent asked questions, which the weasel then translated. They started by asking about my connections to the KLA. I told them that I didn't personally know any of them and that they were just contacts given to me by a person in London. After a few more questions along those lines, they caught me by surprise with a completely different line of questions—or, more to the point, accusations.

The weasel now turned out to be more than just a translator because he was the one who actually started the accusations. He began by saying that they had reason to believe that I was involved with the bombing of the embassy in Nairobi a week or two earlier.

"Are you fucking crazy?" I said.

"Is it not true that the men who were in the house with you last night were associated with Usama Bin Laden?"

The hairs on the back of my neck prickled. Son of a bitch, I thought. Those two-timing sons of bitches at the Agency had finally found someone to tell about me. It was all starting to make sense.

"Let me guess," I said, "You're a liaison to the Agency here in Tiranë, aren't you?"

Now he was the one taken by surprise. I should've picked up on it sooner. His English was more than the garden-variety British English he'd be likely to learn at a university. It was American English, and you pick that up only from living in America or working around Americans. Any uneasiness that I might have had before went out the window. I knew what the game was about and was ready to play. At the very least, the Albanians were turning a blind eye to KLA activities in Albania, if not actually supporting them. The raid on the house was at the behest of the CIA; somebody had told the Albanian intelligence guys that there was something going on between Usama Bin Laden and the KLA guys in the house.

"So let me guess," I continued. "You think I'm the go-between for Usama Bin Laden and the KLA people who were in the house last night?"

Before he had time to respond, the other agent asked him what I'd said. When the weasel answered, he seemed amused and smiled at me. He told the weasel to ask me where I was when the bombing happened. I told him that I was in the States. He then said that I could probably prove that if I had to, and I told him that I wouldn't have answered with that if I couldn't. He turned to the weasel and they started to argue in Albanian; the first guy was obviously taking my side.

"So what are you doing here in Albania? And why were you with the KLA if these things about Usama and the embassies aren't true?"

"Look," I told him. "You obviously got this shit from the CIA. You have probably worked around them for enough time to know the difference between an American and some Arab terrorist. Which one do I look like to you?" Then I took a gamble and played on what I thought I detected from the first agent. Without putting religion into it, I explained how I had came to help the KLA against the Serbs. Why would I do this? The same reason why I'd lost my leg in Chechnya. I showed them my prosthetic. Although they wouldn't get the impression by the way the U.S. government acted, some Americans really just wanted to help for the sake of helping. So what if I had contact with some Islamic figures? Did they think I'd gotten to Albania by working with the Boy Scouts? Then I really started to lay it on thick and went into a speech about how the Albanians were next, after the Serbs completed their genocide of ethnic Albanians in Kosova.

"So why do we have this disturbing information about you?" he asked.

"Why don't you just come out and say that the CIA gave you that information? And that on top of it, it sounds really stupid now that you think about it. Doesn't it?"

The other guy listened to the translation through all of this, and the only thing I could think was that he found it amusing. Now he started to ask some questions. Whether he did it intentionally or not, he gave away the secret when he asked me who Abu Amin was. I thought about it for a second, then figured, What the hell, it would do more harm to deny knowing him. I said that he was just a contact in London who had connected me with the KLA guys. What struck me strongly then was that the KLA guys didn't know him as Abu Amin; he used a different alias with them. The fact that the Albanians knew his name proved to me that the CIA was behind all of this.

In the end it came down to a man-to-man conversation between me and the first agent, or as man-to-man as we could manage through the translator. The impression I got was that the translator never really believed me, but the other guy did. The idiots at the Agency would never understand this; they assumed that no one would ever question them and that they could meddle in the affairs of Third World countries without any sort of interference from the authorities there. At the end of the day, it always comes down to the guys on the ground.

They never did come out and say any names, but the Albanians gave me the impression that someone from the Agency had "leaked" information about a

Bin Laden cell operating in their country. They also said that a dangerous guy who'd had a part in the Nairobi bombing was in their country right now and that no questions would be asked if anything unfortunate were to happen to this person while he was in their custody. Aside from the fact that this was simply the CIA's style (that is, they were too chickenshit to carry out their own vendettas), two events would confirm the Agency's involvement for me a short while later.

Finally we came down to what they were going to do with me. Maybe just put me on the first flight out of their country with a warning? *Au contraire*: instead, the first agent offered me a car and driver to go to Kosova. Oh really? I thought. What a pleasant surprise. I wanted to take his offer but declined for my own safety. These guys didn't have the world's greatest covert tactics, and I was probably already on thin ice with the KLA. I didn't need them to think I was working for the Albanians, and if I had an Albanian cop as a chauffer, it would look fishy. The next issue was my bags. The agents told me that they were at the Interior Ministry Building. I wanted to see just how cooperative these guys were going to be, so I told them that I needed some important medication out of my bags. This was partly true, but I had some in my pocket anyway, so it wasn't really urgent.

The first agent told me that it was no problem and that the guy who had brought me here would take me over there right now. They called him on his walkie-talkie, and he showed up a few minutes later. I got the first agent's phone number and name for future use and left with Raxhab's agent friend. The Interior Ministry Building wasn't far. It was slightly less decrepit than the police station, but not by much. We went to the second floor and into an office where there were a bunch of bags on the floor. I recognized some of the bags from the KLA house, and I also saw mine lying there. I asked the agents if I could take my bags, but they told me to just get what I needed. I told them that I didn't even have any clothes with me, so after they went through it, they ended up letting me take my small backpack. While I was there they asked me about the contents of my big bag, which they'd obviously already examined. They were particularly interested in my Yaesu two-way radios. Whereas my sets were the latest digital models with extended batteries, I'd noticed that the Albanian intelligence guys had old, beat-up Yaesu units. They told me that my two-ways were illegal in Albania. Well, I thought, at least they're being polite about asking for a bribe. I also noticed that my $800 piece of body armor and custom mag vest were missing.

Backpack in hand, Raxhab's friend took me back to the center of town, where he had originally picked me up. He asked me if I had a place to stay. I was tempted to see how far I could push these guys, but I told him it was fine, so he dropped me off at the hotel I'd stayed at the night before. He also gave me his number. As he was leaving, I invited him and his driver up to the hotel's restaurant, which served a pretty good steak, and they accepted. It wouldn't hurt to have a friend or two in Albania.

I called Andy the next day just to let him know I was all right, but he answered with a voice I'd never heard before.

"Aukai, you need to get the hell out of there right now." Andy had always called me Aqil, my Muslim name, and only used Aukai when something was up.

"What do you mean?" I asked.

"Look, just take my word for it, you need to get the hell out of there for your own good."

"I know you're not going to tell me why, but at least tell me what's up."

"You know we can't talk over an open line. The only thing you need to know is that you pissed off the wrong people back East."

"Back East" meant the CIA.

"I can't just leave because they turned nasty on me."

"You don't know what you're getting into."

"That's the sad part. I do know. That's not the kind of shit you're supposed to get from an American organization."

It took a couple of days and a lot of phone calls to London, but finally Abu Amin set up a new contact for me; the first guys never resurfaced. In the meantime I hung out with Raxhab. He was turning out to be okay, and since he was a Kosovar, he had an interest in helping beyond his own concerns.

The new contact was someone named Jaffar, and he was as far away from home as myself. He was from Trinidad but had been living in Malaysia. Abu Amin didn't know a whole lot about him but thought he was probably okay and told me to try dealing with him. I called, and we met a short while later. Jaffar had been in Tiranë for a while now, dealing with the deputy defense minister of Kosova. Now we were getting somewhere, I thought.

Supposedly Jaffar was in with some important people in Malaysia who wanted to donate a large sum of money so that the KLA could purchase weapons. Jaffar was staying with the assistant to the deputy defense minister, who had already visited Malaysia with Jaffar. When I came on the scene they'd been in Tiranë for a couple of months but hadn't made any progress. I asked what the problem was; it seemed that the guys in Malaysia didn't want to part with the money until they knew for sure that weapons were being purchased. The problem was that the KLA didn't have any solid weapons connections, and neither did Jaffar.

After talking about the problem with Jaffar, I sat down with the deputy defense minister and told him that I could arrange for a medium-sized shipment of weapons but that getting it into Albania would be his problem. He told me that he carried enough weight at the airport in Tiranë to get the weapons through customs if I could get the shipment flown in. From there, we went over quantity, price, and what was available. But before we made any weapons deals I needed to get into Kosova and do an assessment. The deputy defense minister said that this was no problem and made the arrangements.

A couple of days later we headed back up to the dam, but this time we were in a private van. I invited Raxhab along to translate for us and to give him a chance to do something for Kosova. The first time I'd traveled this road we hadn't been stopped at a single checkpoint, but on this trip we were getting flagged down at literally every one. I had a visa for Albania, but the cops at the checkpoints were still taking bribe money from us. After about the tenth stop, I got pissed and told Raxhab to ask our driver what the hell was going on. The driver said that our van had German plates and that the checkpoint cops always hassled foreign vehicles. These guys really had their shit together, I thought. They send an American, a black guy from Trinidad, and the assistant to the deputy defense minister to Kosova in a van that is sure to get stopped at all the checkpoints because it has German plates.

Despite all the stops, we eventually made it to the dam and parked the van near some other vehicles on the small patch of land. This time I had a chance to poke around the place a little. The assistant to the deputy defense minister went to make a phone call in the little shack where the guy on my first trip had used the phone. When he came back he told Raxhab that although it wasn't confirmed, the Serbs might be attacking Tropoje today.

There was also the possibility that they might attack the ferry on the river by air, as it was currently the only practical way to get in and out of the area. This added a little excitement to the atmosphere. The few people and vehicles that were going to take the ferry that day got spooked, and most of them left before the ferry arrived.

Just as before, I watched as the ferry nosed around the bend in the river, then came into full view. Just as before, it was overloaded, but this time it was listing dangerously to the port side. It docked with the usual hubbub of conflicting advice and wild gestures. The people got off the ferry even faster than last time, and looking genuinely panicked. As I watched people scramble down the ferry ramp, I noticed an Arab traveling by himself. I knew who it was, but I just couldn't believe my eyes. I ran up and greeted him. "Abu Mujahid, is that you?" he asked as we hugged each other.

"Who else would be going to Kosova after all the Arabs have left?" I said.

It was Salaah, the mujahid who'd mysteriously appeared in Tutsanute when the Russians were surrounding the city and I had to get Ayeesha evacuated. We wouldn't have gotten out of there if it hadn't been for Salaah. The last I'd heard was that he'd been killed while I was in the hospital in Azerbaijan.

Salaah told me he was going back home. The situation in Kosova was very bad, and he'd had serious problems with the KLA. I told him that I had a good plan and asked him to go back up to Kosova with me, but he said there was no way he'd go back up there. Was it that bad? I wondered. One of the wanderers, Salaah had walked all over Chechnya by himself in 1995, just like me, and had been in more than a few tight situations. I was more than surprised that he was going to leave Kosova. So far everyone had told me not to go, but I was still driven to go there.

It was good to see Salaah, but it would be for the last time. I boarded the ferry with the others. A fraction of the people and vehicles accompanied us. Despite the problems that might be waiting for us in Tropojë or even along the river for that matter, it was such a beautiful day that I couldn't really worry much. The sun was shining and the gorge along both sides of the beautiful green river was stunning. It was at least five hundred feet to the peaks of the gorge, and every once in a while you could see a lone house on the steep walls. They were built on little flat spots and looked like they would wash away in a good storm. Every so often the river branched off into another gorge. A person could spend days exploring every nook and cranny of the reservoir. We took our shirts off and sat on the ramp of the ferry and watched the water go by.

A couple of hours later the ferry shuddered as the pilot throttled back. I got up from our tanning deck and looked around. The river had narrowed, and although it continued up ahead, the ferry was stopping here. Another ferry of the same size and shape and general disrepair was beached on the opposite bank. The ferry lurched forward as we came to a stop and then the front ramp dropped. Our merry band of KLA supporters got back in the van and we drove down the ramp.

From the landing area we could see the small town of Bajram Curri nestled in a wide part of the gorge up ahead. I didn't hear any action or see any plumes of smoke coming from that direction, so nothing was happening yet. We drove past the town without stopping and continued in a northeasterly direction. We were far into the mountains, but even now we saw those ridiculous domelike concrete bunkers that seemed to cover the entire countryside, only these were somewhat bigger. After driving for an hour or so, we took a side road up a mountain. It was a rough ride, and the van we were in didn't look like it was going to make it, but finally we got to a point where we could see a group of small buildings.

We'd come to a KLA training facility. The soldiers, dressed in mismatched pieces of camouflage, stared at us as we entered. Some were performing drills, while others were just sitting around in groups. The commanding officer came out of one of the buildings to greet us. After talking to the assistant to the deputy defense minister for a few minutes, he invited all of us to sit down at a table near a campfire. Raxhab acted as the translator, and after speaking with Jaffar for a moment, the officer asked me some questions. I told him that aside from the weapons deal, my primary objective for being here was to fight the Serbs and to assess the situation for my friends back in London. This seemed to interest him more than what Jaffar had to say, and he told me to come with him. We left the other guys at the table and went to one of the buildings. There were a couple of guys sitting outside of it. He spoke to one of them, who then introduced himself in English. He said he was the camp doctor and asked me about my military experience. They got excited when I told them about Chechnya, and they gave me a tour of the camp, which included their armory. The commander showed me a brand-new Steyr AUG .308, a scout rifle that had just been introduced in America. I was surprised that these guys already had one. When I got back to the States, *Soldier of Fortune* magazine had an article about the KLA that featured a photograph of a KLA soldier with the very same gun. I would also find out later, through a distant acquaintance, that the gun's designer had bragged about the fact that it was chosen by the KLA because of its ruggedness. But at the time the camp commander told me that an Albanian KLA supporter living in the United States had sent it to them because it "looked cool."

After the tour the camp commander asked if I wanted to get a look at the Serbs. Of course the answer was yes, so he called for his men. A lot of the KLA shaved their heads and had red facial hair, like me. One of them, a little guy, asked the doctor to ask me if my grandfather was from Albania. Everybody laughed but then scrutinized me. The commander told me that Jaffar and I would go up the mountain with a couple of scouts to get a look at the Serb lines. I didn't have any gear because my bags were at the Interior Ministry Building, and I didn't like the idea of getting into something unprepared. But my clothes were neutral colors. I was wearing trail running shoes, which were a little better than sneakers, and I rubbed mud over them to cover any shiny areas. The little guy and the other soldier were carrying Chinese AK-47s so I asked the commander to give me one, too. Although it had a full mag, I asked for a couple of spares. At this, the commander nodded with a knowing look; it was a test to see whether I knew what I was doing or I was full of shit.

We set out on the road that ran by the camp. I was too excited to walk, so I got the others to move at a jog. We ran along the dirt road for about twenty minutes, to the top of a ridge, before the little guy indicated that we would leave the road here. The road continued down the other side of the ridge and wound off to the left. We could see out over a valley, which was the border between Albania and Kosova on the other side. The terrain was rocky, with heavy brush, and we pushed our way through it for about half a mile, then we stopped on a fairly high point on the ridge. The little guy pointed somewhere. "Serb," he said.

I looked and couldn't see anything. We had a telescope with us, so I looked through that. I could see an observation tower on the other side of the valley. It didn't look well defended. I asked the little guy why, using the universal language of hands and a few common words. He told me to look closer. I did, but I didn't see anything. Later, back at the camp, the commander explained that the Serbs had observation towers every kilometer or so. Each tower had 23mm tribarreled antiaircraft cannons, which the Serbs loved to use as antipersonnel weapons. Before I'd left the States the Serbs had turned one of these guns on a compound of houses that belonged to a large prominent ethnic Albanian family. *Soldier of Fortune* magazine published photographs of the results and reported that about fifty people had been killed. Here the Serbs were using them to protect their observation towers, and each tower was within range of the next tower, so it would be difficult to attack one when you were getting showered with 23mm fire from another.

By the time we got back to the camp my leg was hurting, so I sat down and unzipped my cargo pants. The little guy and one of his buddies watched in amazement. I'd forgotten that they didn't know that I had a prosthetic leg. When I took it off to rest my stump, they all had a look of disbelief on their faces. I'd led the hike and jog most of the way, and now I was taking off a fake leg. In this part of the world, when you lose a limb you pretty much sit in front of your house the rest of your life to watch cows go by. No one asked for my AK-47 back, and it was my habit to not give a weapon back unless they asked for it. Armed is simply better.

After a while I rode with the commander in his jeep to the main barracks, where I met with the commander of the 163rd Brigade of the Kosova Liberation Army. The brigade commander and I spoke for quite some time about the situation in Kosova. A former Serb military officer, he understood Russian, which enabled us to talk without translators at length about what we could do to change the present situation. Up until that time the KLA had been trying to wage a conventional war and were getting their asses kicked by the Serbs. The brigade commander knew that they had to switch to a guerrilla war, but the KLA was having trouble doing this. He pulled a map out and laid out the present situation. The Serbs' main headquarters were inside Kosova with six or seven garrisons spread out around the headquarters. The brigade commander asked me what I would do differently if I were calling the shots. I told him that they should use hit-and-run guerrilla tactics to systematically hit a different garrison every few days. They should never hit the same one twice in a row and they shouldn't use any rhyme or reason to indicate which one would be attacked next. The Serbs would have to reinforce the garrisons with troops from the headquarters, so we could cut their supply lines and draw more troops away from the headquarters. In the end we could concentrate our forces and overrun the headquarters. Once the headquarters fell, the garrisons would be without communications or supplies, and if we moved fast enough we could roll them up, too.

After breakfast I told the brigade commander that I was eager to go out on the front lines. He told me that he was going to send a patrol to the area I'd gone to the day before, but this time down to the border itself. So as Jaffar and the others went back to sleep, I rode with the camp commander back up to the training camp. It had rained all night, and the road, already difficult for travel, was now a muddy mess. When we finally made it to the camp I noticed a few vehicles that hadn't been there the day before. One of the vehicles was an older GMC Jimmy, but the back window and bumper had rodeo association stickers, a COWBOY UP sticker common to trucks in the Southwest, and a bumper sticker for a Texas radio station.

The camp commander took me to a room where they had uniforms stored. They were using mostly Swedish battle fatigues. It had gotten cold overnight, and it was a wet and miserable day, so one of the guys found me a cold-weather set with mag pouches built into the front of the uniform top. Next they issued me extra magazines and two grenades. Outside I saw the little guy from yesterday, who was going on the patrol with us. The commander got two others and this time we all piled into his jeep. At first I thought he was going with us, but one of the guys spoke a little English and explained there was Serb activity down in the valley. Although civilians lived in homes on the Albanian side of the border, the Serbs had been coming across, and the commander was worried. Obviously no Albanian troops were guarding the border, and I began to wonder if this was another Kashmir. Perhaps the Albanians were allowing the KLA to operate off their soil to keep the Serbs busy without risking Albanian involvement. The commander seemed to confirm this when he told us not to engage in a firefight with the Serbs unless we couldn't avoid it. It would be okay if their number was small and we could take them quietly, but otherwise we should fight only if it was unavoidable.

The mountaintops were shrouded in fog that day, and the commander took advantage of this to get us closer to the homes down in the valley. Under the cover of fog, we drove down the road that wound down the mountain until we got to the point where he wanted us to patrol. Then he turned around and headed back up the hill. We moved at a fairly fast pace, and the brush gave way to a section of forest. As we passed a couple of homes on the edge of a small creek, I could see some women working in their yards and a teenage boy standing in the front. He waved and flashed us the V, for victory.

As we neared the border it started to hit me that I was back in the field again. This was the first time that I had been back on the front lines in a military action since I'd been hit in Chechnya. We moved through the forest, slower and quieter now, and I started to feel a kind of fear rise in me. I had been in dangerous situations since Chechnya, and had even killed the Azeri assassin, but this was the real thing. I'd been wondering if I'd be able to do it again. Had I waited too long since Chechnya?

After a while the fear passed and I felt almost exhilarated to be back in my element. Anyone who's ever been there would know the feeling. Walking through the brush with your weapon at the ready, you're aware of every sound and movement. Everything becomes sharper and clearer. A misty fog was drifting through the forest; the underbrush was soaking wet. The soldier walking point raised his fist. We all silently dropped to a crouch and strained to listen. I tapped the little guy on the shoulder and motioned for him to let me take point. He nodded and signaled the first guy. After I was sure that everything was clear, I got up and motioned for the others to follow. This was it! I was back in the saddle again. In Chechnya I'd loved to walk point and had even lost my leg to it, but here I was again. Most fools love war until they experience it. On that day I realized that I was among the strange few who knew war and loved it nonetheless.

We came to the edge of the forest. A rocky hill led down to a river that ran through a little ravine, with a dirt path alongside it. This was obviously the border or right by it. The Serbs and their observation towers must have been only a few hundred meters up the other side of the valley, but because the fog obscured everything we couldn't see them and they couldn't see us. By then my leg was really starting to kill me and I needed to take off my prosthetic for a few minutes. I sat down on some rocks and told the other guys to go ahead to the river. I watched them walk down the hill and follow the dirt path; then the fog enveloped them.

As I sat there rubbing my aching stump I heard voices coming from the opposite direction. I looked over to see four guys walking up the dirt path. I didn't have time to put on my prosthetic, so I hopped over to a larger rock and took cover. I pushed the selector on my AK to semiautomatic and drew a bead on the group of guys. Two were in civilian clothes; the other two were wearing what I assumed were Serbian uniforms and carrying AKs. One of the civilians was carrying a two-way radio.

They were just strolling along casually, discussing where they would have their picnic and whether or not they should use doilies. The pair in uniforms had their AKs slung over their shoulders and didn't seem to be very cautious, considering that this was a known KLA area. They weren't more than fifty meters away. At this range I was sure that I could drop all four of them before they could reach cover, but I remembered what the camp commander had said about noise and debated whether or not I should do it. It was a hell of an opportunity, and aside from just wanting to drop them I didn't want them to catch the three KLA soldiers off guard. And there was another issue: Who were the two civilians?

I waited till they'd gotten past me and put my leg back on. Then I trailed them, hiding from rock to rock. There was some brush running along the bottom of the hill, so I moved down to this to keep out of sight. I had decided that I would tail them as far as I could. If they ran into the three KLA guys, at least I could drop the four Serbs from behind. If they spotted me I would drop them anyway. After tailing the four for a few minutes I saw figures in the brush ahead of me. They were crouched down and watching the four guys also. They were my three KLA buddies. I was moving so stealthily that they didn't hear me until I was right up behind them. They swung around but turned back when they saw that it was me. I took a spot next to them and gestured: What's up? They didn't respond, so I tried to explain to them that we should take the four guys quietly. They understood what I meant but said no. The little guy pointed to the guy in civilian clothes who was carrying the two-way radio and said "Albanian *polesesky*." Not more drama, I thought. What were the Albanian cops doing up here talking to the Serbs? In this light it didn't look like a good idea to kill them.

We waited until the four were out of sight before heading back up the hill. We went back pretty much the same way we'd come. We passed the houses again and made our way back up the mountain to the road. One of the KLA guys had a radio with him but hadn't used it yet. I assumed that they were avoiding radio traffic in case the Serbs were listening. We sat down near the road and he called the commander. About twenty minutes later, he picked us up.

This time we passed the camp and headed for the barracks instead. Back at the barracks, I sat down with the brigade commander and the camp commander and tried to make sense of what I'd seen. The brigade commander told me that the two guys in civilian clothes were Albanian intelligence. He was very disturbed by the idea that we had seen them talking to the Serbs. He also said that they had recently gotten information that the Serbs might try to come over the border in this area to try to wipe out the KLA. The fact that we had seen the Albanians talking to them wasn't a good thing. Sometimes alliances change by the hour in these areas of the world. At the end of the war in Bosnia the Bosnian government had been in on a U.S.-Croat plot that led to the assassination of the top three mujahideen commanders, which effectively ended the jihad there. Following that, the mujahideen who had given their blood for Bosnia were rewarded with an ultimatum from the Bosnian government to leave in thirty days or be arrested.

We spent the rest of the night talking about the situation. The brigade commander thought that they should leave the area before the Serbs could make a move. I agreed with him. These guys were in no condition to defend themselves against a full Serb assault, especially if the Albanians were colluding with the Serbs. Finally the brigade commander decided to decamp, which led to the subject of what to do with me. I could go with them into Kosova and make camp in the mountains, but if I did this I would be cut off for who knew how long. This is what I wanted to do, but Jaffar and the defense minister wanted me to help with the weapons deal. The brigade commander wanted me to go with them regardless of the equipment. The assistant to the deputy defense minister got in the middle and made a veiled threat that he would tell the defense minister if the brigade commander interfered with the acquisition of weapons. I told the brigade commander not to sweat it: I wouldn't be gone for more than a couple of weeks, and my heart was in the fight now. I wouldn't forget him and the others. Besides, I said, if things went well, when I returned I expected him to commission me as an officer in the KLA. He laughed and agreed.

If we were going to leave it had to be right away because the situation could get weird at any minute. Early the next morning we headed back to the ferry landing. It went down the river only once a day and if we missed it we would be there until the next day. When we arrived, however, it looked as if we might not be able to get on. All the refugees were trying to get out of the area, and some people had even camped overnight in order to get on the ferry. By the time we got in line there were about thirty vehicles in front of us, and more kept pulling up behind us every minute. In addition, pedestrians would swarm the ferry once it arrived.

After a couple of hours I noticed a Mitsubishi Montero with dark windows nudging around the vehicles behind us. I don't know why, but this really pissed me off. I figured that it was just some rich gangster trying to get ahead in the line. I opened the side door of the van and was going to get out and harass the guys in the Montero just for the hell of it. I waited till they were starting to try to nudge around us; then I noticed that one of the guys riding in the back looked familiar. The second thing I noticed was that the front passenger had an AK sitting barrel-up between his legs. Suddenly it hit me where I had seen the other guy: he was the little piggy I'd seen in the valley conspiring with the Serbs. As the Montero slowly crawled up, I stood in its way just to be an ass. The driver leaned on his horn and the guy riding shotgun raised his AK slightly. I bent down to play with my shoelaces. When I finally moved out of the way, the guy with the AK tried to give me a tough look. I just smiled at him.

A couple of hours later the ferry came into view. Once it docked and everyone had gotten off, the madness began. People swarmed up the ramp with the vehicles. By the time our van reached the ferry, it was loaded far beyond its capacity. I thought for sure that we wouldn't get on and would have to camp out for the night, but the assistant to the deputy defense minster walked up the ferry ramp and talked to someone who obviously worked on the boat. Somehow he bribed the guy into letting our van on, even though it would barely fit. We crammed into a spot between a dump truck and a bus.

The ride down the river was uneventful. The weather reflected my gray mood. I wanted to stay with the KLA and go into Kosova right away, but I tried to tell myself that what I was leaving for was just as important. This wouldn't be the last time that I would leave a war against my better judgment with intentions to return in a couple of weeks.

We got back to Tiranë just in time to catch some of the chaotic madness for which Albania is famous. The entire country was already tense because of the pyramid-scheme scam, the situation in Kosova, and the upcoming elections. The prime minister at that time wasn't even Albanian but a Greek named Fatos Nano. Some people wanted former president Sali Berisha back. I took a room at the Tiranë International Hotel for a week because there weren't any flights out. On the second day I ran into a group of Western journalists in the lobby who were all agitated about something, so I asked them what was up. Supposedly Fatos Nano had ordered a hit on Azem Hajdari, Sali Berisha's running mate, and the man had been gunned down that morning. The hit man, however, had done a sloppy job, and everything pointed back to the Greek. By that afternoon people were rioting in the streets.

Armed guards showed up in the lobby of the hotel, and all the journalists ran upstairs to their rooms. The hotel staff asked me to stay inside the hotel, but I told them that riots were the best thing happening in Tiranë—I wanted a ringside seat. The hotel looked straight out over the central square of the city, where I figured it would all culminate, so I grabbed my camera and sat down on a bench and waited. A little later I heard a noise that sounded like a freight train approaching from the distance. A mob of people was marching along one of the avenues that led to the central square. I couldn't tell how many there were at first, because I could see only the front of the crowd, but as they started to spill out into the central square it was obvious that there were thousands of people. They didn't seem particularly violent but this was more than your average demonstration. Some carried banners and the roar of the crowd was almost deafening.

A handful of cops were making a halfhearted effort at riot control when the mob started to swarm over the square. I watched the cops rip their uniform tops off and join the mob. There were no soldiers anywhere, so this was obviously bigger than a protest or simple rioting. I looked around to see if the journos had come out yet and saw them on the upper balcony of the hotel. Later that evening it was supposedly confirmed that Fatos Nano had fled the country. Pandeli Majko, a former student activist, then took over as prime minister.

The next day I tried to get my bags back. I called Raxhab's friend the Albanian intelligence guy, and we met for coffee. Later that day he took me to the Interior Ministry Building. Once again I saw my bags, but the ministry still wouldn't release them. The agent with me talked to one of the bosses down the hall and came back a bit agitated. This was Albania: if you have one of their agents on your side you can get back a confiscated load of drugs with the right bribe. But the ministry was acting as if my bags meant something. This made me wonder. Maybe somebody else was pressuring them to hold my gear.

I wanted to see what my former associates at the Agency were up to. It looked like they were starting to act like the crazy woman in the movie *Fatal Attraction,* and I wondered how far they would take it. I tried to call the embassy but couldn't get through. In the lobby of the hotel I heard that something had just happened at the American embassy that morning. An Albanian cop had jumped over the wall of the compound with a gun, and one of the marine guards had shot him in the head. Another mob was gathering outside the embassy.

I finally got through to one of the embassy numbers, which had been routed to a secure compound on the outskirts of the city where the embassy staff members lived. It took forever, but I finally persuaded one of the guys over there to agree to talk with me about my bags. I decided to use the mob unrest as a pretext to go see them immediately, telling them that I had to "flee" Albania. I took a cab up to the compound on the hills around Tiranë. Once we got in the general vicinity, the cabdriver had to ask more than a few people for directions, because the compound's location was a fairly well-kept secret.

Finally we took a small turnoff onto a small bend in the road where there was a checkpoint manned by Albanian police officers. They had a Russian armored personnel carrier parked there, and they all carried AKs. They stopped the cab and told me that I would have to walk from that point. I walked for a few hundred meters, until I reached another bend in the road, where the road went down a small hill. The compound started at the bottom of the hill and stretched up onto the next hill. A big wall ran all the way around the whole thing, which had American-style two-story houses in the middle. Giant concrete blocks were staggered along the road up to the gate so that you couldn't make a straight run for the gates in a vehicle. Inside the gates were sandbags, and as I got closer I saw that a marine in full combat gear had me in the sights of his M203.

As I approached the gate the marine shouted for me to stop and turn around slowly. Then he had me lift up my shirt before another marine came out of the guard shack while the first still had me in his sights. The second one asked me for my passport, then he took it through the gate. I stood there and waited under the gun while the second marine called up to the houses. Once he got the okay to let me in, they performed a weapons search and issued me a visitor's pass.

Inside the compound I could see that these people were expecting serious trouble. They'd dug machine-gun nests halfway up the hill. Another marine with an M60 sat behind some sandbags. One marine escorted me up to the third house in the row, where there was a madhouse of activity. Whatever family had lived here had already been evacuated. Moving boxes lying in the corners were filled with personal belongings. Four embassy staff members sat at computers at their makeshift workspace of the dining room table. Fax machines were plugged in everywhere.

One of the staff members told the marine to have me wait on the couch. He came over a couple of minutes later and introduced himself. He asked me to please excuse the mess; they were pulling out all nonessential personnel and dependents. I briefly explained to him the deal with the bags. He said that he would make some phone calls but that there wasn't a whole lot they could do. He never asked what was I doing in Tiranë. I got the impression that he knew who I was and that something was up with the bags. He told me to call him the next day.

I left the compound with my suspicions pretty much confirmed. When I called the guy the next day, he told me that they hadn't had any luck and I should call back in a couple more days. I knew that they weren't going to get my bags back for me, so I contacted the deputy defense minister of Kosova. I figured that if anyone in Tiranë had enough pull to get my bags, it would be him.

I gave him the number of the intelligence agent that I had been talking to so that he wouldn't have to start from the bottom up. They went to the Interior Ministry Building together the next day. My flight would be leaving the day after, so I assumed that I would be leaving with my bags. But the next day Jaffar and the assistant to the deputy defense minister came to the hotel to tell me that my bags were gone. The deputy defense minister had gone to the Interior Ministry building with the agent, but someone had already taken the bags. In order to take anything from the Interior Ministry Building, you had to sign a logbook. The agent said that he'd looked in the logbook, and somebody with an American name had signed for my bags. In short, the CIA was now engaging in top secret panty raids. I'm still waiting to get my skivvies back, preferably washed.

Still furious about my bags, I caught my flight for London. I met with Abu Amin immediately because I wanted to get back to the States as soon as possible. We met with Abu Ubaidah on the second night to discuss what should be done in Kosova. I gave a report on the situation there and concluded that it was a worthwhile cause. Their response was surprising. The original assessment group that been ambushed continued to say negative things about the KLA. Abu Ubaidah went into a long speech about what constitutes a jihad and what doesn't. In the end he said that it was his opinion that Kosova and the KLA didn't deserve the time and blood of the mujahideen. I didn't get angry at him. After all, I respected him as a fighter who'd done far more than I had. Nevertheless, I made the mistake of stating very clearly that I disagreed. I wanted to help the Kosovars regardless of what he said and couldn't understand why he wouldn't get involved; the Serbs were slaughtering Muslim children again.

Later that night Abu Amin also tried to lecture me about why it would be a bad idea to involve myself with the KLA. I had a major argument with him over this. I told him that he had sent me there to try to salvage the situation and I had done more than that. We now had a solid connection with the KLA, and I could probably even get my own platoon. What more could we ask for? He started to give off strange vibes. It was becoming apparent that he'd sent me to Kosova because he thought I wouldn't be able to accomplish anything, but I'd come back with more than he'd bargained for. Something else had been bothering me about him, but until now I hadn't made an issue out of it. Abu Amin had fought briefly during the war in Bosnia but hadn't been to the front since then. He ran his little make-believe mujahideen group as though he was a field commander, but he never actually fought anywhere. I didn't particularly care about him or his group, but when confronted by the real deal he clearly felt threatened.

We left on tense terms, but he still promised to lend support if I wanted to continue on with Kosova—just as he'd promised to get Ayeesha to London.

He was going to give me some rich Arab contacts in the States and promised to give me a letter of introduction so that they would donate money for the KLA project. This letter was more than important; it was essential for us to be able to continue. I couldn't raise enough money on my own to get the equipment I needed in order to do the kind of operations that I wanted to with the KLA guys.

I caught a flight back to the States and went through the usual humiliation. Every time I've entered the United Stated since 1996 I've been put through the exact same bullshit, regardless of the port of entry. Hand the man at the counter my passport and wait for his face to change when he enters the numbers into the computer. Then wait as another agent approaches with his hand resting on the butt of his gun and instructs me to come with him. Then the baggage search, followed by the strip search. My name has been flagged in their computers for several years now, but the funny part is that during each and every one of these degrading episodes they've never found anything worse than dirty underwear in my bags.

I tried to call Abu Amin when I got back, but I couldn't get in touch with him. This went on for three days, until I received a fax. After reading the first couple of lines I had to stop and make sure the fax had been sent to the right person. I couldn't believe what I was reading. Because of my "behavior" in front of Abu Ubaidah I wasn't welcome to deal with Abu Amin anymore. My "behavior" indicated that I didn't understand anything about Islam and that I had no manners. Of course there would be no letter of introduction to wealthy Arabs. To make it worse, the coward hadn't even had the nerve to tell me this before I left London.

By this time Ghareeb, the little Saudi guy, was back at my house, and he knew Abu Ubaidah well. It took a couple of weeks, but eventually Ghareeb called him and confirmed everything I thought about Abu Amin. Abu Ubaidah was shocked about the fax and said that we disagreed about Kosova but that this was no reason to cut somebody off. Furthermore, he said that he didn't consider my behavior the least bit offensive. In the end he promised Ghareeb that he would come down on Abu Amin for sending the fax. But that still didn't help me with the KLA project.

I was bent on getting back to Kosova, only without the money to do it I was dead in the water. I tried to raise the funds myself but didn't have any luck. The so-called Islamic community in America is so afraid of its own shadow that it won't even listen to a subject that has anything do with fighting. I tried to go to the mosques, but I was known too well as one of the mujahideen, and no one would even listen to me. I laugh when I hear the FBI talk about "terrorist" activities being funded through the mosques in America. I have literally been asked to leave certain mosques because the Arabs there feared me as being too militant. The Muslims of Bosnia, Chechnya, Kashmir, Kosova, and other places have been slaughtered while the Islamic community in America has done nothing more than send letters to the president of the United States, begging him for his help.

After I realized I would never get back to Kosova, I contacted Andy. We had a meeting, and they put me through a debriefing. Surprisingly, after a little bit of paperwork, I was reactivated. A lot of drama had gone on between the FBI and the CIA over the botched Chechnya operation. Andy and I had mistakenly thought that the FBI was standing behind me on the whole matter. I told Andy about the situation with my bags, and he eventually confirmed what I thought all along: the CIA had leaked information to the Albanians that I was an Usama Bin Laden operative and that I'd had a hand in the Nairobi embassy bombing. A CIA agent had also signed the logbook at the Interior Ministry Building in Tiranë when my bags had disappeared. This was just beautiful. Whether intentionally or out of sheer stupidity, the agency had twisted the invitation to Bin Laden's camp into something that it wasn't. It was a classic case of "Are they corrupt or are they inept?" When you start asking questions like this, it's usually a little of both.

Andy and I continued to work our same old angles, but shortly after that Len moved on. For who knows what reason, he decided to go from working counterterrorism to working at the Indian reservations in Arizona. This disturbed me, because I'd thought Andy and Len worked counterterrorism because they believed it was right. But now I saw that for Len it was just a career.

By this time I'd become good friends with Ghareeb. He was living with me at my house, but we went down to Sierra Vista quite often to visit his brother and the other Saudis down there. Andy saw that having Ghareeb around was good for our work because of the contacts he had, which of course were also my contacts now. Looking back, I really don't remember how long this period lasted, but at the time, it seemed like forever. Ghareeb and I fell into a comfortable routine. We always said that we were doing work for the jihad, but at times it seemed as if we were on vacation twenty-four hours a day.

We did a lot of "playing" during this time. We were always going out to the desert and would brush up on tactical things with all of our guns. By now Ghareeb and I had a considerable collection, ranging from AKs to pistols to sniper rifles. At some point during this time, I assumed the lease payments on Ghareeb's brother's car, the Taurus with dark windows. We started to travel to California frequently to visit some rich Arab friends. Ghareeb would hold court about the jihad and occasionally they would fund our little "projects." Andy knew about our travels and didn't care, as long as I reported back every once in a while. For a while I even worked for some crooked Arabs out of Los Angeles. They were paying me almost four grand a month, plus expenses just to do muscle work.

While in Phoenix we would spend time playing with Ghareeb's Arab buddies. We generally avoided the mosques but would occasionally hang out at one of them to meet with other Saudis. One of Ghareeb's friends would later be one of a handful of people who would alter our world forever. I didn't particularly like him when I met him. I didn't have anything against him; I just didn't like him all that much. He was a little scrawny guy, short and maybe 150 pounds with his clothes on. He seemed like more of a follower than anything, the kind who would get caught up in something just because other people were doing it. He was one of many Arabs whom Ghareeb would visit to talk about jihad.

I didn't like how these guys acted. They were what I call "hanky-panky Arabs"; they participated in forbidden activities, like drinking alcohol or perhaps eating hotdogs and screwing around. They lived in America as any other person might but got all excited about jihad stuff when Ghareeb told them stories or brought them videos. Yet you'd never find a single one of them on the front lines. I never saw any of these guys in Chechnya, Kosova, or Kashmir. Ghareeb himself hadn't even been a practicing Muslim when he'd first watched a video about the war in Chechnya, while he was still living in Saudi Arabia. He later admitted to me that one of the things that had inspired him to get involved in the jihad was a guy in the video with a big red beard who didn't speak Arabic. The guy was sitting on the front lines pointing an RPG toward the Russians for the camera. Of course the guy had been me.

The little scrawny guy was taking flight lessons in Scottsdale, right up the road from my house. I'd known some of his roommates before Ghareeb had started talking to him and was good friends with one of them. They were all taking flying lessons, and my friend was already rated for twin-engine aircraft. I myself got into flying at this time. I'd learned how to fly ultralights and wanted to move up to the real thing. Andy was also a licensed pilot, and he was the one who actually talked me into starting my pilot's license course, which I never finished. I was still working for the Bureau at this time and reporting to Andy regularly. Both the FBI and Andy were fully aware of all the Arabs whom Ghareeb and I had contact with, including the scrawny little guy, whose name is widely known now: Hani Hanjoor. Hani Hanjoor would get his pilot's license in 1999 and would fly an American Airlines plane into the Pentagon. They were hardly "deep-cover sleepers," as the FBI is calling them now. They lived very openly, and although I had no idea what some of them would eventually do, they made no secrets about what they thought or believed.

We visited Ghareeb's brother quite a bit. A whole bunch of Arabs were taking courses down there. Ghareeb's brother had worked for Saudi Arabian Airlines and was taking a 747 flight-mechanics course. Some of the other Saudis were taking similar courses and some were taking actual flight training. At the time our world started to center around guns and airplanes. We hit every air show that came to Arizona and even some in California, not to mention that we were also regular features at the gun shows.

Then one day it all started to come to an end. During a routine meeting Andy told me that he would be moving on to work in Washington. I'd thought from the beginning that this guy believed in what he was doing, but now he was telling me that he was a careerist too. The first thing I told him was that it wouldn't take more than a couple of months before things went sour for me. He assured me that this wouldn't happen and told me that he'd handpicked another guy to take his place. But either he was the worst judge of character or he'd lied.

Before he left he introduced me to his "replacement." His name was Pat Flanders, and the first problem I had with him was that he was a civilian. Before joining the FBI he'd been some kind of salesman. For people like Andy and

Len coming from the military, it seemed natural to join the FBI. The reason the three of us had had such success was that we were all military-minded. It was always the civilians that were screwing things up for us. I expressed my concerns about all of this, but Andy was too set on his career to listen to me. To make things worse, the next time I went in for a routine meeting, Pat showed up. He told me that Andy had already left for Washington.

Looking back, I can honestly say that I tried to make it work with Pat, but he never got the big picture. To make ithings worse, he was a born-again Christian, and for some reason he thought that his beliefs had something to do with our work. Andy and Len were both Christians, but that was personal business that didn't spill over into our work. But Pat had been "born again" yesterday, and that meant that there was something wrong with being a Muslim, which in turn meant that Islam was the problem, and not terrorism.

This would eventually lead to the end of my relationship with the FBI. It wasn't more than a couple of months later—just as I'd told Andy—before Pat started to imply that I was holding back information in regard to the Islamic community in Phoenix. He also wanted me to stay in town more to focus on the mosques. I guess he thought he could stick it to the Muslim bastards by starting where they worshiped. I'd told him from the beginning that there wasn't anything worthwhile going on at the mosques. All of the good stuff I'd generated with Andy and Len came from Arab contacts who specifically avoided the mosques. This became a source of conflict between us that finally came to a boil.

Pat asked me to meet him with and the boss, Jonathan Canter, for a nonroutine meeting at a hotel in Tempe early in 1999. When I got there, it was not only Jonathan and Pat but a third guy whom I'd never liked from the beginning. This was odd, three of them to have a meeting with me. It was never more than two special agents for routine stuff. I had never been particularly friendly with Jonathan, but we hadn't had any problems either. This day, however, he was in a sour mood. We hadn't been talking for more than five minutes when the accusations started.

When Jonathan said that Pat believed I was holding back "specific information," I immediately blew up.

"What information?" I demanded. "If it's so specific, then what is it? What specifically makes you think I'm holding back?"

The meeting went on like this until the third guy accused me of being a terrorist. I gave each of them the one-finger salute and walked out the door. Nearly three years of work ended over that idiot's comment.

But to me it was more than just a comment. I'd started working for them with honorable intentions. I never considered myself a traitor, although many Islamic figures will view me that way. I considered myself to be a mujahid, and I thought that working with them would be a way to fight the real terrorists of the world, the cowards who have never spent a single minute on the front lines and then go and kill unarmed civilians and call it jihad. Nothing was being done about this in the world of Islam. Real mujahideen, like Khattab in Chechnya, who fights enemy soldiers and not their women and children, have done far more for the jihad than I can ever hope to accomplish. But that doesn't change the fact that they don't do anything about the real terrorists, who give the jihad a bad name. I never succeeded in my goals, but my intentions were good. Once it became clear that the FBI considered everything I believed in as "terrorism" I could no longer work for them in good conscience.

I went home and activated my contingency plans. I destroyed all documents, files, photographs, and anything that the FBI might try to come back and use to prove that I was a "terrorist" later. I also told Ghareeb that he needed to get out of the country immediately. As far as I knew, he'd never done anything illegal, but I wanted him to get out before the FBI had time to get as vindictive as the CIA. He was on a flight two days later, and I would never see him again.

Chechnya Revisited

1999-2000

FOR THE FIRST COUPLE OF MONTHS it was weird to not be working with the FBI. I felt like a cop who'd suddenly lost his job. I'd grown accustomed to the structure in my life, but then it was gone. I had a few talks with some people at the Bureau, and they even had Andy call me to see what was going on, but they never apologized. At first I was worried about what I would do for money, but I'd been doing a few side jobs while helping the FBI and had been able to save a little. For the next few months I went back to a somewhat normal life with my wife and children. My son, Saifudeen, was walking by then. We had always been close, but I really started to enjoy being home and watching him run around the house.

Chechnya started to heat up again in August 1999, just as I was settling down to a somewhat normal life. By September the Russians had invaded again and I felt a sudden, desperate urge to get back to Chechnya. Not only did I want to go and fight but I was also concerned about Ayeesha and Nusaiba. Abu Amin had scammed me with the passport deal, and because I had gone to Kosova and not Chechnya the Islamic court had granted her a divorce. I hadn't heard anything from her since then. Hundreds of thousands of refugees were fleeing Chechnya under the Russian onslaught, and I didn't want her to be caught up with them.

While using a search engine to find Web sites related to Chechnya, I came across one for Robert Young Pelton, the author of *The World's Most Dangerous Places*. Tracy, the CIA case officer, had given me the book in Tysons Corner, Virginia, while we were waiting to start the Chechen operation. After I'd posted a few messages on his site, someone in the military sent me an e-mail saying that Robert was a decent guy and that he was knowledgeable about Chechnya, so I sent him an e-mail and then we started talking by phone. Robert was also thinking about going to Chechnya, so I told him about the problem with Ayeesha. He said that if I wanted to go with him, he would get her out while I stayed and fought.

We were set to go by mid-November. Grozny was under siege, but the mujahideen were holding it. I'd missed the first two battles for Grozny and had vowed that if there was a third battle I would be there. It was an especially painful good-bye because Saifudeen and I had gotten so close. When Robert and I got to the airport in London, we waited for his journalist friend Sarah, who came in on a New York flight about an hour later in a bright orange jacket. I told her she should get something a little less conspicuous, but she would eventually take her bright orange jacket all through the trip. She would be going with us, along with a Turkish cameraman named Sedat. In another twist of fate I ran into Raxhab, the Kosovar Albanian, in London. He'd come to England for political asylum.

A couple of days later we left for Istanbul. The Chechens had a number of organizations there, and Robert was using one of them to get us in to Chechnya. I was enjoying our trip because I was getting an inside look at the world of journalism. I'd had a low opinion of journos up until then, and I can't say that has changed much, but it was interesting to get a look at their world. To my mind they were big-hair opportunists who traveled in packs, ducking and running and taking pictures while other people died for a cause. Additionally, they didn't seem to understand Muslims or the jihad as I've tried to explain it here, and they didn't care to learn either. Even now they don't understand what's happening in the Middle East, or why so many people around the world hate America, and if the journalists don't understand, how can the American people understand?

Before leaving Turkey for Tbilisi, Georgia, we met the Chechens who would be coming along with us on the trip to Chechnya. It was an amusing flight. We took a Turkish Airlines puddle jumper. They must have removed the original seats and replaced them with smaller ones for the little Turks because Robert and I had a hard time fitting into our seats. It was funny because all the people on the flight were either Turks or Georgians, neither of which are particularly big people. Robert is tall, and I weighed a good 220 pounds on that trip. Everyone on the flight was staring at the two big American guys sandwiched next to each other. During the flight, someone told me that Ayeesha and Nusaiba were safe somewhere in Turkey, which was a big relief. Robert also told me that one of the Chechens had identified me as a CIA agent, and that I would be shot as soon as I got to Chechnya.

We entered Georgia without any complications and were met by the Chechen contacts that Robert had arranged. Then we spent some time in a Turkish hotel in Tbilisi, waiting and waiting to take a trip north up to the Caucasus Mountains to the Argun River Gorge, which led down to the plains of northern Chechnya and the capital, Grozny. When we reached the border of Chechnya, Robert and Sarah talked to the Chechens about their plans. I noticed that one of the meaner-looking ones standing off to the side was staring at me. I didn't like the expression on his face. He had a full beard but also a crazy kind of look like the not-so-religious Chechens that I had learned to look out for in the first war. The way he was staring at me gave me the idea that he had already heard the rumors that had started with the CIA.

A couple of things worried me about this situation. The first problem was that with the exception of a knife, I wasn't armed yet. The second problem was that although the Chechens who'd driven us from Tbilisi to the border knew me from the first war, I was a stranger to everyone in this camp and they could get away with just about anything before I could establish that I was a veteran mujahid. This left me with no choice but to confront the guy staring at me while there were still others here who knew me.

"What's up?" I asked the guy in Russian.

"Nothing, why?" he replied.

"Because the way you have been staring at me. Did you heard the story about me being an agent?"

His expression changed a little with that. "Yes, I heard that," he said.

"Well," I asked. "Do you think that it's true?"

"I don't know," he replied.

"Think of it this way," I said. "I'm here standing with you in the Argun Gorge trying to get to the front to kill Russians."

I got a nod out of this. "This is true," he said.

"I left my wife and kids in America to come here and die in Chechnya. If you believe the bullshit story, then do what you have to do, because it makes no difference to me. Death is death."

"Okay," he said.

I didn't know whether I'd convinced him or not, but at least it gave him something to think about. Then there was a commotion around Robert and Sarah and the other journalists who had appeared out of nowhere. At first the plan was that all of us would be spending the night here. Everyone had put their bags into the back of one of the vans parked here for the night. I'd also put my big bag with the others but had kept my small backpack with me. I had already pulled out my uniform and was trying to find a place to put it on, because I didn't want any of the Chechens to think I was a journalist.

But then all of a sudden the plan changed. There was a rumor that the Russians were going to paratroop into the gorge, so the Chechens told everyone to get their bags out of the van to move to another spot for the night. In the commotion my big bag was thrown into a jeep under everyone else's stuff. All the journalists were getting paranoid about being separated from one another and were all trying to pack into the jeep like sardines.

Not really caring if I got into the jeep or not, I waited for everyone else to pack themselves into it. This turned out to be not such a good idea, because in the end there wasn't enough room for me. The Chechen in charge of this camp told me that I would ride with his driver in one of the vans parked here and follow Robert and everyone else to wherever it was they were going. From experience I always try to not get separated from my gear, but I was unable to get my bag out from under the pile of all the other bags. Panic is contagious, and everyone sitting in the back of this jeep looked pathetic. No one was willing to get up for a second to help me move the bags so that I could get to mine, so I just let it slide. Little did I know at the time that I wouldn't see Robert for almost another week, and that I would never see my bag again.

As the jeep drove off down the river, I was suddenly hit with the seriousness of the situation. It was pitch-black in the gorge, but we couldn't turn the headlights on. A faint glow emanated from the doorway of the shack that was up against the sheer cliff behind it, but there were no other lights anywhere. The roar of the river and the howling of the wind made it difficult to hear anything at all. One of the Chechens told me to sit down in the van, that the driver would be out in a minute and that we would leave to follow the others. Then he disappeared and I was left standing in the darkness next to the van.

When I sat down in the van my mind started to play with me. Had my confrontation worked? He was nowhere to be seen now, and I started to think that he was inside the shack telling the commander to whack me. I felt a growing fear rising in me. I almost became sure that any second a guy was going to appear next to my window and "give me nine ounces," as the Russian saying goes. Although I'd never run from anything in my life, I had to fight the urge to get out of the van and set off back toward the Georgian border. I had my GPS with me, and I had saved the position of the border post where I had exchanged gifts with the Georgian border guard. But as with every other time in my life, when I wanted to run from something I couldn't seem to do it; something inside just wouldn't let me.

About half an hour later one of the Chechens came out of the shack and got in the driver's seat of the van. He fiddled with some things in the van for a second before speaking. "So," he said, "are you ready?"

"Yes," I said. "We're going to the same place as the others, right?"

"Oh sure," he said in an almost sarcastic tone.

I looked over my shoulder, now that the interior light of the van was on, to see what we were carrying. The van was full of combat boots and winter gear. It didn't mean anything to me at the time, but if I'd known what battalion these guys in the gorge belonged to, I might have asked more questions about our destination.

The road that ran along the river was actually just parts of the walls of the gorge that the Chechens had bulldozed into a rough road. A short distance after the camp there was a massive Russian bulldozer parked against the edge of the cliffs. My driver pointed at it. "The Russians bomb the road by day and we fix it at night," he said. Not much farther past the bulldozer I saw what he meant. There was a massive crater in the middle of the road. There was barely enough space between the edge of the crater and the edge of the swiftly moving river to pass through with the van. As we edged around the crater, the back end of the van started to slide toward the water. Just as I thought that we were going to lose it and fall into the river, the driver punched the gas and we made it back up onto the road.

The whole trip down the infamous Argun Gorge was like this. When the road became too narrow on one side of the gorge, it would simply switch over to the other side. The river wasn't that wide, probably not more than a few meters at the narrow spots, but the water was moving extremely fast. I remembered from the first war how the Chechens always managed to cross the most wicked-looking rivers with the worst vehicles, but I still couldn't help but think that we were going to be swept away at these crossings.

As the gorge started to widen and become more of a valley, the sides of the road were littered with the mangled hulks of earth-moving equipment that had been destroyed by Russian bombs. At narrow spots in the valley parts of the cliffs had collapsed onto the road from Russian heavy bombs, and we had to skirt the piles of dirt and boulders. It was very clear that the Russians were trying extremely hard to shut this road down, as it was the only operating supply line going into Chechnya at the time.

I looked around the van for weapons but didn't see any. I asked the driver why we didn't have any arms with us and he said we did. "Where?" I asked.

"Right here," he said as he pulled a pistol out of his waistband.

"You're telling me that we are traveling through the Argun with who knows how many Russian paratroopers waiting to ambush us and all you have in this van is your pistol?"

"Of course!" he replied cheerfully. Nothing like being back in Chechnya, I thought.

After a while we finally got out of the Argun Gorge. The moon was about half full, and I could see the Chechnya of my memories passing by outside the van window. It brought back a wide range of emotions all at once. It brought feelings of joy, like the kind you feel when you have been away from home for a long time and finally see your house as you turn down the street you live on. But at the same time it brought feelings of fear and dread. For all the good times I'd experienced in Chechnya and all the love I felt for this place, I'd also experienced the most frightening and painful moments of my life here.

The miles passed by as I reminisced. Occasionally we'd pass through one of the countless mountain villages, but something seemed different this time. The villages seemed more lifeless than during the first war. No lanterns burned in the windows. No teenage boys sat outside the gates of their houses smoking cigarettes and talking about Hollywood movies. The deeper we got into Chechnya, the spookier it became. We stopped in one of the bigger villages— Shali or Argun, I forget—which I thought was our destination. When we pulled up in front of one of the houses I half-expected Robert to be waiting outside, but Robert wasn't there. It turned out to be my driver's grandmother's house, and he only wanted to stop and have some tea. I had tea with them but didn't really enjoy it because I was growing anxious to get wherever it was that we were going.

Once we got going again I noticed from my GPS that we were continually heading north-northeast. I still didn't stop to think that our destination was anywhere else other than where Robert and the others were. The first hint that we might be headed somewhere else was when we came over a hill and I looked down into the moonlit valley. Wait a second, I thought to myself, this valley looks kind of familiar. Roads from three different directions met here and crossed the river running through the middle of the valley. From here you could go east toward Dagestan, back south toward the Argun Gorge, or north to Grozny. As we came down the road into the valley, I could just make out the bridge that crossed over the river. The bridge was completely destroyed. The approaches leading to each end were heavily cratered, and the bridge itself, a fairly substantial structure, was broken in two in the middle, with both halves sloping down into the river like an inverted drawbridge. Farther down the river, off to one side of the valley, I could see a series of lights zigzagging back and forth. When the driver headed in that direction I realized that the lights were headlights. In true Chechen fashion, when a bridge is destroyed you simply go around it. It was going on something like one o'clock in the morning, so I was surprised at the number of lights trying to cross the river.

The river was very wide here and the water wasn't very deep. There were dry stretches in the middle, like sandbars, and the river would flow around these. Jeeps, trucks, and even a few cars were trying to cross the shallower parts of the river, going from sandbar to sandbar. Most of the traffic was coming at us from the opposite way, leaving the plains and heading to the mountains.

We almost got stuck a couple of times even though our van was a Russian military type with four-wheel drive. As we came up and over the road on the far side of the valley, the driver stopped the van for a moment and shut the lights off. He sat forward in his seat and looked skyward through the windshield. "Once we leave the mountains we have to move fast," the driver said. Leave the mountains? I thought. Robert and the others wouldn't have moved to the plains this early in the trip.

Not more than half an hour later we were leaving the last of the hills and the road became flat. We were surrounded on all sides by vast fields. The driver had shut off the headlights and had the gas pedal down to the floor as we flew down the road. Despite the cold outside, I rolled my window down. "Are you crazy?" he said. "It's too cold. Close the window."

"Your grave is going to be colder if we can't hear what's out there," I replied.

A few minutes later I heard a faint buzzing. "Airplane," I shouted at the driver. He had enough experience to not hit the brakes but let off the gas and pull off to the side of the road and into the grass as we rolled to a stop. The driver killed the engine and we both sat there with our heads cocked like a couple of curious dogs. "Where is he?" I asked. The driver lifted his hand and pointed in front of us. "Reconnaissance," he said. "Must be over Grozny."

Then it started to sink in. The plane couldn't be that far off even though we couldn't see it. So that meant Grozny couldn't be that far off. We waited a minute to make sure that we didn't hear anything else; then the driver mashed the gas down and we took off again. Not more than a few minutes later I saw one of those large concrete Soviet-style signs on the side of the road. I'd never learned to read Cyrillic but I could make out some of the letters in the alphabet, and as we passed by this sign I made out the letters G-R-O.

"Did that sign we just passed by say 'Welcome to Grozny'?" I asked the driver.

"Of course!"

Of course.

Before I knew it tall, pitch-black buildings loomed in the near distance. It was truly strange to approach the large, modern city in the middle of the night and not see a single light anywhere. The buildings that hadn't been pounded to rubble stood like silent ghosts, just lurking there and watching us. It might be hard to imagine a building as something spooky, but in Grozny they were. For every building that was left standing there was one that was nothing more than a pile of rubble. The streets were literally covered in debris: bricks and slabs of concrete from exploding buildings, piles of dirt and rubble kicked up from the endless bomb craters, blown-up vehicles, and even broken chairs.

As we drove on through this once-beautiful city, I would occasionally see shadowy figures dart between buildings. The driver saw the look on my face and told me not to worry; those were our guys. Sometimes the driver had to turn on the headlights for a brief second to see enough to maneuver around a pile of debris blocking the road. When he did this, the headlights illuminated packs of now-wild dogs that roamed the city looking for something to eat. The dogs never ran away when people or vehicles approached. They'd always seemed to just stand there staring at you with weird eyes that seemed to say, Why the hell are you here? Can't you see that this is a place of death and destruction? Flee while you still have your soul. And that's exactly what I wanted to do, just as I had back at the border and just as I would almost every minute of the coming days.

We traveled through the downtown area to the other side of the city. The tall buildings and apartment blocks gave way to factories surrounded by long walls and other industrial-looking buildings. The driver suddenly turned toward a set of big iron gates at the entrance to one of these factories. He stopped in front of them and flashed the lights. When nothing happened, he flashed them again. When still nothing happened, he started honking the horn in frustration. A moment later a young Chechen guy came out of the doorway of a six-story brick building that was just inside the gates.

"What were you doing, masturbating?" the driver yelled.

"I was downstairs in the bunker," replied the young guy as he came to open the gates.

The driver pulled in through the gates and parked the van under a stand of trees in the courtyard of the building.

"What is this place?" I asked.

"Our battalion," he said.

"Whose battalion?"

"*Our* battalion."

I followed him through the doorway of the brick building, where the young guy now stood holding a flashlight so that we could see. We walked down a set of stairs that led to a long concrete hallway. At the end of the hallway we passed through a large steel door, which led to a small entryway with another large steel door on the other side. The doors had massive locking bars on them. Some rooms opened up off the hallway, and I could hear the noise of a small generator coming from one of them.

We passed through the second steel door and into what would be my home for the next few days. It was an old Soviet-era nuclear fallout shelter. There was a small room with two nonworking bathrooms off to the side as you came in. Through a doorway was a much larger room, a dormitory complete with wooden bunk beds. At the far end of this were a couple of smaller rooms. At first the bunker made me feel a little better about being in Grozny, but on closer examination the concrete looked old and brittle, and I guessed that a direct hit from a bunker-buster would land right in our laps.

The driver introduced me to the battalion commander. He seemed nice enough but looked at me a little oddly. He obviously didn't know me, and there wasn't any way that he could have known that I was coming. The commander and the driver knew I only spoke Russian, so they started speaking in Chechen. I listened intently, trying to gauge their tone of voice and body language, and it didn't seem like they were saying anything negative. The longer they spoke, the more I got the impression that the commander seemed confused about what was going on.

I asked the driver why we hadn't gone where Robert and the others went and he told me that he didn't know where they were. So I asked him why we came here and he said that the commander back in the gorge had told him to take me here. When he first said this I felt a little sick to my stomach. Maybe they did plan to kill me after all, I thought. But then I thought about the fact that they hadn't sent anyone else other than the driver with me. The commander started asking me questions that wouldn't normally be asked if they were just going to kill me. I still didn't toss out the possibility of something bad happening, but I relaxed a little bit and decided to wait and see what was going on.

The commander basically just wanted to know what the story was. I told him that I came into Chechnya with some journalists but that I was here to fight. My plan was to find my old group or commander from 1995 and join up with them. The more we talked, the more I understood what was going on. The commander back in the gorge had sent me here because he was part of this battalion and he was doing what most Chechens do—whatever they want to. There really wasn't a reason for it other than that the guy in the gorge thought that I should be in his battalion, so he'd sent me here. I told them that I really didn't have a problem with all of this but that there was the issue of my bag and I still needed to see Robert before I settled down somewhere. The commander told me that they would take care of my bag and also get on the radio and see where Robert and the others were. Neither of which they ever made an effort at.

By now it was something like four in the morning. We had been traveling since the early morning the day before and I was completely exhausted.

The commander told me to take the first bunk in the row and lie down. I figured total exhaustion would put me to sleep immediately, but it was actually a while before I could doze off. Even though I was scared shitless and lying here alone in the middle of Grozny, I also felt exhilarated. I felt as if I'd snuck into a lion's den while he was asleep and lain down next to him. It was probably the worst place on earth that I could possibly be, but the fact of the matter was that I had the balls to do it and I was still alive. What happened when the lion woke up was another story.

We all lined up outside the bunker for a kind of loose inspection and to go over final assignments. Since we were expecting the Russians to advance on our position today, the commander was trying to get us to carry as many rockets for our RPGs as possible. The Russians who were supposed to attack were units from an armored division. There were only two RPGs in the group, but every person that could carry extra gear was holding one or two extra rockets for those two launchers. We needed all the tank-stopping power we could get. Aside from the RPGs, the heaviest weapons we had were a couple of PKM light machine guns. The rest of us were armed with AK-74s and a few Krinkovs. Not much stuff for stopping half an armored division from rolling straight over us.

About ten of us lined up that afternoon in front of our headquarters. It was time for a shift change. Three of our guys would stay at the bunker during the shift change, while the ten of us went to the front lines to relieve the ten already there. Three days on, three days off—that was how the frontline positions were manned. All of twenty-three mujahideen made up the Noor Allah Battalion. Twenty-three soldiers would constitute an undersized platoon, not a battalion of 400 soldiers. I never bothered to ask the guys if they were what was left out of a battalion or if they just used the name for morale. Whatever the reason, that's what stood between half a Russian armored division—over 5,000 troops—and the northwest approach to Grozny.

Before getting into the jeep the commander asked how many guys had gas masks. About half of us said we had one. The Russians had been using chemical weapons heavily this time around in Chechnya, and this disturbed me, because I didn't have a mask. Since I was a guest, the commander told one of the guys who did have a mask to give it to me. He offered it to me without the slightest hesitation or complaint, but I refused it. I made an expression of holding my breath and then tapped my watch and said, "No problem." Everyone laughed, but inside I was scared, scared, scared. Later, leaving Grozny, I would wish that I had accepted the mask.

There wasn't enough room in the jeep for all of us, so the rest walked to our forward position in the industrial sector of Grozny, which was only a couple of kilometers from our bunker. This sector was filled with factories and refineries and stuck out of the northwest part of Grozny like a finger. Our position was located in some fields and orchards just outside of this area. A couple of kilometers farther the plains turned into a shallow valley, and we could see the Russian armored division sitting on the other side. Within minutes our jeep had cleared the last structures of the industrial sector and was bouncing and sliding along a very muddy dirt road between two orchard fields. About a kilometer down the road we slid to a stop.

"Dismount!" the commander yelled. Then he turned to me. "Hurry, Abu, follow the others. If the Russians see you before you reach the trenches you'll meet Allah sooner than you thought."

The trenches were about two hundred meters away. Everyone set off at a light jog down a worn path through the field, which had at one time been an orchard. What few trees remained were bare because it was wintertime, and the field was littered with knocked-down trees and gaping craters. The ground was muddy, but the frost firmed it up enough for us to get around. The commander turned the jeep around to park it in one of the only tree stands left intact. As I trotted along behind everyone else, my stomach tightened and my breathing was labored. I seemed to be the only one who was worried about passing through open terrain under direct observation by a Russian position. The others were joking and laughing as we approached the trench. One of the guys looked back at me. I must have looked scared.

"Don't worry, Abu," he said cheerfully. "It will be dark in a few hours. The Russians are too worried about finding a place to hide for the night to be bothered with us. The Nokche Bores—Chechen Wolves—feed at night. In a few hours the Russians will be cowering in their holes and bunkers."

Despite our circumstances, his confidence calmed me a great deal. Outnumbered or not, we were still the hunters. When we arrived at the trench the relief crew greeted the guys who'd been here for the last three days. I hardly noticed the hugging and handshakes as all of the guys laughed and joked with one another. Now that I had the relative safety of the trenches, I had time to take in my surroundings. I was almost overwhelmed by the sight laid out before me. We were in the middle of a vast section of fields. With the exception of a tree here and there, the fields were muddy, barren, cratered moonscapes. Even though it was late afternoon, the sun seemed too far away as it cast a very pale light over the land. There weren't any clouds in the sky, yet everything seemed dim, as though even the sun was afraid to get too close to Chechnya.

Our position consisted of a network of trenches and bunkers dug out of the muddy earth. It reminded me of all the old footage of World War I I had seen. Now I was right smack in the middle of no-man's-land. One of the guys called my name, snapping me out of the trancelike state I'd lapsed into. "Come here, Abu, the others want to meet you," he said. After three cold days on the front, the last thing the other shift had expected was an American volunteer, and they were all staring at me with a kind of amused expression. Following the warm greetings and the usual questions about where I was from and why I'd come there, I asked a question of my own.

"So," I said as casually as I could in Russian, "what is the purpose of this position—just out of curiosity, you know?"

Everyone, and I mean everyone, looked at me at the same time, paused for a moment, then in unison yelled enthusiastically, "*Kamikaze!*" When they saw the surprise on my face they all started to laugh.

"Just look over there, Abu," one of them said. "Those Russians are going to come over that hill and through that valley any time now. We only hope to slow them down long enough to give the other groups enough time to get here and avenge our deaths!"

During my first war in Chechnya, back in 1995, I probably would have been a little more enthusiastic about such an idea. But this time all I could think of was my son, Saifudeen, back in Phoenix. I walked around for a bit to see what kind of a defensive setup we had. The network of trenches and bunkers was spread out over an area of about fifty square meters. The trenches were shallow and very narrow. We had to walk crouched over to get our heads below ground level, and our shoulders almost touched the walls as we walked through. They'd dug individual fighting holes into the front of each trench and spaced them out so that a direct hit wouldn't take everybody out at once. They also had a large bunker for sleeping, in the middle. All in all, I wasn't pleased with the setup. For starters, the earth was very soft here. We didn't have any antiaircraft capabilities, and a couple of well-placed two-thousand-pound bombs from an Su-24 would turn our whole position into a giant mud pie with hamburger toppings. The most obvious flaw was that we were sitting in the middle of a muddy field. Where the hell were we supposed to go if we had to pull back? But I knew the answer to that question: there wasn't going to be any pulling back from this position. We were an expendable position and were supposed to buy time for the larger groups, who would mount a counterattack when the Russians advanced.

After going over the layout of the trenches I walked to the farthest side of our position, then to a couple of small trees about thirty meters past where our trenches ended. I wanted to get a good look at the terrain between us. I stopped at the trees and steadied a sniper rifle in between the V of the branches. There wasn't much between us. I'd barely started to scan the terrain through the scope when I heard a distant shot. "That was aimed at you!" one of our guys called out. "Get back to the trenches before the next one gets you." At first I thought that he was just playing around, because I hadn't heard a bullet strike anywhere. But as I continued to scan the terrain I felt the air move near my right ear as a bullet whizzed past my head, followed by the second report. I lurched backward in surprise and slipped in the mud. The Chechens started shouting: "Stay low! Get back to the trench!"

I got up and started to run toward the trenches but fell on my back in the mud again. This probably saved my life, because a third shot sounded just as I hit the ground. A Russian sniper had me in his sights and seemed determined to kill me before I could get back to our lines. The Chechens were trying to see where the shots were coming from, but there really wasn't much they could do. I got up again and managed to make it back and into one of the trenches without falling.

The second in command greeted me when I got back. "Tsk, tsk, tsk. Look at my rifle. I told you to take care of it and you bring it back *covered* in mud!" Everyone started laughing, including myself. It was kind of comical if you thought about it. But it also reminded me that this was the front. You can't screw up too many times like that and make it out of here.

A short while later the sun started to go down. One of the guys stood up and began the call to prayer. I looked up and watched as the fading sunset framed his silhouette. It was a moving sight. He stood on the edge of the trench and called us to prayer with an AKM slung over his shoulder. Prayer time always gave me strength in Chechnya. The Russians had come to destroy Chechnya because of its Islamic faith, but even in the worst conditions we stopped to fulfill our commitments to that faith five times a day. Praying within shooting distance of five thousand Russian soldiers who were waiting to kill us gave me an unexplainable feeling of contentment. Many people like to talk about God's will, but few have any understanding of it. Here in the middle of this insanity, on this cratered battlefield, we were experiencing the will of God firsthand. Only He could stop the Russians from plowing us into these muddy fields.

As we started to pray I heard the rapid *whoomph whoomph* of Grad missiles as they left their launchers. Moments later the earth began to erupt around us as the missiles impacted almost on top of us. I had an almost uncontrollable urge to run for the cover of the trenches, but the Imam didn't stop his recitation of the Qur'an. You are not allowed to stop praying before the Imam signals the end of prayer. As the dirt rained down on us from the explosions of the missiles, the Imam raised his voice so that we could hear him over the deafening explosions that threatened to consume us. As he calmly called out the last words to signal the end of the prayer, all of the guys jumped into the trenches with an unusual serenity. No one moved with the sense of urgency that you would expect of people who were under a rocket barrage.

"What was that all about?" I asked one of the guys while kneeling in the trench.

"They do that every time we break for prayer," he replied. "But we haven't lost anyone yet. Allah truly is the protector."

All I could do was nod my head in agreement.

Now that the sun had gotten out of the line of fire and had dug in for the night, the cold really started to creep into my bones. During the night two or three of our guys would man the light machine guns; we'd rotate through the duty in shifts. I made it through that first night on the lines in nothing less than misery. An occasional minute or two of sleep would creep in between bouts of uncontrollable shivering. To make matters worse, the usual pain in my leg was compounded many times over by the chilling cold and the amount of walking that I had been doing.

The other difficulty that I was just now learning was that muddy terrain and prosthetic legs don't go together. I was remembering how exhausting it could be to pass through a particularly muddy area. The mud would accumulate on my boots until it started feel like I was walking with lead shoes, but it was nearly impossible to walk through mud with a prosthetic leg, and running was out of the question. A disturbing thought nagged me. It wasn't as if we had anywhere to run anyway, but if I had to run, what would I do? This just fed the sense of helplessness I'd been feeling since arriving in Grozny.

I didn't understand these feelings of fear and helplessness that were threatening to overcome me. During my first trip to Chechnya I'd occasionally experienced the terrifying moments that come with any war, but I'd generally felt strong and confident; we were always the hunters, not the hunted. But this time was different. I don't know if it was because an entire army had surrounded us, or if this was the natural result of not having the proper faith. The whole concept of jihad was based on faith. Without faith there was no jihad.

Since the first war in Chechnya my faith had definitely declined, for reasons that I still don't understand. I'd still come back to Chechnya, because it was the right thing to do, but I couldn't help thinking that maybe this time I was on my own. Had God put me in the middle of this insanity and death to test my faith or to punish me for my transgressions? It wasn't for me to answer this, but for whatever reason I didn't feel anything like I had in the first war.

The next morning the same pale, eerie sunlight hung over the battlefield. Aside from the occasional booms of incoming rockets and artillery rounds and bursts of heavy-machine-gun fire, everything was dead quiet. That was one of the creepiest things about Grozny: the awful silence of the city with all of its high-rise buildings and apartment blocks, its wide avenues with trolley lines. My mind strained to hear the sounds that were supposed to be emanating from the city; in fact, my mind came close to somehow providing them, like some sort of haunting present memory, but there was nothing there, of course. No honking horns, no traffic. Just the awful, eerie, overwhelming silence that hung over everything.

I was thinking about this as I stood in one of the trenches when the roar of jet engines broke the silence. Naturally I ducked below the trench as it passed over. Someone shouted that a second one was coming. I looked up in time to see the guy who had shouted point his PKM toward the sky and start firing. The second jet, an Su-24, was climbing out of an attack run and was just starting to bank as it passed right over our position. The little 7.62 x 54 rounds from the PKM were plinking harmlessly off the heavily armored bottom of the Su-24, but the guy who was firing them seemed to be enjoying himself immensely. He was grinning and shouting *Allah-u-Akbar! Allah-u-Akbar! Allah-u-Akbar!* If we'd had something heavier we might have brought the plane down, simply because it was so close, but the only indication that the pilot even knew he was getting hit was a slight waggle of the wings as he banked away. After the plane was out of sight I walked back to the bunker to wait for the rocket barrage that would surely come once the pilot called in our coordinates.

I hadn't seen or heard anything about Robert, Sarah, or Sedat since we'd been split up near the border. I kept asking my commander about them, but he wasn't able to find out anything either. Then one evening my commander told me that he had heard over the radio that Robert was in Grozny at the house of another field commander. We waited until sundown and headed for the house. The Russians were very near by now, and moving at night could be extremely dangerous because of Russian commando ambushes. My commander fiddled with his Russian night-vision goggles so we could drive around blacked out.

Driving through Grozny at night would be described by some as terrifying, by others as wickedly fun. You could, and at times had to, drive anywhere you wanted. Up on the sidewalk, over curbs, through the front yards of houses even. And everywhere you looked something was on fire or smoldering. As we neared the neighborhood of the house where Robert was supposed to be, we started to hear the scream of incoming missiles. The commander stopped the jeep, and we took cover in some rubble near the road, and watched as incoming Grad missiles leveled an apartment building across the street. The detonations worked their way up the street like footsteps, and pretty soon the entire block was in flames. We waited a few minutes, then kept going.

When we got to the house Robert wasn't there, but a mujahid told us he'd be back soon. I saw that Robert had left his satellite phone, and one of the Chechens had been talking on it.

"You just got the neighborhood flattened with that," my commander told them. The Russians monitored all of the radio and satellite-telephone communications coming out of Grozny. They would triangulate the coordinates and send cruise missiles or rocket barrages wherever they detected satellite-phone communications because they knew Chechen commanders would be in that area.

About an hour later we heard people outside and then Robert, Sarah, and Sedat came in. Sarah still had her bright orange jacket but hadn't been shot yet. Robert was cheerful and joking, as usual, but Sedat looked like a woman on the verge of a nervous breakdown. Later, Robert told me that Mr. Hardcore Combat Photographer had really freaked out while they were in Chechnya. It was good to see everyone again, and my commander invited Robert to come visit our position and fight the Russians, but Robert wisely declined. Instead, he gave me one of his digital video cameras and asked me to bring him back some footage, which I was more than happy to do. We all said, "See you tomorrow"—there are no good-byes in Chechnya—and the commander and I headed off toward our bunker.

We took a detour through the central square on the way back. The civilians who couldn't get out of Grozny—the poor, the crippled, and the blind—went to the market there but only at night. It could still be hit by a random bomb or rocket attack, but at night the sadistic Russian jet pilots couldn't deliberately target it. It was an odd sight to see people shopping by candlelight at the little stalls lining the street. Chechens don't fear the Russians, or even death, so no one really looked afraid. They more resembled individuals who were caught in the path of a slow-moving bulldozer and couldn't get away. As I walked around the marketplace everyone stared at me, presumably wondering why I'd willingly entered such madness.

Food was scarce in Grozny, and the market sold whatever had reached the city that day. One stall offered cooked cuts of meat, which steamed in the freezing air, and I bought a whole bag full of them to share with the other mujahideen in our group. The woman selling them was a young lady who was probably in her early twenties. She had beautiful blond hair and piercing blue eyes. When she saw me looking at her, she managed a smile. For a moment it was almost as if we weren't standing in a city that had been bombed to pieces and surrounded by the Russian army. Instead of an AK-74 in my hand, maybe

I was carrying a newspaper, or even a bouquet of flowers. Instead of a chest full of magazines and grenades, maybe I was wearing a stylish shirt. And instead of being in the street in the middle of the night because we were hiding from Russian MiGs, maybe we were out to see a movie or walk in the park. Painful memories filled my mind as I stared at her. My thoughts drifted back to a sunny day years ago at a market stall in Kerchaloy. That day I'd stared at Ayeesha. We were at war then too, but everything was different. We had been able to move about freely during the day, almost thumbing our noses at the Russians. Now they attacked anything that moved. The last war had been brutal, but this time the Russians were saying "Fuck it, we'll just kill the whole damn country and be through with it once and for all."

I wanted to talk to the woman but couldn't bring myself to do it. I know the situation is bad when I won't even go after a beautiful woman. I asked one of my companions about her and he said, "*Ana Russkieya.*" She's Russian. Grozny had had whole Russian neighborhoods for as long as anyone could remember. The Russians too had nowhere to flee, but the Russian army didn't care; they were determined to kill everything in Grozny. As we left the marketplace I wondered what would happen to the beautiful Russian girl and all the other civilians when the Russian army finally pushed their way into Grozny. The only thing between the Russian army and the civilians were a couple of thousand lightly armed mujahideen. God help us all.

The next morning we had to go back to the same downtown area before heading out to the front, but something didn't seem right as we drove through Grozny's ruined streets. The air was more ominous than usual, and the other mujahideen stared at us strangely as we drove past their positions in the city. We turned onto one of the main avenues downtown and headed for the central square, but we hadn't gone a block when one of the buildings in front of us suddenly disappeared. One second it was there and the next it was gone. A massive explosion rocked the little Lada we were traveling in; then a cloud of dust rolled up the street in front of us like a tidal wave. Bricks and pieces of concrete went flying everywhere. Our driver stomped on the gas and headed straight into the mess.

"What are you doing?" the other guy in the front seat yelled. "Turn around before they hit again!" As we turned around and raced back down the avenue, I stuck my head out of the window and looked for jets. This sucks, I thought. You can't even fight against this. I wanted Russian soldiers to come down the avenue. Hell, even tanks would be better than this. At least you had a fighting chance with tanks.

We took another route and came out near the central square, where a crowd of hard-core people were milling around. They'd come out just because they wouldn't let the Russians control their lives. About a month earlier the news had reported that two hundred people had been killed in a Russian cruise-missile attack at the marketplace where I was standing now. The Russians claimed that two Chechen bandit groups had been fighting each other when a box of ammunition had exploded in the crossfire, but that didn't explain why two hundred innocent civilians had died there. The Russian army had murdered them, but the Western news media never questioned any part of the Russians' story. I felt a terrible rage swell up inside of me toward the media and even the West in general. Two hundred dead Chechens had no entertainment value; it wasn't like watching a white Ford Bronco drive around southern California. I doubted whether the central Asia bureau chief for any of the major news organizations could locate Chechnya on a map. I thought about all the hack stories the major newspapers regurgitated on their front pages while the destruction of entire cities, civilizations even, were relegated to a paragraph or a few chance sentences tucked somewhere in the back of the Sunday paper. Where was the moral outrage? Where was the horror at the loss of innocent life? Were the people who lost their lives of such little consequence? Does it matter what the whole world thinks of us? What would it take for America or the West to take notice?

I stood around staring at the scene in front of me as the others in our group talked with the civilians and other fighters who were milling around.

"Come here, Abu," one of the guys shouted.

"What's up?" I asked as I walked over to him.

He made a motion with his hands as though to say That's it—it's all over. "The Russians have taken the last approach to Grozny; we are surrounded."

"Come again?" I said in English. "I thought I just heard you say we were surrounded," I continued in Russian.

"You heard right."

Aw fuck, I thought. This *really* sucks. I felt sick to my stomach, and my head was pounding. No one else really seemed bothered by the news, but I couldn't even pretend to be macho about it.

"What," one of the guys said, "don't you want to be *shaheed*?"

It wasn't that I didn't want to be martyred; that's why I'd come. But the idea of being surrounded freaked me out. It just added to the overall sense of helplessness I had been feeling since entering Grozny.

Before I could feel any sorrier for myself, someone called out "Airplane!" We all looked up to see an Su-24 lining up for an attack run. The plane was fairly close, but no one conveyed any sense of urgency in the way they we moved for cover. I ran through the doorway of the nearest building with some other guys, and we waited. The roar of jet engines filled the air, followed seconds later by the scream of an incoming bomb. There was a deafening boom as it hit one of the buildings across the street, then the sound of debris raining down. Everyone casually walked back into the street and looked around for more airplanes, but there weren't any for the time being. At just about any time during daylight hours you could hear bombs going off somewhere in Grozny. Jets constantly prowled overhead, looking for someone to bomb.

Now that we were surrounded, our commander called us on the radio and told us to look for food. He wanted us to buy anything we could find. We spent most of the day stopping at the occasional stall that was bold enough, or defiant enough, to stay open during the day. There wasn't much left in the city, but by the end of the day we'd managed to fill up the trunk of our car with food, mostly canned goods. Despite being surrounded by the Russian army the people in the city were fairly cheerful. We passed by several groups of mujahideen, and they would all yell *Allah-u-Akbar!* as we drove by. But we also spent most of our time dodging the Russian jets that were constantly circling overhead. Eventually it became routine and I stopped worrying about it. When someone spotted a plane that was close enough to be a threat we'd stop the car, get out, and find cover.

We did this until the afternoon, when we had to travel to one of the suburbs on the edge of Grozny. To get there we had to cover a couple miles of open road. Playing dodge with Russian jets was one thing in the middle of the city, but out in the open we would be extremely vulnerable. When we got to the exposed stretch the driver floored it, and we flew down the road at top speed. I stuck my head out the window to search the sky for jets. One of guys joked that I was going to get bugs in my teeth like the front of the radiator grille. Another car that was trying to run the gauntlet approached from the opposite direction. As it flew by we saw that it was full of civilians. Then I saw it, just a shiny glint at first. The glint turned into an Su-24 that was traveling in the same direction as the car we'd passed. My heart sank. Can't you fuckers just leave us alone? I thought. The driver slid to a stop and we all scrambled out, but there really wasn't anywhere to take cover, so we just stood there. I thought for a minute that we were done for, but then it looked as though the pilot hadn't really noticed us; the jet was following the car full of civilians for target practice.

"He's gonna hit that car," I shouted at our guys. We jumped in our car and turned around in the road. Just as we started to head back in the other direction we saw the puff of smoke as the Su-24 fired its rockets. The other car was way up ahead, and when the rockets impacted we couldn't tell if they'd hit it or not. A cloud of dust started to rise from the explosions.

The car was stopped on the side of the road; maybe the driver had tried to pull over at the last minute, but the occupants hadn't been able to get out in time. The car hadn't taken a direct hit, and it didn't look all that serious. But as we got closer we could see the damage. All the windows were blown out and there were holes in the car just about everywhere. Everyone inside was slumped over. The driver of the car was a man. There were two women in the front seat and four women crammed into the back. It looked like a man, his wife, their three daughters, and Grandma. None of them moved. There were no moans or screams of pain. Just silence. There was no cell phone on which to dial 911. No ambulances would come to help us. One of the guys shouted that the old woman in the middle of the back seat was still alive. They pulled her out and laid her on the ground. She was just starting to regain consciousness but was obviously in shock. Blood oozed out of entry wounds in her calf and her head.

I'd looked around to see if the jet was coming back when I heard the stuttering of antiaircraft fire coming from the city. Some of the mujahideen there had a truck-mounted 23mm antiaircraft cannon and were firing at something. I hoped that it was the jet that had just killed these people. We actually caught sight of the Su-24 for a second. It seemed busy with whoever was firing at it from the city. We put the old woman in our car and took her to Grozny's central hospital.

It wasn't a happy occasion, but when I saw the hospital staff I couldn't help but feel overjoyed. It was the same crew from the field hospitals in Benoi and Tutsanute who had taken out my appendix and operated on my leg. The last time I'd seen them was the day the Russians had surrounded Tutsanute and Salaah had helped me escape. Now we were together again in the middle of Grozny. "Abu!" all the doctors and nurses yelled when they saw me. One of the nurses asked, "What are you doing back again?"

"What do you think?" I said. "How could I not come back again?" We hugged and then sat down for tea. Leila wasn't there, but her sister was. One of the doctors whom I'd particularly liked was missing, so I asked where he was. They told me that he'd been killed at a Russian checkpoint when the latest war started. All of the doctors and nurses were surprised to see that I was missing my leg now. They were even more surprised to see me back in the war again with a prosthetic.

The Chechen minister of health was there too. We had a conversation that would eventually lead to my departure. Umar explained how desperate they were for medicine and supplies and suggested that I could do more good by going back to America to get these. I told him that I wanted to stay to defend Grozny this time, but Umar insisted that it was more important for me to help them with medicine. They had plenty of soldiers but no one to get medicine. Over the next couple of days the battalion commander became involved in this discussion, and in the end the two of them persuaded me to return to America long enough to raise money for the medicine they needed. I didn't want to leave, but the commander made it almost an order so we tried to figure out how I could get out of Grozny.

I still had Robert's digital video camera, and one morning we were standing out in front of our bunker taping some stuff when there was a massive explosion. Everyone hit the deck as the shock waves from the impact swept over us, and the ground moved under our bodies as though we were on a ship in the ocean. No one really knew what was happening, but a mushroom cloud rose from just behind the building that housed our bunker. I gave the camera to one of the guys, and he ran to the top of our building to shoot what was happening. The whole building next door had been leveled; all that was left were a couple of outer walls and a pile of twisted steel and concrete. That was too fucking close, I thought. Our commander was always yapping on his radio, and the Russians had finally gotten around to targeting us with a cruise missile.

About a week later the commander made arrangements for me to get out of Grozny. One of the other groups had found a weak spot in the Russian line on one of the hills overlooking Grozny. Late one afternoon a car showed up at our building. I bade everyone farewell and promised that I would be back soon. It was relatively calm as we drove through downtown Grozny because the weather was thick and overcast and the Russian jets couldn't attack us. At one of the main boulevards, we saw a man hanging by his neck from a light pole. He was well dressed, with a stylish trench coat and an expensive Russian fur cap. A sign was attached to his ankles: TRAITOR. Grozny was going insane, and I had to get out before it consumed me.

We stopped briefly at a house occupied by another group of mujahideen. There was a hill behind one of the last neighborhoods on the outskirts of Grozny, and we were going to try to go over it. As we neared the neighborhood the clouds started to lift, and within minutes we could hear the jets prowling over the city again. When we came to the edge of the village, where the hill began, the driver let us out and took off without saying a word. Now I was alone with the younger guy who'd picked me up at the bunker and an older guy we'd picked up at the house. The car hadn't been gone two minutes when the sound of jet engines broke the silence.

"Where is he?" I yelled at the younger guy.

"I don't see him yet," he said as he looked around frantically. I started jogging toward a drainage ditch about twenty meters away as the noise from the engines grew louder.

"There! There!" the younger guy shouted.

The older guy had started running in the opposite direction and was out in the open.

"*Get down!*" I yelled at him. I spotted the jet, an Su-24, it was coming in low over the neighborhood. Damnit, I thought. The old guy isn't going to make it to cover in time.

"*Get DOWN!*" the younger guy shouted. He'd followed me to the ditch. The pilot fired off a volley of rockets. *BOOM, BOOM, BOOM*, the rockets impacted about a hundred meters in front of us. He's dead for sure, I thought. But when I stuck my head up from the ditch I saw him smiling at us. The rockets must have hit not even fifty meters away from him, but he didn't have a scratch.

"Allah doesn't want you," the younger guy yelled at him.

We ran toward a muddy road that went up the hill and through the forest before the jet could come back around. Once in the forest we walked slowly for a minute.

"We need to follow this road up the hill, but the Russians are on both peaks," the younger guy said, pointing ahead and to both sides. The walk was very difficult. The road was extremely muddy, and we slipped constantly. Neither of my companions was armed, and I was worried about what would happen if we ran into an ambush. I walked with my AK at the low ready, straining to listen for any noises. About halfway up the hill we heard a jeep coming from the direction of the neighborhood, but it was just another group of mujahideen trying to do the same thing we were. The jeep was having trouble making it up the muddy road, but it still looked easier than walking. I hoped they'd stop to give us a ride, but as the jeep passed, I saw that it was packed full. About ten minutes later another jeep came up the hill, followed by a third. So much for our secret escape route. The noise of the jeeps would probably alert the Russians, but the jeeps would be gone by the time the Russians got here. That would just leave us walking through the forest. Finally another jeep stopped, but it had room only for one. My two companions told me to take it because of my leg, and I said I would wait for them at the top of the hill. As it happened, I didn't have to ask the driver to stop at the top, because he ran out of gas. The driver and the other fighters got out and walked on while I sat down on a log and waited for my two companions. The sun had set, and it was getting painfully cold. My leg wasn't doing well, and when I took my prosthetic off I found that I'd rubbed my stump raw climbing the hill. Unfortunately, the walk was far from over.

It was nearly pitch-black when I heard my companions moving up the road. Climbing down the other side of the hill proved to be more difficult than going up. The road was deeply rutted, and I fell down every few steps. I considered stopping for the night, but it was so cold that I thought we might freeze to death. Besides, I didn't want to be this close to the Russians when dawn came. The road ran through a ravine, and we could just make out the top of the hill to our right about a hundred meters away. All of a sudden we saw lights coming from the peak directly above us, and then we heard voices. The Russians soldiers were right there. We wouldn't stand much of a chance in a firefight, but I figured I could take a few of the pigs out with me if it came down to it. Somehow we made it down the hill without being seen or heard.

At the bottom of the ravine, we came to an open field where the mud was nearly knee-deep. My two companions practically had to drag me to the other side. The field was at the end of a valley, and on the ridges of the valley we could see several lights. The Russians were up there in force and would probably sweep the valley at dawn. This is going to be a long night, I thought. We came to a small village and found a jeep that would give us a ride. We drove through the village and continued to the other side of the valley. As we came to a clearing we saw that the lights couldn't be more than half a mile away. The whole countryside was crawling with Russians. One of the locals got out of the jeep with his flashlight and jogged in front of us. Our headlights were blacked out, and he was guiding the driver. Somehow we made it to a city; I think it was Shali. My younger traveling companion was supposed to have a contact here who could get us a ride, but he was unable to find the contact, so we walked through the city to the main road that led back to the border with Georgia. I started to recognize landmarks; we'd passed through here on the way to Grozny. When we got to the destroyed bridge over the Argun River, we managed to scramble down one of the giant concrete slabs and up the other. While we were climbing across the bombed-out bridge I noticed a faint odor of something like rotten eggs. It drifted in and out on the breeze that ran through the valley.

"You smell that?" I asked the younger guy.

"Yeah," he said. "Chemicals."

It was mustard gas. The Russians were gassing everybody. I didn't know if running would do any us good, but it made sense to try to get away from the odor as fast as possible. We ran all the way across the part of the bridge that was still standing, nearly falling through the gaping holes.

About a mile up the road we stopped to rest. I was exhausted and suffering extreme pain in my leg. We had no water and were coughing from the mustard gas we'd inhaled back on the bridge. But we had no cover here, and the Russian jets would surely be working the valley at dawn, so we couldn't rest for long. We could hear the deep, buzzing drone of a Russian reconnaissance plane and watched as giant flashes emanated from it as it passed overhead. With each flash we heard a curious *whoomph, whoomph.* What the hell is that? I wondered. Giant flashbulbs to take nighttime surveillance pictures? Anything seemed possible with the Russians.

The road ahead was paved, a rarity in Chechnya, and I lay down in the middle because it was the only dry spot I could find. A couple of jeeps packed with mujahideen came by, but neither had any room for us. We were starting to get worried about the approaching dawn when a jeep with some extra room stopped. We rode the jeep to a mountain village, where they dropped us off at a house. It turned out to be the older guy's brother's house, and we stayed the night there. I was woken the next morning by the rattling of windows and the deep, hollow detonation of bombs. I scrambled to put my leg on and grab my AK before heading out the door. My companions were crouching in the court-yard of the house, along with the family that lived there, a man, his wife, and three small children. The children were crying and clutching at their mother.

The air roared as another Su-24 ripped through the sky overhead. It dropped its bombs right smack in the middle of the village, a few hundred meters away from us. Miniature mushroom clouds rose from where the bombs hit. Let me guess, I thought. The Russians are cleansing the village of "terrorists." I looked at the children crying and holding onto their mother, and I wondered how the Russians could do this to women and children. How they could drop bombs on houses they knew were full of civilians?

I guess it would take the same mentality as it would to fly an airplane into a building full of people, but these people didn't matter to anyone. Their deaths would spur no outrage or aid packages. The Russians would call them terrorists, and the media would repeat this mantra, chapter, line, and verse. I started to get pissed off. Fuck the people who give the orders to bomb these villages, I thought, and fuck the pilots. Fuck the people who fail to report these crimes against humanity. Fuck the world.

For whatever reason, we had to spend the day in the village. The bombing went on all day long. Every fifteen minutes or so the jets would appear, drop their loads, and fly off. Over and over again. The villagers had nowhere to go, so between bombings they tried to occupy themselves with daily chores. Watching the children was the most disturbing thing. They seemed to almost forget about what was happening around them when the jets left, and they would begin to play, only to run screaming to their mothers fifteen minutes later as the ground shook under them. It was like trying to get accustomed to having someone around you shot every fifteen minutes. I could only imagine what it was doing to their poor little brains.

As the day went on I watched group after group of ragtag mujahideen walk toward Grozny with nothing more than automatic rifles and grenade launchers. Five in one group, twelve in another, and so on. I couldn't see how anyone would regard them as anything less than heroic. They were on their way to defend a city that was surrounded by seven divisions of the Russian army.

The younger guy was able to arrange a ride for us, and as night fell we started off toward the Georgian border. Amazingly, the road was even more damaged than when I'd traveled on it on my way into Grozny. A couple of times the driver was barely able to inch around giant craters that took up almost the whole road. I kept my AK at the ready because Russian paratroopers were dropping into this gorge almost daily. There was a faint, glowing light on the walls of the gorge, and at first I thought it was evidence of Russian soldiers. But when we stopped I realized that the mountains were smoldering with dying fires. Later I would learn that Robert, Sarah, and Sedat had escaped Grozny before it was surrounded and that when they'd passed through this very spot, the fires were blazing. Apparently, the Russians had tried to burn down the mountains.

We stopped at the little camp carved into the side of the gorge where I'd first been split up from Robert and the others. The little group there had been battling with the Russian paratroopers to keep the gorge open. This was the only open road in or out of Chechnya, and the Russians had intensified their efforts to shut it down. I spent nearly a week there. We were deep inside the gorge and relatively safe from jets, but helicopter gunships would sometimes try to come up the gorge to drop bombs with delayed fuses, attempting to close the road.

Chechen civilians were piling up in a bottleneck where the gorge entered Georgia. The Georgians weren't letting adult males from Chechnya cross the border, which was a problem for me. It was bitterly cold and snowing, and one day the Georgian border guards decided to delay a minibus full of women and children. All of the kids were sick, some of them wounded. One small boy about two years old had had his right eye blown out, and he desperately needed medical care. I treated him as best I could with my medical kit, but it wasn't much. The bus had no heat, and the people wouldn't last the night out here. Some of the mujahideen walked up to the Georgian border guards and threatened them.

"Look," one of our guys said. "you wouldn't let your dog stay out in the cold like this."

Another chimed in, "We don't want any problems with you, but if you don't let these women and children cross your border, we will attack you." Within minutes the minibus was waved ahead.

The commander of the gorge camp also needed to travel to Tbilisi, so one day we tried to cross by hiding my prosthetic leg and saying that I was wounded. The trick didn't work, but the Georgians knew that my new traveling companion was a Chechen field commander, so they turned a blind eye. Eventually we made it to Tbilisi.

Robert was long gone, and since I hadn't planned on leaving Chechnya again I didn't have money for a ticket back home. I called Sumaya who had to borrow money from some friends and wire it to me in Tbilisi. I spent a week alone in a hotel room waiting for a flight back to the States. I was on the edge, tormented by what I'd seen in Chechnya. I would cry for no apparent reason. Whenever I dozed off the noises on the street would startle me awake, and I would crouch on the floor waiting for the bombs to hit. I was wearing the same clothes that I had been in for weeks and must have looked like some kind of madman on the long flight to London and then on to Los Angeles.

This time it was bad. I didn't really want to be home, and I couldn't get Chechnya out of my mind. I couldn't talk to Sumaya and spent my time trying to raise money to get what I needed for the Chechen health minister. As always, the American Muslims wouldn't have anything to do with helping Chechnya because it was a jihad. I became frustrated, and when my frustration turned into anger I began to have problems with everyone. Chechnya began to consume me. I couldn't see what was happening to my relationship with Sumaya.

I started working a bodyguard detail with some local guys so that I could stash some money away and get back to Chechnya. One evening the day-care center called to tell me that they were closing and that no one had picked up our kids. I collected them at the day-care center and went home to find an empty house. Sumaya had left me with the kids and taken off.

Everything went to hell. A couple days after Sumaya left, one of the bodyguards I was working with—a friend—was killed. It wasn't a big deal compared to what I had already been through, but it was the last thing that I could deal with then.

September 11, 2001

I STRUGGLED FOR ABOUT A YEAR to get my work and family life together. I started to develop a career as a bounty hunter specializing in south-of-the-border apprehensions, a description of which would require at least another book. One of these operations took me to Mexico for a couple of weeks, where I chased a drug dealer who was wanted for failure to appear in court in Maricopa County. Eventually I found out that the information someone had given me was bogus, so I went back across the border to negotiate another contract in Phoenix. On September 10, 2001, I decided to stop off in San Diego and spend the night. The next morning I woke up and went on-line to check out the latest postings on the Black Flag Café, a message board on www.comebackalive.com, Robert Young Pelton's Web site. Someone had posted a message saying that the World Trade Center had been attacked and that it was on fire. Yeah right, I thought. A lot of people post weird stuff like that on the Internet. After browsing through the other messages, I turned on the news. That's when I saw that the message posted on Black Flag was serious, and that the World Trade Center really had been hit.

As more of the story came out, I contacted the FBI and told them I was ready to go back to work. They didn't call back for a few days, but when they did we made arrangements to meet at the Phoenix office to have a little chat. By this time some of the details were coming out about the people who were alleged to have taken part in the hijackings, and it was apparent that a few of the guys were known not only to me but to the FBI as well. I was full of hope as I sat down to offer my assistance. I offered to go to Afghanistan, to talk to people I knew, or to help the FBI in any way. But my hopes proved to be naive. When FBI agents have absolutely no information, they don't grasp at straws; they rely on fear and intimidation. They immediately started in on me as though I were a suspect. I even took a voluntary polygraph to clear up any crazy ideas they had about the remote chance that I'd had any advance knowledge of September 11.

I was very mistrustful about the fact that Usama Bin Laden's name was mentioned literally hours after the attack. When I combined this with the fact the FBI had no apparent desire to accept what I brought to the table, I became very skeptical about anything anybody said about what happened, or who did it. I thought back to when I was still working for them and we had the opportunity to enter Bin Laden's camp. Something just hadn't smelled right. There were also the details I knew personally about Hani Hanjoor, one of the "hanky-panky" hijackers on the Pentagon flight. He wasn't even moderately religious, let alone fanatically religious. And I knew for a fact that he wasn't part of Al Qaeda or any other Islamic organization; he couldn't even spell *jihad* in Arabic.

Within hours of the attacks Muslims all over the country were being rounded up and being held as supposed "material witnesses." In the end nearly a thousand Muslims, mainly of Arabic origin, were sitting in jail cells across America. How could nearly a thousand people keep a secret about something of that scale without leaking it somehow?

To this day I'm unsure who was behind September 11, nor can I even guess. But one thing is apparent: Bush and his so-called war on terrorism are doing the world far more harm than good. At this writing, the authorities have apprehended neither Usama Bin Laden nor even a single important terrorist. For all the talk of secret terrorist cells lying dormant in the United States, we haven't seen evidence of a single one yet.

Someday the truth will reveal itself, and I have a feeling that people won't like what they hear.

INDEX

A

Abbas, 41–43, 116–17, 119–21

Abdullah, 4–5, 171

ablutions, 24

Afghanistan, 16

  crossing border, 20–21

  leaving, 38

  map of, 15

  Russians in, 9

  training camp, 21, 23–37

  trek to, 18–20

  U.S. attack on, 181

AGS-17 automatic grenade
  launchers, 85

Ahmed Omar Saeed Sheikh. *See*
  Umar

AK-47s, 11–13, 16–18, 24–25, 33,
  79, 82–83, 88, 189, 200

AK-74s, 55–56, 107–8, 110

Albania

  American embassy, 208–9

  Bajram Curri, 186–87, 199

  Interior Ministry Building, 195

  riots in, 207

  Tropojë, 186, 197

Albanian cops, 189–90

Albanian intelligence agent,
  191–95, 205–6

Al Qaeda, 9, 175–76

American World Wide Relief,
  41, 48

Amin, Abu, 165, 183, 217

  Albania, 190, 194

  association with KLA, 185, 210

  conflict with Collins, 173, 211

  introduction to Ghareeb,
    179–81

  introduction to Jaffar, 196

  meeting Abu Ubaidah, 176–77

  meeting Collins in London, 170

  visa extension to Collins, 126

Amman, Jordan, 116

appendicitis, 61–63

Argun River, 242

Argun River Gorge, 219,
  221–22, 244

Arizona Boys Ranch, 140

surrounding areas and
  map of, 155

training camp, 163–64

arms embargo, 4

arm-wrestling, 33

arthritis, acute, 39

Aryan Brotherhood, 140–41

AsSalaambeck, 72–77, 85–86, 91,
  93, 97, 111

Attiquallah, 42

Awazik Russian jeeps, 49, 101

Ayeesha, 87, 93–94, 102–3, 105–15,
  123, 126, 151, 160–61, 177,
  217–18

azan, 3, 24, 27, 163

Azerbaijan, 43–44, 46, 117
  border crossing, 113–15, 118
  See also: Baku, Azerbaijan
Azeri driver, 128–30
Azeri police, 47–48
Azzam, Abdullah, 9

B

Bajram Curri, Albania, 186–87, 199
Baku, Azerbaijan, 44, 46–47, 79,
  115–16, 118–20, 122, 127
Baltimore, Maryland, 169
Basaiyev, Shamil, 59, 63
Battle Dress Uniforms, 50
Benelli Super-90 shotguns, 184
Benoi, Chechnya, 59, 61, 103
Berisha, Sali, 207
Bin Laden, Usama, 9–10, 21,
  126, 193
  and Abu Amin, 170
  funding of Harakut-ul Ansar, 33
  and Ibn-ul Khattab, 57
  opportunity for Collins to meet,
    175–78
  and September 11, 2001, 248
  U.S. embassy bombings, 181
Black Flag Cafe, 247
Black Shark helicopters, 91–93, 98
BMP combat vehicles, 69, 93, 108
Bosnia, 4–7
  map and surrounding areas of, 7
  treatment of jihad, 205
bounty hunter, 247
Bradley, Bob, 133
Bradley, Geraldine Faye, 133–35,
  137–38

Brandon, 138
Braveheart (movie), 115
BRDM armored reconnaissance
  vehicles, 27
bribes, 197
Britain
  influence on Islam, 4
British Airways, 119
BTR personnel carriers, 27, 85, 93,
  107–8
  ambush of, 76–78
Buddenovsk, Russia, 59, 63
Bumble Bee, Arizona, 163
burial rituals, 29–30

C

Cairo, Egypt, 150
California
  growing up in, 134–35
  See also: Los Angeles; Maricopa
    County; San Diego
California Youth Authority, 116,
  134, 140–41
Canter, Jonathan, 158, 164,
  167, 215
carouge, 8
Caspian Sea, 44, 47
Caucasus Mountains, 219
Cecin, Chechnya, 70–71, 80, 83
Chechnya
  American embassy, 147–50
  bandits, 80–83
  Cecin, 70–71, 80, 83
  character of people, 106
  crossing border, 51–54, 118
Dargho, 59, 109

front lines, 59–60, 231–32
Grozny, 41, 63, 84, 217–42
Gudermes, 111
Kerchaloy, 86–87, 93, 97–98,
    102, 109
leaving, 243
mafia, 52, 79–80, 84, 114–15, 117,
    151, 160
Russians in, 41, 243–44
surrounding areas and
    map of, 45
training camp (See Khattab's camp)
Zandak, 54–55, 58–59, 65, 71,
    74–75, 78, 84, 110–11
chemical warfare, 227, 242
childhood of Collins, 133–43
CIA, 21, 48, 194–95, 212
    Chechnya operation, 166,
        168–69, 173–75, 178
    computer surveillance, 165
    first contact with, 148, 150
Clinton, Bill, 181
Collins, Asiya (daughter), 46, 165
Collins, Ayeesha (wife).
    See: Ayeesha
Collins, Nusaiba (daughter), 151,
    160–61, 217–18
Collins, Saifudeen (son), 162, 167,
    179, 181, 217, 229
Collins, Sumaya (wife), 40, 42–43,
    46, 116, 155, 157, 245–46
Collins, Tammy. See: Collins,
    Sumaya (wife)
Colt M-16 rifles, 25
comebackalive.com, 247

computer surveillance, 165
concealed weapon badge, 189
converting to Islam, 142–43
Cosgrove, Leonard, 158, 160, 162–
    63, 166–70, 172–73, 212
C-130 transport planes, 183
Cyrillic, 224
CZ75 pistols, 128

D

Dagestan, 47–48, 71, 110, 113, 118
Dargho, Chechnya, 59, 109
Dean, 136
Degtyarev 30 machine guns, 26
dhal, 25
Dragunov sniper rifles, 25, 57
DShK machine guns, 26, 64, 68
dysentery, 8, 31

E

Enfield 303 rifles, 25
explosives, 28–29

F

fake IDs, 113
Fatal Attraction (movie), 208
Fatih, Sheikh, 58, 78–79
FBI, 8, 42, 212, 247
    Chechnya operation, 173–74
    and CIA protocol, 150–51
    differences with, 178–80
    end of relationship, 215–16
    working with, 156–59, 162–65
ferry, 187, 198–99, 206

F-9 grenades, 82
Flanders, Pat, 214–15
flight lessons, 214
FN FAL rifles, 25
FN MAG machine guns, 26
food, 25, 31
Fort Huachuca, Arizona, 179
Frankfurt, Germany, 6
FSB Russian intelligence agency,
    172–73

G

al-Gama'at al-Islamiyya, 150
Genghis, 115
Georgia, 218–19, 244–45
Ghareeb, 179–81, 211–14, 216
Gibson, Mel, 115
"Gladiator School," 141
graves, 30
G3 rifles, 25
Grozny, Chechnya, 41, 63, 84, 218,
    224–30, 232, 234–36, 238
    leaving Grozny, 240–42
Gudermes, Chechnya, 111

H

hadiths, 29
Hafs, Abu, 110–11
The Hague, 176
Hajdari, Azem, 207
Hamza, Abu, 126–28
hand-to-hand combat, 28
Hanjoor, Hani, 214, 248
Harakat-ul Ansar, 33, 36

Harakat-ul Jihad, 8–16, 38
Harry, 165, 168
Hawaii, 136–38
HEAT rockets (high-explosive anti-
    tank), 35
helicopter-gunship rockets, 84
Hell's Angels, 134
Hikmartry, Golbudeen, 42
Hisham, 116
hospitals
    in Azerbaijan, 115
    in Chechnya, 103–7, 239
    in Jordan, 116
hostages, 36, 39
Hoxa, Enver, 184

I

Ibrahim, 3–4
India, 13–14
Indiana, 133, 139
Inter Services Intelligence Agency
    (ISI), 13–14, 35–36
Ishiguro, Tom, 151–52, 154–59
ISI (Inter Services Intelligence
    agency), 13–14, 35–36
Islam, 4–5, 27
    burial rituals, 29–30
    Collins conversion to, 142–43
Islamabad, Pakistan, 8, 10, 15–16,
    38–39
Islamic community
    in America, 212
Islamic Information Center of the
    Americas, 5
Issa, 71, 80, 83–85

Istanbul, Turkey, 43–44,
160–61, 218

J

Jaffar, 196–97, 199–200, 202,
205, 209
Jaffar, Abu, 47
jamats, 3, 24
Jihad
principle of, 4
prophet Muhammad and, 5
Jihadwal camp, 21
Juglarge, 84–85, 94, 106

K

Ka-50 Charney Akula helicopters.
See: Black Shark helicopters
Kaneohe Marine Corps base, 133
Karachi, Pakistan, 8
Kashmir, 8–10, 12–14, 36
map of, 15
Kerchaloy, Chechnya, 86–87, 93,
97–98, 102, 109
Kesacee, 142–43
Khalid, 29–30, 34, 37
Khalid, Commander, 10–15
Khalid Bin Whalid camp, 21
Khambiev, Umar, 63
Khamil, 3
Khattab, Ibn-ul, 47, 67, 70, 102,
162, 175
betrayal, 147
CIA interest in, 166
FBI interest in, 155

first time meeting, 55–57
helping Collins leave Chechnya,
110–11
Khattab's camp, 65–66, 68–70, 109
Kiffah, 41–44, 55, 67, 127
Kosova, 203
CIA, 210
crossing border into, 186–88
deputy defense minister, 196–97,
205, 209
entry, 198–99
getting weapons for, 197
surrounding areas and
map of, 182
Kosova Liberation Army, 168,
204–5
and Abu Amin, 177, 184–86,
210–11
Albanian intelligence office,
192–95
crackdown on, 188–89
need for weapons, 197–98
163rd Brigade, 201
situation in Kosova, 173
training camp, 199, 202
Krinkov assault rifles, 58

L

Laith, 8
landmines, 85
Lee, Bruce, 86, 115
leg amputation, 159–60
leg injury, 100–107, 115, 117,
123, 163

Leila, 63, 104
Lindh, John Walker, 33
London, England
  and Abu Amin, 181, 210
  FBI agent in, 178
  infiltration of Pakistanis, 169–72
London Pakistanis, 166, 169
Lori, 138
Los Angeles, California
  airport, 151–54
  Islamic community in, 4
loti, 23
Lufthansa airlines, 120
Luqman, 64–65, 111

M

madrasah, 17, 19, 170
Majiko, Pandeli, 207
Makarov pistols, 27, 48
Makhachkala, Dagestan, 52, 112
Malaysia, 196–97
Malik, Abdul, 170–71, 173,
  175–77, 179
maps, 15, 45, 155, 182
Maricopa County, California, 247
Masjidul Noor mosque, 3
Mecca, 30, 47
Mi-24 "Hind" helicopters, 98
Miram Shah, Pakistan, 17, 19,
  32, 38
mongooses, 31
mosques, 158, 212
  Masjidul Noor, 3
MP5 rifles, 184
Muhammad, Abu, 65

Muhammad, Umme, 43, 58, 65, 78
Mukha rockets, 57, 69, 76, 92,
  98–100
Musa, 85–86, 91, 94, 97–100, 106
Mushakil, Abu, 67
mustard gas, 242

N

Nairobi embassy bombing, 193
Nano, Fatos, 207
nashids, 47
news media, 236
Nokche Bores, 106, 228
Noor Allah Battalion, 227–31
North-West Frontier Province
  (NWFP), 16, 19, 32, 37–38
Nozhai-Yurt, Chechnya, 58–59, 78

O

OMON (Russian military police),
  74–75, 79, 108

P

Pakistan, 9, 11–13
  Harakat-ul Ansar group, 33, 36
  Harakat-ul Jihad, 8–16, 38
  Inter-Services Intelligence Agency
    (ISI), 13–14, 35–36
  map of, 15
  origin of Tabliqis, 4
  training camp, 12–14
Palestinian Authority, 162
Pashtuns, 16
Payson, Arizona, 140

Pearl, Daniel, 39
Pelton, Robert Young, 217–20,
    233–34, 247
Pentagon
    attack on, 248
peroneal nerve, 115
Peshawar, Pakistan, 42
Phoenix, Arizona, 116–17, 156,
    179, 213
PKM machine guns, 11, 25, 33–34,
    41, 57, 70, 76, 101, 233
prayers, 30
    Salaatul Fajr, 23
    Salaatul Jama'a, 28
    Salaatul Janazah, 29
    Salaatul Maghrib, 3
prophet Muhammad, 29

Q

qibla, 30
Qur'an, 12, 24, 37, 142

R

raka'at, 30
rappelling, 124–25
Raxhab, 190–91, 195–97, 199, 218
Reno, Janet, 164
Robert, 244–45
RPGs (rocket-propelled grenades), 11,
    26, 34–35, 57, 74, 76, 79, 227
RPKs (automatic weapons), 100
Ruby Ridge incident, 164
Rukshan, 118
Ruslan, 85–86, 91–92, 96–97, 101

Russia
    in Afghanistan, 5, 26, 42, 57
    cause for Chechnyan conflict, 41
Russian-Afghani War, 42, 57
Russian military police (OMON),
    74–75, 79, 108
Russian PPS rifles, 25
Russian soldiers, 59, 69–70
    ambush of, 76–77, 100–101
    attrocities of in Chechnya, 61
    bribes, 48–50
    bunker attack, 95–97
    in Chechnya, 87–89
    converting to Islam, 73
    defectors, 72, 74
    sparing Ayeesha, 108

S

Saifudeen, Abu, 44, 46
Salaah, 108–9, 198
Salaambeck, 72–77, 111
salaat, 24
Salaatul Fajr prayer, 23–24, 97
Salaatul Jama'a, 28
Salaatul Janazah prayer, 29
Salaatul Maghrib prayer, 3
Samoans in Hawaii, 137
Sanchez, Andy, 156–60, 162–63,
    165–67, 169–75, 177–79, 196,
    212–14
San Diego, California, 116
    author's youth in, 139–40
    Islamic community in, 3–5, 39
Sarah, 218, 233–34, 244
Sarajevo, Bosnia, 6–7

satellite-phones, 234
Saudi Arabia, 123, 125
Saudi Arabian muslims, 47
Scottsdale, Arizona, 214
Sedat, 218, 233–34, 244
September 11, 2001, 248
Serbs, 4–5, 173, 176, 200
    and Albanians, 205
    garrisons, 202
    observation towers, 201, 203
shahaadat, 73
shaheed, 29, 39
Shaheed, Mufti, 9, 15–16, 38
Shali, Chechnya, 242
Shamil, 115, 117–22
shawal kamece, 12, 35, 124
Shilka antiaircraft guns, 26
Sikh commandos, 13–14
SKS rifles, 24
Soldier of Fortune magazine, 200–201
Somalian muslims, 40
Soviet-Afghan War, 26, 42, 57
Spetsnaz Russian special force,
    60, 98
Stetckin automatic pistols, 63
Steyr AUG rifles, 200
Stinger antiaircraft missiles, 5
Sudan
    U.S. attack on, 181
Sudanese Muslims, 6–7
Sumaya, 163
SU-24 Russian bombers, 64, 233,
    237–38, 240, 243
SwissAir, 183

T

Tabliqi Muslims, 3–4, 8
Tajikistan, 25, 34, 36, 38, 57
Taliban, 16, 39, 181
    rise to power, 17
Tbilisi, Georgia, 218–19, 245
terrorist acts, 150, 181, 193, 248
Tiranë, Albania, 181, 183–85, 188,
    190–91, 207
Tokarev 9mm pistols, 89
Toyota trucks, 25
Tracy, 166, 168–69, 172–73, 176–77
training camps
    Afghanistan, 21, 23–37
    Arizona, 163–64, 181
    Chechnya (Khattab's),
        65–70, 109
    Pakistan, 12–14
Tropojë, Kosova, 186, 197
T-72 tanks, 66–67, 91
T-80 tanks, 91
Turab, Abu, 67–68
Turkish Airlines, 43, 218
Tutsanute, Chechnya, 101–2, 107–9

U

Ubaidah, Abu, 176–77, 210–11
Ulbi, 58–61, 63, 71–76, 78–80
Umar, 5, 31–39, 65, 103, 239
Umar, Abu, 124–25
United Nations, 6
United States
    arms embargo in Bosnia, 4

support of Afghanistan, 5
UNPROFOR card, 6
Urdu language, 31, 35–36
Uthman, 70–71, 109, 111

V

Van Damme, Claude, 115
Vedeno, Chechnya, 59, 64, 68, 110
Vienna, Austria, 6, 8

W

Waco incident, 164
Wall Street Journal, 39
Washington, D.C., 169
weapons, 11–12, 25, 57
*The World's Most Dangerous
    Places,* 217
World Trade Center, 247
wudhuu, 24

Y

Yaesu radios, 195
Yemen muslims, 47

Z

Zacharia, 78–79
Zagreb, Croatia, 6–7
Zaid, Abu, 68, 70
Zakaria, 55, 58
Zaky, Muhammad, 5–6, 8, 41, 44,
    64–65, 68, 111
Zandak, Chechnya, 54–55, 58–59,
    65, 71, 74–75, 78, 84, 110–11
Zelemkhan, 104–5, 107–9
Zubair, Abu, 72, 110–11, 170
Zubair, Abu (of Khattab), 122–23,
    125–26